WORD
FOR
WORD

Also available in Large Print
by Andrew A. Rooney:

Pieces of My Mind
A Few Minutes with Andy Rooney

WORD
FOR
WORD

Andrew Rooney

G.K.HALL &CO.
Boston, Massachusetts
1987

Published in Large Print by arrangement with
G. P. Putnam's Sons

G.K. Hall Large Print Book Series.

Set in 16 pt Plantin.

Library of Congress Cataloging in Publication Data

Rooney, Andrew A.
  Word for word.

  (G.K. Hall large print series)
  1. Large type books.   I. Title.
[PN6162.R6334   1987]   814'.54   87-8625
ISBN 0-8161-4315-3 (Lg. print)

*With thanks for good help
from Jane Bradford and Neil Nyren.*

CONTENTS

PREFACE

Writing is difficult. That's why there's so little of it that's any good. Writing isn't like mathematics where what you've put down is either right or wrong. No writer ever puts down anything on paper that he knows for certain is good or bad.

When I was in The Albany Academy, I won a writing prize and, because I was not otherwise a good student, it was the academic high point of my years there. Several years later, I came home from college and looked at the things I'd written to win the prize in high school and winced. They were so bad.

In college I was a prolific contributor to the school literary and humor magazine. When I got out of the Army, four years after college, I reread what I'd written in college and couldn't believe I'd ever been so young or written so badly.

In the Army, I was assigned as a reporter to the newspaper, *The Stars and Stripes*, and spent three years covering World War II and learning from the great war correspondents like Hal Boyle, Bob Considine, Homer Bigart, Dick Tregaskis and Ernie Pyle. It seemed to me I was finally growing up as a writer.

In several boxes in my basement I have every issue of *The Stars and Stripes* printed during the time I was on the staff and they contain hundreds of stories I wrote. I like having them as mementos but I'd be embarrassed to have anyone else read them.

All this self-criticism of what I wrote in the past seems like a not-unnecessarily modest attitude on my part but lately it has worried me. When do I get good? How come what I wrote last year, last month, last week and even yesterday, doesn't seem quite right, either? How come every day I think that for the first time I'm beginning to get the hang of writing but when I reread it the following day I realize I still have a ways to go? When do I arrive as a writer?

I have finally come to the sad realization that I will never write anything today that looks as good as it should to me tomorrow. It's the writer's albatross.

The syndrome is common among writers and, to some extent, it protects them. If writing wasn't difficult and often even demeaning, more people would be doing it. The competition would be greater. In motion pictures, television, newspapers and book publishing, there are hundreds of producers, directors, publishers, editors and salesmen standing around waiting to get what the writer has put down on paper so they can change it, package it and sell it. Producers, directors and editors don't become writers. Writers, seeing where the good life and the money are, become producers, directors and editors. It's so much safer.

It's the writer who makes a fool of himself and

reveals how shallow he is by putting every thought he has on paper, where everyone can see it, read it and put it away to read again tomorrow. Those who merely speak their thoughts are safe. The spoken word drifts away and evaporates in the air, never to be held against the speaker.

"You know what I mean?" the speaker asks, as a substitute for thinking it out and putting it down on paper.

The writer may not think much but he has to know what little he thinks to get it down on paper at all. If someone knows what he's doing, he ought to be able to tell you, and if someone knows what he thinks, he ought to be able to write it down. If he can't, the chances are he doesn't have a thought.

The computer people are trying to make writing easier but they won't succeed. They make computers with writing programs, just as if there was some kind of magic that could help. All a writer needs is something to say, a blank page and an instrument with which to mark words on it. No word processor with a "writing program" will ever help a writer have something to say. No program ever designed will help make writing any better. It may make typing easier, the page neater and the spelling perfect but it won't improve the writing. Writing can't be turned out by machine, doubled, divided, added to and subtracted from, the way numbers can. The English language is more complex than calculus because numbers don't have nuances.

Several years ago someone wrote me asking if I understood how lucky I was to have my opinions printed and read by other people. I said I did appreciate it. I find something ridiculous about it, too. I even try to forget it. If I thought about how many people were going to read what I wrote every time I sat down at my typewriter, I'd freeze. Who is this person so presumptuous as to think anyone gives a damn what he has to say?

If writing is difficult, it's also one of the most satisfactory jobs in the world. Before I won that prize in high school, I already knew what I wanted to be when I grew up. I wanted to be a writer. I wish I was a better one ("were a better one," if you prefer, I don't) but I enjoy being the one I am. If I was forced to choose between appearing on television and writing the words to appear on paper, I wouldn't hesitate for a second. I'd give up television.

Igor Stravinsky, the musician, said, "I experience a sort of terror if I sit down to work and find an infinity of possibilities open to me. No effort is conceivable. I stand on nothing. Endeavor is futile."

Stravinsky said that what he grabbed for on such occasions were the seven notes of the scale. With the limitations they imposed, he could go to work.

A writer needs boundaries too, or he can't get to work. This book isn't a play, a novel or a history. I've set out to write a series of short essays. Within the boundaries of that form, I can go to work.

I hope the essays look okay to me tomorrow.

I

BODY SHOPS

BODY SHOPS

My car and my body are in about the same shape. Both have quite a few miles on them but they're running well and I haven't had any serious trouble with either. All that's needed is some preventive maintenance.

I don't know which is harder, taking my body to the doctor or my car to the garage. Both worry me. I'm always afraid they'll find something I didn't know about. The only advantage to taking my body to the doctor over taking my car to the garage is that the doctor never asks me to leave it overnight.

When you consider how really important our bodies are, compared to our cars, it's surprising how many similarities suggest themselves in their treatment.

Most of us are vaguely nervous about catching something else in a hospital or a doctor's office and, similarly, a car often comes out of the garage with more problems than you knew it had when it went in.

The advertising for help for your body and your car is surprisingly similar, too. I feel extraordinarily lucky that neither my car nor my body seems to suffer from any of the ills you hear so much about on radio and television.

3

I don't have trouble with engine knock, dirty spark plugs or hemorrhoids. This morning on the radio they were saying something like, "More doctors recommend Metamucil." We're always being told what doctors recommend but I have never heard a doctor recommend any commercial product, let alone Metamucil.

I'd be plenty suspicious of any doctor who advised me to take Metamucil, too, because I don't suffer from whatever they say it cures.

I feel the same about Metamucil as I do about AAMCO, the transmission specialists who advertise so much on radio. AAMCO says they fix more transmissions than anyone else and that you can go right in and have one fixed without an appointment. It sounds like a good deal, but in thirty-five years I suppose I've owned twenty cars and I never had any more need to have my transmission overhauled than I've had to take Metamucil. They're advertising both those products to a stone wall when they talk to me.

The other thing that makes me think of cars and bodies at the same time is that insurance companies treat them in many of the same ways. You pay about $1,500 for an appendectomy or a new right front fender but the insurance company doesn't believe either costs that much so they only reimburse you for half.

My office in New York City looks down at the entrance to the Cadillac service garage. At the opposite end of my building, people can see the entrance to Roosevelt Hospital. At Roosevelt Hos-

4

pital the waiting room is crowded with people waiting for personal attention, and in the street outside the Cadillac place, cars are lined up around the block at seven-thirty every morning.

If the people about to buy Cadillacs in the new car showroom in another part of town could see how many of them need fixing, you'd think it might hurt Cadillac sales . . . although there's just as long a line outside the Ford service center a block away.

It's hard to get anything fixed, animate or inanimate. It doesn't matter whether the arteries leading to your heart are shot or your toaster-oven is broken. It's difficult, costly and time-consuming to have them checked over.

We need a new kind of shopping mall where, instead of buying things, we could get things fixed. The doctors, the dentists, the optometrists, the tailors, the shoemakers, the specialty repair shops of all kinds would be right there together where we could get two or three jobs done at the same time . . . without moving the car.

FEAR OF DOCTORS

Doctors have some funny ideas about why people don't like to come to their offices. Some doctors think people are afraid of them. Some think it's because of the probing questions they ask about personal matters. None of these is the reason.

People don't like to go see the doctor because they know they're going to have to take their clothes off.

In spite of all the appeal nudity has for us in certain forms, most people are fully aware that they don't look as good as they ought to naked. Most people think they look worse than most other people naked.

They must have courses in medical schools about how a doctor should tell the patient to take his or her clothes off, and each medical school recommends a different method.

A few doctors just say something direct like: "Take your clothes off." I always figure they went to a Dominican Republic medical school.

Other doctors try to break it to you gradually. They say, "Strip to the waist, please." This is good news because you figure you can at least leave your underpants on, but if you have any experience at all going to doctors, you know it's only temporary. There's bad news coming.

Some doctors try to be discreet. They say, "All right now. Let's take our clothes off, shall we, and see what we have here."

It sounds as though the doctor's going to take his clothes off too.

I don't know whether men doctors treat women patients any differently than they treat men or not, and I certainly have no information about how women doctors treat men patients.

I doubt very much if you'd catch one of them saying, "All right now, let's take our clothes off."

Doctors are used to all this because they see a lot of patients. Patients aren't used to it because they only see one doctor.

It has occurred to me that to be on equal footing with the patient, it might be a good idea if the doctor did remove his or her clothing to set the patient at ease.

I know, though, that in real life this wouldn't work out very well. After all, doctors know just as well as anyone else that they don't look great naked.

No matter how the doctor breaks the news about undressing to a patient, he tries to make it sound matter-of-fact, professional and like an ordinary, everyday kind of thing to do. Well, taking all your clothes off in a stranger's office is not a common, ordinary kind of thing for most people to do, and there's no way for a doctor to phrase it to make it sound as though it were.

Some doctors are cowards. They have their nurses do it for them.

"If you'll remove your clothes," she says, "Dr. Carter will be with you in a few minutes."

If it's ten minutes before the doctor comes, there's almost nothing for a patient to do in the interim. Doing nothing is twice as hard if you don't have any clothes on. If the doctor's license is hanging on the wall, you can read that but if you didn't think the doctor had a license you wouldn't have come to him in the first place . . . and, anyway, you aren't used to reading naked.

Usually a patient just stands there once he's

undressed, and it can be a long stand. The patient can't sit down because the small side chair in the inspection room has a fake leather cover on it that is no doubt sanitary but is also cold . . . especially to sit on.

If doctors want patients whose blood pressures don't rise to abnormally high levels when taken in their offices, they've got to find a way to diagnose patients' illnesses without making them undress.

WAITING ROOMS

One of the reasons everyone would like to be king or president is that he wouldn't have to sit around the waiting room in a doctor's office. If you're either of those, the doctor takes you right away.

Waiting for the dentist or doctor can be almost as unpleasant as being sick enough to need one in the first place.

I've never had to go to any doctor much but I've hated every minute I've ever spent in a waiting room. For one thing, if you suspect there is something wrong with you or know darn well there's something wrong, you aren't interested in reading a magazine article while you wait that gives you nine exciting new ways to decorate your bathroom.

In a doctor's waiting room, I always find myself sneaking glances at the other patients. Each patient ought to have his own little cubicle to wait in privately so people like me can't sneak glances. I find myself wondering what they have. I worry about whether I could get whatever it is. Being in a room with a lot of people who have something wrong with them is no fun at all.

What you really feel like doing in a waiting room is to sit there and stare. You want to worry. You don't want a lot of distractions that take your mind off your problem.

In most cases, it takes half a day to go to the doctor, even though you're lucky if he actually spends twenty minutes with you. Doctors have learned a little something about mass production in the past twenty years. They used to have one office, one examination table. They took patients one at a time. Now many of them have several little places where they store and examine patients. The nurse puts you in one, and you sit there naked while the doctor is in one of his other offices with another patient. He comes in, gives you a few minutes and disappears to go to the next little room. He plays medical chairs.

Every day thousands of hours are lost by people who are "at the doctor's." You hardly ever get through a week at work without looking for someone who isn't there today because "he has a doctor's appointment." Translated, that means "forget it."

Major employers, like the automobile companies, report hundreds of thousands of lost hours each year because workers have to go to the doctor's office. Sometimes they may be out in the

9

woods hunting deer but people do get sick and have to see a doctor.

Most large employers have a company cafeteria, a cashier, a carpentry shop, an electrical shop and a personnel office but they don't have doctors.

Maybe large companies ought to rent office space to private doctors so that employees could go to the doctor and lose an hour instead of all day.

Some companies have medical offices with a consulting doctor who spends twenty minutes a week there, but I don't know of a company that rents space to private doctors.

If a worker who wanted to see a doctor could remain on the job until he or she was called by the doctor's office to come down the hall and take his or her clothes off, it would save years of time in hours wasted waiting. It would save time getting to and from the doctor's office in some other part of town.

Unfortunately, we are divided between people who call the doctor every time they get a hangnail and people who won't call one until it's too late for the doctor to help.

Doctors, like hypochondriacs, must occasionally get sick too. I wonder if doctors have to wait when they go to the doctor.

THE URGE TO EAT

No number of books or magazine articles detailing the kind or amount of food I should eat to lose weight will ever convince me that I'm not a person who is just naturally overweight.

I don't have a potbelly or great globs of fat hanging from me anywhere in particular. I'm just overweight. There's too much of me everywhere. Right now I'm up around 210. That may not sound bad but I'm not six-foot-three.

No one has ever been able to prove the extent to which we can alter the course of our lives by resolve. Nine times a year I promise myself to lose weight, but at the end of the year the chances are I'm going to weigh more or less what I weighed when the year started. That's if I'm lucky.

Years ago I remember thinking I had found the answer. I had read a good book by a doctor who taught at Harvard and he convinced me that the problem of weight was a simple one. You are fat for just one reason. You take in more calories than you burn. The doctor conceded that some people burn calories faster than others and that differences in our rates of metabolism make it harder for some to lose weight than others. The fact remains, though, he wrote, that if you weigh too much, it's because you eat too much. There are a few medical exceptions to the rule but they don't involve enough people to be worth talking about.

What the doctor didn't talk about, because he was a nutritionist and not a psychiatrist, was some faulty wiring in my brain and the brains of a lot of overweight people that affects the appetite. My appetite keeps me going back for more long after I've had all the food I ought to consume. Food keeps tasting good so I want more and am unable to control my urge to take it.

I hate to be in a room with cigarette smokers but I'm sympathetic to them. I've never smoked cigarettes but I understand how difficult it must be to give them up. If I can't give up ice cream, I've got no business feeling superior to someone who can't stop smoking.

There have been periods in my life when I've lost weight. I can overcome my urge to eat for short, intense periods when I devote practically my whole life to trying not to, but it doesn't last. Overeating is as much a part of my personality as blue eyes and wide feet. I can no more keep from eating too much over a period of years than I can change the Irish look of my face.

When I look at those weight charts in a doctor's office, I laugh. According to them I ought to weigh 145 pounds. They'd have me lose a third of what I am. I'll get down to 145 pounds the day the doctor starts making house calls for ten dollars a visit.

Many things about overeating are too depressing to contemplate. Butter is certainly one of the purest, most delicious foods ever made. It's made with such a wholesome and natural collaboration between man and cow, too. It seems unfair to farmers who have so much of it, and to good cooks who love to use so much of it, that butter should be high on the list of things we shouldn't eat.

Years ago I learned that bourbon was fattening. All alcoholic beverages are high in calories. It seemed incredible to me that two things as different as butter and bourbon could produce the same deleterious effect on the system. I recall wondering whether the fat produced on my frame by bourbon would look any better or worse than that produced by butter.

Everything about being fat seems so unfair.

THIN FOR CHRISTMAS

I'd buy a new suit if I wasn't about to lose weight. There's no sense buying a new suit and then having it hang on me after I've lost twenty pounds. That's about what I'll probably lose, twenty pounds.

Unlike some people, I know how to lose weight. I'm not going in for any crazy diets. I weigh too much because I eat too much. It's that simple. I'm not going to count calories or watch carbohydrates, fats and proteins. I'm just going to cut down on food.

It's time I did something. All my shoes seem a little short and not as wide as they were when I bought them and I think it's because I have more weight on my feet. The extra weight makes my feet longer and wider.

The only thing I'm going to cut out completely is ice cream. I may have a dish of ice cream after dinner tonight but after that, that's it. No more ice cream until I drop twenty pounds. Or bread. I know who makes the best loaf of bread in America and I eat too much of it. No more bread, either.

Another thing I'll do is cut out second helpings. When I'm asked if I want more, I'll be strong. "Couldn't eat another bite," I'll say.

It's the middle of December. The average person would probably wait until after Christmas to start losing weight but not me. Those people don't have any strength of character. I'm going to start right now . . . tomorrow, probably.

I read that it's a good idea to drink a glass of water before a meal, so I'll start doing that. Maybe I'll drink several glasses because I want to drop off some weight in a hurry. The kids will all be home for Christmas and I don't want to hear them saying, "Boy, Dad, you've really put on some weight since summer."

What made me decide to lose all this weight I'm going to take off, beginning tomorrow, is that for the second day in a row I popped the top button on my pants, the one right above the zipper. It might be that I just happened to get two bad buttons but I don't think so. Anyway, I'm not taking any chances. I'm going to make it easier on the pants.

For the past few months I've been wearing wider ties because my suit jackets don't come together and button the way they used to. The wide tie helps fill the gap so that people don't see a big expanse of shirt in front. Thank goodness I'll be able to go back to wearing thin ties again pretty soon.

It's going to seem funny being as thin as I plan to get. Some people probably won't even recognize me, I'll be so thin.

"You look great, Andy," everyone will be saying.

The least I ever weighed after I got out of college was 183 pounds. The most I ever weighed was yesterday when I hit 221 without even my socks on. I don't develop a great paunch that sticks out, I gain weight all over. Even my ears are heavier.

It's easy to see why a lot of people aren't as successful at losing weight as I'm going to be. They go for some crazy scheme that doesn't work. Not me. I'm going to do it the old-fashioned way and simply cut down on everything. After I've lost twenty pounds, I may write a book about it.

Come to think of it, later today I may call my publisher and ask if they'd be interested in a book about my weight loss. *How I Lost 20 Pounds in 20 Days*, I may call it. That would be a good title, give or take a few days.

15

It might even be a good idea if I started a diary the same day I start losing weight. Maybe I'll start the diary tomorrow, too, then I'll have the book done at the same time I'm twenty pounds lighter.

Of course, I don't want to get too thin. I don't want to look drawn. Doctors advise against going up and down too fast, so I don't want to overdo it. Maybe I'll have an occasional dish of ice cream. It might be better if I didn't try to get too thin too soon. If I lose weight gradually, it might be a good idea if I didn't start the book right away, either. I wouldn't want to finish the book before I'm finished losing weight.

RUNNERS ANONYMOUS

The company offered a free blood test a few weeks ago, so I went down to the medical office and gave them a little tube of my blood. Needles are a lot better than they used to be and you don't hear so many horror stories about nurses or doctors who couldn't find someone's vein.

Yesterday they called and said I should come down to the medical office to attend one of a number of group sessions they were having. They would explain the results of our blood tests, the nurse said, and it would take "about forty-five minutes."

If I drop dead of a heart attack tomorrow, I know what they're going to say. "He could have avoided that if he'd come down and talked to us about his results. He told us he didn't have time . . . and now he has all the time in the world."

That's what they'll say because that's what I told them. "I just don't have forty-five minutes to hear about my blood today."

The question is, how much time should we spend trying to live longer? There are certain basic steps we should all take but I don't have a lot of patience with people who worry full-time about their physical condition. The value of regular exercise has been established beyond any doubt but I can't bring myself to exercise for its own sake. If there's a purpose to exercising, like chopping wood or some friendly competition in a tennis game, I like it, but to go to a gym and lift weights or to run endless miles on the same path every day is something I don't understand. It seems to me runners and alcoholics are afflicted with the same symptoms of disease.

Anyone who runs regularly ought to be asked these questions:

—Do you run socially, or do you find yourself sneaking out to run when no one's looking?

—Does it bother you to go a day without running?

—Do you often find that you can't stop running once you start?

If you answer yes to all of the above questions, you ought to think of joining Runners Anonymous.

The trouble with trying to get your body in

shape is that it has more muscles than you have time to exercise. If you use weights, you can increase the size of your biceps easily but what about some of the obscure muscles? Most of our muscles aren't ones that need to be any bigger than they are. Big biceps look good on a man in a short-sleeved shirt but they aren't the most important muscles. If you use weights to give your legs more strength, the chances are you increase the size of the wrong muscles. The leg muscles we all need most are the ones we use for walking, and these aren't usually the ones we build with weights.

You run into all kinds of health nuts and all of them can make a good case for their particular form of health business. There are people who gulp down vitamin pills to ward off colds and flu viruses. There are the natural-food people, many of whom are very fuzzy about what is "natural" and what isn't. Spaghetti colored green with a little spinach is "natural"?

A medical expert on age said last week that it won't be long before the average life expectancy at birth will be eighty-five years. That's an amazing figure when you think of all the people who pull the average down by dying early. I like the idea of living as long as possible but I wish the doctors could work it out so that all our years are healthy ones, even if there are not so many of them as we wish for.

PSYCHIATRISTS

There are days when everyone in the world seems strange but me. I seem normal, average, regular. The rest of you are a little off center.

I was pleased to have my suspicion confirmed, in part at least, by an announcement of a study by the National Institute of Mental Health that reports one in every five people in the United States has a mental disorder of one kind or another. Obviously, they understate the case, but it's a start.

According to the statistical table of this $15 million government-financed study, 29,400,000 of you (not me) are at least a little bit off your rockers. It doesn't surprise me one bit. You should understand that among the Americans who must be suffering from some kind of mental disorder are the people who decided to conduct this survey.

Saying one out of every five people has a mental disorder is like saying the average person is crazy. The average person isn't crazy. He or she may act crazy sometimes but that's all part of being normal. The average person is average. If being a little crazy is part of that, so be it.

The first findings of this report were published in the *Archives of General Psychiatry*. The study, conducted by psychiatrists, was based on interviews with ten thousand average people. That's like having automobile mechanics take a survey on whether or not the average car needs work.

About a year ago, the people working on the study said that only 16.6 percent of us had a screw loose. This year they've added another two percent of us to their list.

The psychiatrists I've known have been particularly interesting and bright, but all of them have spent so much time trying to unravel the mysteries of the human mind that they don't recognize a normal one. They've done too many mental one-and-a-half back somersaults with a half twist. They've lost their reference point from which to judge normality.

Psychiatrists, like most medical specialists, see the world in terms of their specialty. The orthopedist sees all our ills in terms of skeletal defects that affect our posture, which in turn affects our digestion, which in turn affects our general health.

The heart specialist is worried about the old ticker. If you go to a thoracic surgeon, he's going to be most worried about the condition of your lungs. If each group of specialists spent $15 million to come up with a report on the performance of those parts of our bodies they were familiar with, our scores wouldn't be any higher than they were in the psychiatric study.

The practice of psychiatry has been a medical disappointment. Not a failure, but a disappointment. It held such promise, but now it seems likely it ought to be moved out of the field of medicine and be considered a separate science.

There's no question of the value of studying the aberrations in the performance of the human brain, but there's a big question about whether or not psychiatric medicine has been any substantial help to mankind in alleviating the ills it set out to treat.

If psychiatry were as effective a branch of medicine as surgery, we wouldn't have any alcoholics. The psychiatrist could find out what it is in a person's brain that drove him or her to drink and develop a cure. None of us would be overweight if we delivered ourselves into the hands of a psychiatrist if psychiatry was as effective as it once promised to be.

How much would it cost to find out whether more or less than one out of five psychiatrists have mental disorders?

THE HIGH COST OF CHEWING

First, I'll give you some idea of what kind of dentist I have. The last time I went to him he had to remove the old work another dentist had done to get at some decay under it.

"Boy," he said enthusiastically, as he worked away, "you've had some very good dental work done in the past. Whoever did this did a nice job."

How many professional people do you know, in

any field, who compliment the work done by anyone else?

It had been at least five years since I'd been to see my dentist. I'm one of those who doesn't go until it hurts, at which point, of course, it's too late. Many years ago I'd had a tooth removed toward the back on the left side. A bridge had been fixed to the teeth on either side of the hole and it was so strong and comfortable that I'd forgotten I ever lost the original tooth.

On my first trip my dentist took X rays.

"You may have to have root canal work," he said as he looked at the pictures.

I winced.

He got out his drill, stretched my mouth out of shape and started to clean out the bad stuff. Finally he stopped, inspected the crater he'd dug and said, "You may be lucky. It didn't go down as far as I thought."

He put a temporary filling in the holes and sent me off with a numb mouth and warning not to bite myself while the novocaine was still working.

Toward the end of the second visit, he was in my mouth with his jackhammer when he said, casually, "How are you going to pay for this?"

He has a naive, open way about him, and obviously this is standard practice for him. He doesn't just send you a bill when he's finished, he talks to you about it. They must have classes that address this problem in medical and dental schools now.

No matter how they do it, I'm always a little

put off when a doctor mentions money. I have such high regard for anyone in the medical profession that I think of them as being more concerned with my health than their fee.

"The company has a dental insurance plan," I said, trying to speak clearly with the vacuum tube in my mouth. "Do I pay you or do they?"

"Why don't you give me a check," he said, "and they'll pay you."

Sure they will, I thought to myself.

On the third visit I brought him a check for $1,000, which he estimated would be about half the bill. I forgot to bring the insurance form for him to fill out.

During the periods when his hands or his machinery weren't in my mouth, I talked to him about dentistry and money. I don't think he's getting rich.

"The money's in things like this bridge I'm making for you," he said, true to form. "I see a lot of patients who only have their teeth cleaned. There's no money in that."

On my fourth visit I brought the insurance form. He said he'd fill it out and mail it. The total bill was $1,972.

Because of Christmas and the time it took the laboratory to make the new bridge, I didn't have another appointment to see him for ten days.

On about the sixth day I came home and, much to my surprise and pleasure, found a check from the insurance company. I hadn't even paid him for everything yet and I was getting the check from my dental plan. The bad news was that they were allowing me $945 of my $1,972 bill. The remaining $1,027 was on me.

It's difficult to put anyone's income in perspective in relation to our own. We expect raises ourselves but are invariably surprised to find anyone else getting them. This skilled professional saw me six times and did a good, important job for me. I do have the feeling, though, that it must be easier for a doctor or a dentist to charge double when he knows that someone other than the patient is going to pay half the bill.

Medical insurance has probably done more for doctors than for patients. I'm not complaining, just stating a fact.

INSURANCE COMPANY ARITHMETIC

People in the insurance business are good letter writers. Every time I mention insurance companies and include some negative remark, I'm inundated with intelligent mail from them defending their industry. Insurance agents ought to understand by now that being attacked by people who don't like them is part of the risk they assume when they go into the business. Call it an occupational hazard. Of course, the average red-blooded American hates insurance companies. They have things arranged so they never lose. People in the insurance business ought to smile condescendingly at our negative comments and take our checks to the bank. With their money, why do they need our love?

In the past two years I had a good radio ripped from the dashboard of my car, which was parked on a New York City street, and a fender dented on my second car by a taxi in a minor collision. The cab driver left before I got his license number.

The insurance company paid me $778.64 to have the radio replaced and the dashboard repaired the first time. For the dented fender, which needed straightening and painting, the insurance company paid $437.46. It's unusual for me to be involved in two such incidents so close together.

I ignore a lot of mail from insurance companies because the one thing you can be sure of is that if they really mean it, they'll write again. I hadn't realized it but apparently my car insurance came up for renewal during the summer. On August 26, I received this letter from my insurance agent. He seems like a straight guy.

"Here at long last is the renewal . . . of the policy covering your two vehicles . . . ," he begins. "I apologize for this late delivery of the contract but we have simply had a very difficult time having the Insurance Company of North America issue this renewal.

"I must bring to your attention," he continued, "the fact that because of two losses that occurred this past year, both in New York City, the company has renewed this policy with a $500 deductible on the fire, theft and collision coverages."

No one likes to be thought of as a bad risk, and when I got the letter I was mad.

"In your letter of August 26," I wrote the agent, "you explain you had difficulty getting the insurance company to renew my policy because of what you called 'two losses that occurred this past year.'

"I wonder if you could provide me with the figures on how much I have paid in premiums since I've been insured with that company and how much they've paid us in claims?"

Well, sir, my faith in my insurance agent was well-placed. He didn't avoid a sticky question. He got the information from the insurance company and sent it to me.

Dear Mr. Rooney,
We originally wrote this contract back in 1982, and since that time you have paid a total of $9,379.00 in premiums to the company. Of this amount, $3,904.00 represents the cost of the Fire, Theft and Collision coverage under which both these claims have been paid.

He went on to say that instead of using the word *loss* for the insurance company, "perhaps a better word should be *incident*."

You see now, all you letter-writing insurance company people, that's why you are not much-loved in America. We rank you with funeral directors. We know we have to have you but we don't have to like you.

I paid the insurance company $9,379 in premiums during a period in which they paid me a total of $1,216.10 and they're reluctant to renew the policy because I'm a bad risk.

It might be interesting if everyone who ever owned automobile insurance checked into how much he or she has paid the companies compared to how much the companies have paid them.

What we need is some kind of seat belt that would protect us whenever we run into an insurance company.

NO INSURANCE ASSURANCE

There's no such thing as living without taking some risks, and if you take risks, the law of averages makes it certain that you'll lose every once in a while.

It's too bad we ever got the idea we could insure or assure ourselves against all bad things that might occur to us. The idea has created a legal monster for the court system and a financial monster of insurance payments for all of us. We refuse to accept the fact that some things happen to people for which there is no recourse. There is not money enough in the world to pay for all the sadness we suffer. There isn't gold enough in the ground to make everyone who has ever been permanently disabled feel better about it. And yet that's what judges and juries keep trying to do by handing out million-dollar liability judgments.

The insurance situation is out of hand. It's natural and popular to blame the insurance companies but it isn't usually their fault, it's our own. We have a disease that's become an epidemic called "litigiousness." The carriers of the disease are lawyers. There is a certain small group of lawyers who encourage people to sue any individual, company, institution or government that might conceivably be to blame for something that has happened to them.

Several months ago I bought a football helmet for a piece I was doing for television. I was shocked that the helmet cost $150.

Why was the helmet so expensive?

"About one-third of that price," the manufacturer told me, "is for insurance premiums. There are lawyers who go to high-school football games just to see kids get hurt. Then they go to the boy's parents and suggest they have a case against the school or the makers of the equipment for negligence."

The lawyer doesn't charge the parents a fee, instead he takes as much as half of any winning judgment. His interest isn't justice, it's money.

Ladder companies are frequent targets for lawsuits. There is a small company that makes ladders on a road I travel frequently in the summer, so I called and talked to the president. Who knows, I thought, maybe I can get rich. Three years ago I fell off a ladder when I did a really stupid thing that was totally my own fault. Maybe I can sue, I said to myself.

"Last year," the president told me, "we were sued by someone who fell off a ladder we made thirty-five years ago when my father was president of this company."

Ski resorts are charging twenty-five to thirty-five dollars for a lift ticket for one day because their insurance costs them so much.

In Yellowstone National Park, people can no longer hike on a quarter of the good trails and all the bears may be removed from the park because someone who was attacked by a bear on one of those trails is suing for millions.

Doctors in the United States hardly dare practice some areas of medicine because of the cost of malpractice insurance, and there are communities where a woman can't have a baby delivered because obstetricians have been forced out of business by the high price of malpractice insurance. Even insurance companies have been put out of business by malpractice suits. It's hard not to smile.

In hundreds of little towns, taxpayers are putting out more money this year for insurance premiums than they are for police and fire protection. There's something wrong there.

Jurors are handing out million-dollar judgments

every day. Twelve people, faced with the sad fact of one life at least partially destroyed by accident, usually vote in favor of the individual and against the impersonal company, city or institution. It's natural for compassionate people to do that.

The fact of the matter is, though, it is not the company, the city or the institution that is paying the million dollars. The victims are us.

II

REAL ESTATE

REPAIRMEN

Making arrangements to get work done on a house is full-time work.

First, you decide who you'd like to have do the job, then you call the number listed under his name in the phone book.

He isn't in. He's never in.

If his wife answers, you leave your number. She says he'll call back. He does not, of course.

Anyone who knows how to do anything has more work than he can handle and obviously doesn't need you.

When you finally reach him, he says he'll come over and look at the job Thursday morning before he goes to the job he's working on now. If he doesn't come then, he says, he'll come late in the afternoon after he's finished.

You wait around all day, and, as we all know, he doesn't come at all.

After several attempts, you finally get together.

The paint is peeling badly on the sunny side of our summer home, so we had a painter come over and look at it. We went through the same familiar dance getting him to come. When he finally got there, the estimate he gave us to paint the house was about half what the house is worth. I figure that to fix everything that needs fixing would cost us roughly forty-seven times the value of the house.

The painter hopes he can get at it by September. He's got a lot of work to do, he says.

The routine you go through once the painter comes is as predictable as the routine you went through to get him there.

"Boy!" the painter always says, shaking his head. "Who painted this last time?"

I always want to be a smart aleck and say, "You did, fella," but you can't kid with someone who's going to work for you.

"He must have used latex instead of oil paint," the painter says, picking off a big piece of peeling paint that I wanted left where it was.

"I dunno," he says, shaking his head. "You let this go too long. I coulda done the job a year or two ago for half what it'll cost you now. I gotta go right down to the wood. Look at those sills."

It doesn't matter what job you want done, it's always the same. Things are worse than you thought. I wanted two electrical outlets put in the garage a while back. The electrician came, looked around and shook his head just like the painter had. They all shake their heads the same way.

"Who did this job for ya?" he wanted to know as he looked at the wiring already in the garage. "If he'd done it right in the first place, this would be a simple job. I could do it for ya in twenty minutes, but look at how he's got this. I gotta do the whole thing over to give you them two outlets."

The first thing anyone does who inspects your house for repair is ask who did the original work. Someday, I'm going to drop dead when the man says, "Whoever did this for you did a beautiful job. He was a lot better workman than I am. Used better materials than I do, too. The way he's got this makes my job real easy. It's gonna cost you less than I thought."

At home in Connecticut, we had the kitchen fixed up several years ago, and there were quite a few nice, decorative tiles left over. Margie decided it would look nice if we had them put on the wall behind the kitchen sink in the country.

After several false starts, the tile man came to look over the job. It seemed to me that the job was so small he could have showed up ready to do it, not just to look at it, but he doesn't work that way. Whatever their work habits are, you have to go along with them.

He stood looking at the wall behind the sink for a few minutes, then he picked up one of the tiles.

"You got a problem here," he said. "See how the edge is on this tile? Well, when you try to fit that in here up against this part here, you're gonna have to cut them and that'll leave you with an open edge."

Sometimes I think houses should be built to evaporate after twenty-five years. Getting anything repaired is too hard.

THE HITCHHIKER

Six weeks ago I picked up a young man hitchhiking between two small towns in Connecticut. It wasn't like picking up a stranger on the highway, and I used to do enough hitchhiking myself so that I feel sorry for anyone trying to get somewhere without a car or money.

The young man told me he was going to work at a gas station on the other side of town. He had a regular job, he said, but he was trying to buy a pickup truck and needed some extra money. It sounded good to me.

"What do you do?" I asked.

"I work for a contractor. I'm a mason," he said.

It just so happens that for twenty years I've wanted to put down a layer of smooth cement over the rough concrete floor in the basement of my house to make it easier to sweep.

"How would you like to do a job for me in your spare time?" I asked.

Before I left the hitchhiker at the gas station he agreed to come to the house the following day to look over the job.

The next day, Saturday, he didn't show up.

Two weeks later, I had almost forgotten about him when he appeared at the kitchen door. We went down to look over the job and he sounded as if he knew his business. He asked for a hundred dollars to buy materials and I gave it to him.

"I'll pick up the stuff later today and drop it off here tomorrow," he said. "Would it be okay if I put it over there in the corner of the driveway?"

He was unnecessarily specific about where he'd put it.

The next day he didn't put it anywhere because he didn't come.

Ten days later I came home from work and found a five-gallon plastic pail of something in the middle of the driveway. It was to be used to make the new cement stick to the old.

Last Saturday he showed up in his new truck with a small load of sand, a shovel and some cement and went back to his truck with a piece of paper and pencil.

"Here's the whole thing," he said, after some figuring. "You owe me another forty-six dollars for materials and one hundred fifty dollars in advance for the labor." I gave him forty-six dollars in cash, all I had, and a check for one hundred fifty.

"I'll be here at eleven o'clock tomorrow," he said. "Is eleven okay?"

"Great," I said. "I'll move everything I can lift into the back half of the cellar."

"Hey," he said, almost as an afterthought as he started to leave. "Do you have a couple of aspirins?"

It seemed like a strange request, and I had the

feeling I was being set up for his failing to appear the next day. He was going to call in sick.

I got up at six-thirty the next morning and worked my tail off until eleven, getting the basement ready for him. I moved file cabinets, boxes of no-doubt priceless old papers, tools, high chairs, broken chairs, Christmas-tree ornaments and all the things that accumulate in a basement.

At eleven-fifteen I went upstairs to get a cold drink and looked wistfully out the kitchen window for signs of his truck.

At one-thirty I had some lunch and then sat down to watch some sports events on television. He never came. He never even called to use his aspirin setup.

At six P.M. I drove to the gas station where he worked. When I asked the manager if he still worked there, the manager shook his head with a gesture that said more than no.

"Did he cash my check for one hundred fifty dollars?" I asked.

"He tried to but we didn't do it," the manager said. He was still trying to tell me more than he was saying.

Monday morning I got to the office early. I couldn't wait. At three minutes past nine I called the bank and asked them to stop payment on the one-hundred-fifty-dollar check.

"The charge for a stop payment will be nine-fifty," the woman said.

"Stop payment," I said.

It's worth $9.50 to me. I don't think the young

38

man is dishonest. He's just one of those people who doesn't show up. Stopping payment is the least I can do for all the people who have waited all day for the guy who says he'll come at eleven and never comes.

Anyone want to buy a small amount of sand and some cement cheap?

"CARPENTRY FOR LADIES"

"CARPENTRY FOR LADIES!" the little headline in my newspaper said.

"Beginning Monday, a course in basic carpentry for women will be held," it went on to say. (I'm not clear whether it was the newspaper or the people giving the course that made the switch from "ladies" to "women" but the word "ladies," I feel, makes an editorial comment that isn't necessary.)

"The series of twelve lessons will cover the care and function of tools, how to make a toolbox, how to mend broken furniture and how to build shelves and storage units."

I've been a woodworker for thirty years and I'm plenty suspicious of that outline.

For one thing, "the care and function of tools" sounds like a bad start. You know perfectly well the kind of woman who's going to take this course. She's got a mind of her own. She's either single or she's sick and tired of being dependent on some guy she can't get to hammer a nail to hold the house together, so she's going to take matters into her own hands. She's going to learn how to do it herself.

This is no woman to give a condescending lecture on the function of a hammer.

I wouldn't spend much time showing women how to use a screwdriver or a quarter-inch drill, either. What I'd teach them about tools is where to put one when they were finished with it so they could find it next time they needed it. Finding the tool is often half the battle. Men have never mastered this art.

If I were teaching the course, "How to Build a Toolbox" is one of the last things I'd get into, too. No woman wants to learn how to build a toolbox. If she wants a toolbox, she can buy one. Making a toolbox is a make-work project for a man trying to avoid actually doing something. How to carry the tools from here to there to do a job is not a major problem.

There's only one important thing to teach women about how furniture should be repaired. My lecture would go like this:

"Good morning.

"Today we will take up the broken chair. The thing to do with a broken chair is this. First, carefully carry the chair to the driveway and put it in the back of the car. Next, get in the car and take the broken chair to someone who knows how to fix it. Ask how long it will take. On the day it's supposed to be finished, return with a great deal of money. The chair will not be finished that day. Keep returning until finally the chair is fixed. This is how to repair a broken chair. Broken chairs may also be taken to the dump."

Shelves, I concede, are something anyone ought to be able to learn how to build in twelve days. The most important thing to know when you're building shelves is that some books are taller than others and the chances are that once you have your shelves built, with one shelf separated from another by a fixed distance like twelve inches, you will almost certainly get a fourteen-inch book for Christmas.

Women who take up carpentry in this course should also be advised that knowing woodworking is not going to save them money, it's going to cost them money. If they add up all the money they spend on tools and materials over the years and then put a fair price on those, they'll find it cost them twice what it would have to get a carpenter to do the work.

Women carpenters aren't going to be any more satisfied with their tools than men are. They're shoppers, too. No handy home-repair expert ever has enough tools. If I have a job that would cost me $107 to have done by a professional, I look it over and decide to do it myself. The first thing I do is go out and spend $84 on materials and $137 on tools I think I'll need.

My final advice to women on carpentry is the same as it would be for men: If it needs doing, call someone and pay to have it done.

REAL REAL ESTATE

When the real-estate people talk about space in houses, they put too much emphasis on the number of bedrooms and bathrooms and too little on how much stuff the kitchen counters will hold.

If we ever have to move out of our house it would be because we've run out of places in the kitchen to put all the pots, pans and electrical appliances we've bought or been given for Christmas. Things are approaching the crisis stage now on our kitchen counters. I don't buy sliced bread, and it's getting very difficult to clear enough space to operate with a bread knife.

In addition to running out of counter space, we're running out of places underneath the counter to put pots, pans and a wide variety of culinary miscellany. When we had the kitchen redone five years ago, we made sure we had plenty of storage space for pots and pans under the counter, but that was five years ago. The pots have expanded to fit the space available to them and now we have more.

It's the odd-sized, odd-shaped pots and pans that are most difficult. There are things we don't use more than twice a year taking up valuable real estate under the kitchen counters but I don't know what to do with them. Where do you keep the fluted cake pans, the cookie cutters, a pressure cooker, Pyrex dishes, big baking pans for the turkey, a fondue pot, the cast-iron popover pan and the muffin tins?

We need double the number of electrical outlets on the back wall of the counter.

Let me see if I can make a list of the major items on the counters without going upstairs to the kitchen to look. The kitchen counters now hold: a toaster-oven, a blender, a heavy-duty mixer, an electric can opener, one orange-juice squeezer, a Cuisinart, a radio, one small black-and-white TV.

Don't tell me some of these items are repetitious because I know it, but if you're given a Cuisinart you can't throw it away even if you have a Mixmaster and a Waring blender.

In addition to these electrical devices, there are, below the counter, a pancake grill, a waffle iron, an egg poacher that hasn't poached an egg in twelve years, an electric fry pan, a deep fryer we never use and a small ice-cream freezer. Pushed to the back is an electric knife that I've only used twice although it was given to us by a relative who now has been dead for nine years.

It's apparent we need either a great deal more counter space in the kitchen or we need someone to invent a compact combination radio–TV–toaster-oven that would open cans, squeeze oranges, whip egg whites and mix cake batters.

I have my house, but my advice to anyone about to buy a new one is to ask some questions beyond how many bedrooms there are. Don't think you're smart because you've asked about the type of heating and the amount of insulation. Ask the real-estate salesperson some really hard questions. Ask, for instance, how much room is left on either side after you've put two cars in the two-car garage.

Have the real-estate salesman demonstrate how to put the vacuum cleaner away in a closet that's already full of heavy winter coats and leaves for the dining-room table.

Ask the person selling you the house where you're going to put the wheelbarrow and the snow tires and try to figure out where you'd hang the leaf rakes and the shovel.

Look at the new house carefully and estimate how far you're going to have to carry the garbage can to get it to a place near the road where the garbagemen will take it . . . then figure out where the garbage can is going to go when it isn't by the edge of the road. Measure the distance between the big outside garbage can and the little inside garbage can that you have to empty into it.

Measure everything and make sure you know where you're going to be able to store the screens and the screen door when you replace them with the storm doors and the storm windows.

AROUND THE HOUSE

Wherever you spend time, you get to thinking about the things you see. I've been spending the last ten days at home:

—We have a dining room but I'd almost always rather eat in the kitchen if we aren't having company. I was brainwashed by my sister when I was growing up, though. You don't leave a bottle of milk on the table, even when you eat in the kitchen. (Of course, you don't leave a bottle of milk anywhere anymore because milk doesn't come in bottles.)

—Scientists ought to turn their attention to inventing a better vacuum cleaner. Vacuum cleaners are absolutely unsatisfactory. Anyone who thinks he's cleaning the house when he's vacuuming is kidding himself. They're clumsy and inefficient. If they didn't make so much noise, people wouldn't use them at all. The noise they make gives the impression they're doing more than they are.

—Dusting has gone out of style. You don't hear of people dusting much anymore. Any one of my working daughters would laugh at the idea of dusting. Dusting is mostly just spreading the dirt around.

—Making a bed is an art that escapes me. Even when I try, I can't make a bed that looks good enough to sleep in.

—The soap they tell you to use in dishwashers has more to do with getting the dishes clean than the machine does. Dishwasher detergent is so strong that if you use it in the sink or in a dishpan, dishes get just as clean as if you use it in the dishwasher, and quicker.

—I always wash a glass before I use it after it comes out of the dishwasher. It may look squeaky clean but too often the glass tastes like detergent.

—Homemade strawberry jam is often a disappointment. It's either too sweet, too runny or it has an artificial thickener in it. Certo wouldn't call it artificial, but I do.

—I don't know anyone who makes homemade orange marmalade. If you do, don't send me a jar.

—We must have twenty-five chairs around the house but only three of them are comfortable to sit in. Someone went to a lot of trouble to make the one in the bedroom but I only sit in it for thirty seconds a day to tie my shoelaces.

—It's good if the lock on the door you use most works easily with the key to it. If it doesn't, it's a constant pain in the neck.

—All garages should be two feet longer and four feet wider.

—At some point, the radio gets irritating.

—People who eat out of deep freezers a lot don't eat very well.

—Clipping food coupons is the all-American time waster. Some people spend hours doing it every week to save a total of $1.19. They're working for about $.27 an hour.

—Making mayonnaise is fun.

—I hate it when we have people in for dinner right after the garbageman comes. It means we're stuck with a lot of garbage for several days.

—The trunk of the car is as good a place as any to keep an umbrella.

—It's pleasant to sit in the yard on a summer evening and have a drink before dinner but the news is on television then, so we sit in the living room.

—I hate cleaning the pan I've made scrambled eggs in. Fortunately, we don't have scrambled eggs very often. It's been pointed out to me that I'm not usually the one who cleans the pan if we do.

—We don't have the newspaper delivered in the summer because we don't want them piling up in the yard when we're away. As a result, I don't have the morning paper at breakfast. I read yesterday's afternoon paper or yesterday morning's. They're still good. I always hate to throw a newspaper out because I've never quite finished it.

—It's funny that you can't take a cold shower even on a hot day.

These are the kinds of thoughts that keep my mind off world problems.

THE STOLEN HOURS

Have we ever taken a vote on Daylight Saving Time?

Is there really great support among the American people for artificially taking an hour of natural light from the first hours of the day and adding it, instead, to the last?

Over the weekend I moved the hands on an old Hamilton railroad watch, two wristwatches and five clocks in various rooms of the house. I reset two clock radios and a timer designed to turn the light on and off automatically in the living room. (This is a convenience we provide for burglars. If they break in at night it will provide them with light so they'll be able to see their way around the house when we aren't home.)

Whose idea is it to steal an hour from morning people? It's obviously the idea of night people, that's who. It is a widely accepted fact that morning people are better, nicer, more ambitious and more honest than night people. Why, then, do the wishes of these basically inferior people of questionable integrity prevail over us virtuous morning citizens when it comes to this matter of time?

The very name, "Daylight Saving Time," makes me angry. Does moving the hands of a watch or clock in an arbitrary fashion save any daylight? It does not. Call it what time you like, the hours and minutes that darkness endures are as rigid as the revolution of the earth about the sun.

The month of April, up until the unfortunate time change takes place, is the most pleasant of the year for those of us who enjoy getting up in the morning. My clock radio is set to go off at 5:37 A.M., but in April it never got to wake me up. Morning after morning I awakened by 5:20 or 5:30 with an appetite for life and an urge to take a shower and start the delightful experience of living again.

Who are these people who are denying me this hour in the morning so they can add it to their night? Night people hate the morning. They're trying to cut it short out of spite because they hate us, too. We know their kind.

Night people not only hate morning, they don't even like evening much. The evil of the pitch dark of night is what they like. Why are they saving light for early evening?

If we have this vote and morning people win, we'll make some big changes. We'll get even. We'll not only eliminate Daylight Saving Time, we'll do just the opposite. We'll add an hour of light to the morning by moving the clocks back instead of ahead at this time of year. It will become light not at six as it does with Daylight Saving Time, not at five as it did with Standard Time, but at four, as it would with our Bright and Early Time.

With Bright and Early Time in effect all winter, we could rise in sunlight the whole year around. An unlit gray or black morning is gloomy, cold and unnatural. There's nothing gloomy or unnatural about a dark evening. That's what's supposed to happen as the day starts coming to an end. Sunset. The light fades and we wind down the day's activities and huddle by the fire with good drink, hot food and friends. Sunlight is not a necessary ingredient.

There's no evidence that Daylight Time does anyone any good. During the oil crisis in the mid-1970s, there was a movement to make Daylight Saving Time last twelve months a year in order, proponents claimed, to save energy. It turns out that Daylight Time saves nothing! It may cause us to use more energy. People often have to turn their lights on to dress and have breakfast in the morning because it's dark. In the evening they do more driving because it's still light out. Of course, they consume energy in their cars.

This is a case of morning people versus night people, pure and simple. It's time we resolved the Daylight Saving Time issue once and for all. Are there more night people than morning people? I cannot bring myself to believe that about the country I love.

Let's take a vote and then put the clocks back where they belong.

DIARY FOR A PERFECT SUNDAY

5:45 A.M. Awoke as usual. Realized didn't have to go to work. Went back to sleep.

8:00 A.M. Woke again to warm aroma of delicious coffee, bacon and hot muffins arising from kitchen downstairs.

8:15 A.M. Breakfast ready for us when I come downstairs. Fresh orange juice and one Sunday paper at each place. We don't have to fight over which parts of Sunday paper we get.

9:15 A.M. The maid clears away breakfast dishes. We linger over newspapers and third cup of coffee

9:15–10:00 A.M. All four children call from various parts of the country. None of them have any problems with anything. It's wonderful to hear from them and learn life is going so well.

10:55 A.M. Two teenage boys arrive at back door, as arranged, to help with odd jobs.

11:00 A.M. We clean out garage, wash and wax both cars and take a load of junk to dump. Boys rake leaves, clean out gutters and put grass seed down on few areas where lawn is bare.

12:45 P.M. Back in house to watch football game on television. Someone has prepared corned-beef

51

sandwich on rye bread for me and has put it on tray with ice-cold beer, which I take to living room just in time for kickoff.

4:00 P.M. After football game, which we win big, I lie down on couch and take short nap before awakening for second football game and some of last World Series game.

7:00 P.M. We have pleasant dinner, watch *60 Minutes*, read, talk politics.

10:00 P.M. And go to bed after relaxing day.

That's my Sunday diary as I'd like to be able to write it. How did it really go?

Sunday Diary for Real:

5:37 A.M. Music radio went off at usual time because I forgot to change it. Couldn't get back to sleep.

7:00 A.M. Got up. Went down to kitchen. Discovered we finished can of coffee last night. Had to make it with instant. Coffee poor anyway because our water's no good at this time of year. Oranges too expensive for orange juice. Have rest of unripe melon we cut yesterday. Terrible breakfast.

7:30 A.M. Go out to get Sunday paper in driveway. Not there. We stopped paper for summer and haven't started it up again. I go get paper at store. Gas low in car. Drive two miles to gas station. Gas station closed.

8:15 A.M. Sit down to have second cup of bad coffee with paper. Coffee's been thrown out, pot washed.

9:00–9:30 A.M. Call four kids, one after the other. All have problems with children, house, boyfriend, girlfriend or job. Who needs it? Got enough problems of my own.

10:00 A.M. Go to office in basement to answer some mail. Elastic part controlling typewriter carriage return snaps. Dig out old emergency typewriter, unused in several years. Needs new ribbon. Takes half hour to change ribbon. Interest in answering mail wanes.

11:00 A.M. Go to garage to clean up, throw out.

11:05 A.M. Realize dump is closed Sunday. Can't throw out. No sense cleaning up garage if can't get rid of junk.

11:10 A.M. Get ladder to clean leaves out of gutters for winter. Realize so many leaves still left on trees, only wasting time. Put ladder away.

11:15 A.M. Think about seeding lawn, raking leaves, washing windows, waxing car, greasing garage-door rails, replacing cracked pane in cellar window.

12:30 P.M. Return to kitchen. Look for something for lunch. Nothing good. Take crackers, old piece of cheese and previously opened bottle of Coke to living room.

12:45 P.M. Turn on TV to watch football game. Discover something's wrong with TV set.

1:00 P.M. Miss kickoff fussing with TV. Can't get picture. Take small black-and-white TV out of bedroom. Giants have one of their few good games and I'm watching on set the size of matchbox.

An honest diary would hurt too much to keep.

THE BIG SHAKE-UP

The President is shaking up his staff. He's moving people around from one job to another, taking on some new people and letting some others go altogether.

That's what I'd like to do. I'd like to shake up my staff. I'd like to move some of my staff members from the jobs they're doing now to new jobs. I'd like several of them to resign so I could appoint new staff members who are more efficient.

The trouble is, of course, I don't have a staff to shake up the way the president does. Bob Forte, Jane Bradford and I have each other. We've worked together for fourteen years now but we don't shake each other up. We each go about our business. That isn't what I want.

What I want is a staff of flunkies. When I say, "Jump!" I want people around me who'll yell, "How high, sir?" I want a staff of ten people who do what I tell them to do whether it makes any sense or not. Bob and Jane are troublemakers, always questioning me.

I take the train to work most mornings but several times a month I drive. Driving is quicker, more private and in some ways more convenient, but adding two hours of driving to the working day is too tough. I need a staff chauffeur. In his free time, he'd do the mechanical work on the car, wash it, fill it with gas and oil and keep the trunk free of debris.

My staff would include a live-in couple. The fellow would be a handyman. He'd be a combination carpenter, plumber, electrician and gardener. He'd shovel the snow and cut the grass. When something went wrong in the house, he'd be right there to fix it. When a bulb burned out, I'd call him and he'd change it. If it was in the hall, he'd get the ladder out of the garage and put the ladder back when he was done with it. He'd take the garbage out and bring the cans back in. I wouldn't have to do any of these dirty jobs. If the television set broke or needed adjusting, he'd know how to fix it. If the toilet wouldn't stop running, he'd adjust that.

The first job I'd give this staff jack-of-all-trades would be to build a new addition to our house. It would be a little apartment over the garage for him and his wife to live in.

His wife would be a wonderfully pleasant and able person who loved to wash windows, make beds, cook and do the dishes.

There would be at least one staff member who worked full-time on my clothes. This person would be in charge of making certain that I'm impeccably dressed. I'd always have matching socks, a clean shirt and underwear. In the morning my clothes would be freshly pressed and laid out for me. There'd be no loose or missing buttons.

Another staff member would be an accountant. He'd handle all my money matters. He'd make sure I had enough quarters when I left the house in the morning, and if I needed to cash a check for one hundred dollars for the weekend, he'd stand in line for me at the bank. He'd keep track of all my receipts for tax deductions and, in April, he'd save me huge amounts on my income tax by knowing all the loopholes.

I'd want a diplomat on my staff. It might be someone like a former ambassador to the Soviet Union who'd be willing to handle all my diplomatic affairs. The diplomat would remind me to call my relatives. He'd write thank-you notes for me and serve as an intermediary between me and my boss.

There'd be a staff doctor, a staff lawyer and a special staff security expert who'd make sure I didn't forget anything. He'd also see to it that the door was locked when I left the house. He'd handle all the keys. The staff security man would guard the house and take care of the dog while we were away. We don't have a dog now because if we want to go somewhere, there's nobody to take care of one.

After I had assembled my staff, I'd appoint one person to be the chief of staff. The chief of staff would do nothing but handle all the problems that came up with my staff, so I wouldn't have to worry about that, either.

Having a staff must be one of the reasons people want to be president.

THE LONG SHORTCUT

This morning I drove to work and took a shortcut. I got to work twenty-three minutes later than when I take the longcut.

Ever since I was a kid on Partridge Street cutting through the Mannings' orchard to get to Western Avenue, I've been using shortcuts that take longer. I'm always looking for that magic path that will cut travel time in half. It's a character flaw I share with a lot of other people looking for the same thing. We almost always find a different route to take but it's hardly ever shorter or quicker. Often the people who leave at the same time we do are already there when we arrive. It's one of the great disappointments of my life but I can't change.

There's something to be said for shortcuts, though, even when they aren't any shorter. A shortcut is more fun. It's more interesting and you're more likely to find adventure on one than on the road most traveled. There have been times when I've gotten off a six-lane highway just because I couldn't stand it anymore. Sometimes the road I get off on isn't even headed in the same direction I'm going. Driving on a highway in a heavy stream of traffic makes me feel like a canoe on the Niagara River headed for the falls.

When I drive from my house in Connecticut into New York City, the traffic often grinds to a halt because someone has a flat tire or there's road repair. When traffic jams up like that, I get off and make my way on local streets. Usually those streets bring me back onto the highway ten miles or so farther along. I can't guess how many times I've marked my position in the line of traffic by noting some distinctive truck or car. I get off, weave my way along the streets and avenues, making what I feel is good time, firmly convinced I'm beating the crowd. Nine times out of ten when I reenter the highway, I find my marker truck or car within a few cars of me. The driver has patiently waited out the slow-moving line of traffic and made better time than I have.

If you hold your shortcomings up to a strong light and look at them from every side, they have less of a hold on you, and I've done that with my propensity for choosing the shortcut. I think where I make my mistake is in trying deliberately to be different. It's almost always true that the way everyone does things is the right way to do them.

The road everyone takes is the best road to take. I wouldn't have the heart to teach that to a child but it's true.

Being different doesn't turn out to be much of a virtue. You have to close your mind to the possibility of new ideas most of the time. They aren't worth the time it takes to look for them, considering how infrequently you find a good idea.

Successful politicians have closed minds. They've decided what they think about everything. They know where they're going and how to get there. They're not interested in being diverted from their direction with alternative routes. The dedicated politican isn't distracted by detours or shortcuts that might temporarily look better to someone less experienced at getting where he's going.

Whenever I pass a school or college, I'm depressed when I look at the symmetry with which the cement paths in front of the school or around the campus are laid out. Kids are not naturally inclined to turn perfectly square corners. They would usually prefer to cut kitty-corner across the grass but the walks were laid out for them to go the long way around, and most of them go that way. It always seems as though it would make more sense if the contractor waited to see where the young people walked naturally and then, after a year, when their walking patterns around the school were established, laid his cement over them.

People who take shortcuts may get there last but they enjoy the trip more.

GOING NEWSPAPER WISHING

A painting bought in 1971 at a garage sale for twelve dollars by a Connecticut man, Andrew Rooney, was sold at auction yesterday at the Sotheby Parke Bernet Gallery for $647,000.

Rooney, who bought the dirt-covered painting because he admired the wood in the frame, put the painting in his basement. Several weeks ago, while cleaning out a storage area between the washing machine and his workbench, Rooney brushed some of the dust off the old picture and realized it was a genuine oil painting. Inspecting the grime-covered surface of the picture more carefully, he noticed a signature in the bottom right-hand corner.

The painting proved to be a rare early work by August Flambeau, the great seventeenth-century Dutch master.

Asked what he's going to do with the money, Rooney replied, "I'm not sure. Maybe I'll spend it staying two nights in a New York City hotel."

A homeowner's attempt to reposition a piece of flagstone in the walk leading from his home to the street led to an important discovery yesterday.

Andrew Rooney, a writer, lifted the heavy stone with a pry bar and was about to shovel sand under the stone in an attempt to level it when he noticed the corner of a metal box sticking out of the ground under the walk.

Rooney dug carefully around the box and, after unearthing it, discovered that it contained more than a million dollars in five-, ten- and twenty-dollar bills. He said there were also a lot of one-dollar bills he didn't bother to count.

Although the money appeared to be more than fifty years old, it was in perfect condition. After counting it, Rooney took his find to the local police station and turned it over to the sergeant on duty. Police officials said that if the money was not claimed in an hour and fifteen minutes, it would be turned over to Rooney.

Asked what he would do with the money, Rooney said he was thinking of turning it over to a home for tired writers.

———

In 1971, a local resident, Andrew Rooney, bought three acres of land in the northeast section of the state, thinking he might someday build a house there. Rooney paid $375 an acre for the land at that time.

Yesterday, the Acme International Machine Tool and Computer Corporation announced its plans to build its new $400 million headquarters complex in a two-square-mile area there. Because Rooney's three acres lie in the middle of the proposed construction site, work cannot begin until Acme can negotiate a sale price for the purchase of his land.

"I want to be fair," Rooney said when questioned by reporters. "I'm asking $125,000 an acre."

———

A Circuit Court judge has ruled that more than $2 million that has been accumulating interest in a dormant savings account for more than sixty years belongs to Andrew Rooney, of this city.

The money, which was deposited there by Joshua Reynolds, a second cousin of Rooney's great-grandfather, has increased greatly in value over the years because of the accrued interest.

A bank official said that just as soon as one of the tellers was free, the money would be counted. It is estimated that, with interest, the amount will exceed ten million dollars.

While Rooney never knew his benefactor, the court decided he was Reynolds' closest living relative. Asked yesterday how he felt, Rooney said that he felt good. He went on to say that, even though he never knew Joshua Reynolds, he felt that if he had known him he would have liked him very much.

Because of a little-known provision in the tax law governing such funds, Rooney will receive the money tax-free.

I read these stories, but never about me.

HOW TO PUT OFF DOING A JOB

February is one of the most difficult times of the year to put off doing some of the things you've been meaning to do. There's no vacation coming up, there are no long weekends scheduled in the immediate future; it's just this long, grim February. Don't tell me it's a short month. February is the longest by a week.

Because I have so many jobs that I don't like to do, I've been reviewing the notebook I keep with notes in it for how to put off doing a job. Let's see now, what could I use today?

—Go to the store to get something. This is one of my most dependable putter-offers. If I start a job and find I need some simple tool or a piece of hardware, I stop right there. I put on some better clothes, get in the car and drive to the store. If that store doesn't have what I'm looking for, I go to another. Often I'm attracted to some item that has nothing whatsoever to do with the job I was about to start and I buy that instead. For instance, if I go to the hardware store to buy a new snow shovel so I can clean out the driveway, but then I see a can of adhesive spray that will keep rugs in place on the floor, I'm apt to buy the adhesive spray. That ends the idea I had to shovel out the driveway.

—Tidy up the work area before starting a job. This has been useful to me over the years as a way of not getting started. Things are such a mess in my workshop, on my desk, in the kitchen and in the trunk of the car that I decide I've got to go through some of the junk before starting to work.

—Make those phone calls. There's no sense trying to do a job if you have other things on your mind, so get them out of the way first. This is a very effective way of not getting down to work. Call friends you've been meaning to call, or the distant relative you've been out of touch with. Even if someone is in California, Texas or Chicago and you're in Florida, call. Paying for a long-distance call is still easier and less unpleasant than actually getting down to work.

—Study the problem. It's foolish to jump right into a job before you've thought it through. You might be doing the wrong thing. There might be an easier way to accomplish what you want to do, so think it over carefully from every angle. Perhaps someone has written a how-to book about the job you have in front of you. Buy the book and then sit down and read it. Ask friends who have had the same job for advice about the best way to do it.

Once you've studied the problem from every angle, don't make a quick decision. Sleep on it.

—Take a coffee break. Although the term "coffee break" assumes that you are drinking coffee in an interim period between stretches of solid work, this is not necessarily so. Don't be bound by old ideas about when it's proper to take a coffee break. If taking it before you get started is going to help keep you from doing the work, by all means take your coffee break first.

—As a last resort before going to work, think this thing over. Is this really what you want to do with your life? Philosophize. Nothing is better for putting off doing something than philosophizing. Are you a machine, trapped in the same dull, day-after-day routine that everyone else is in? Or are you a person who makes up his or her own mind about things? Are you going to do these jobs because that's what's expected of you, or are you going to break the mold and live the way you feel like living?

Try these as ways for not getting down to work.

TILTING AT WINDCHILLS

During the terrible recent cold spell, radio and television weather reporters kept referring to "the windchill factor."

"The windchill factor" is a fitting phrase for our time. People like to use it because it sounds good, but it doesn't mean much. There's simply no way to put a number on how cold we feel.

It's typical of our penchant for overstating things. I kept hearing weather reporters say, "The temperature in Chicago is minus nineteen degrees but the windchill factor makes it feel like minus sixty-five degrees, so bundle up."

It's as though nineteen below zero didn't sound cold enough. We have to find some way to make it sound even worse than it was. That's twentieth-century hype. You can't just say what something is. The plain and simple facts of the matter don't sound good enough or bad enough. To produce the desired effect, we exaggerate.

Why in the world would anyone have to exaggerate a temperature of nineteen degrees below zero?

The final insult is when the weather reporter tells us to "bundle up." Does he think we'd go out barefoot in our shirt sleeves if he didn't tell us how to dress for below-zero weather? How dumb does he think we are? It's like the advice some mothers always give their children before they leave the house.

"Be careful, dear."

In all the history of children, telling a child to "be careful" has never made a single one of them any more careful, but mothers never quit hoping it will help.

Because the windchill factor irritates me so much, I made several calls to three offices of the National Weather Service in New York, Kansas City and Washington. My question to each of them was this:

"Does the windchill factor have any effect on the temperature at which water freezes?"

I got a variety of answers but there was general agreement that it did not.

"The windchill factor is a lot of garbage," the U.S. weatherman who answered the phone in New York told me.

That was the most unequivocal statement I ever heard a weatherman make.

"Then why are they always giving it out?" I asked.

"Because the television people are always asking us for it," he said. "It was invented by Admiral Peary at the North Pole years ago. No one used it for a long time and then someone discovered it and now they're all hung up on it."

In Washington they were ambivalent about whether water freezes faster if the windchill factor is lower. They said that if the water were in a bottle it wouldn't matter, but if it were exposed, the wind would cause evaporation and that would lower the temperature.

"The degree, though, is infinitesimal," they told me.

Your face feels colder with the wind blowing in it because the moisture evaporates from your skin.

Windchill reporting has become so popular for weather reporters in the winter that we can look forward to the reverse of it next summer.

"It's ninety-two out there, folks, but with the sun shining and no wind blowing, it feels like one hundred twenty-four . . . so wear light clothing."

None of us expects miracles from weather forecasters. We understand that it isn't an exact science. All we expect is a guess that is better-educated than our own. Nothing tastes as bitter or as sweet to one person as it does to another. No pain hurts two people exactly the same. Give us the temperature but let us decide how cold it feels. I expect that if you tell me it's five below zero out there, it'll feel the way I've always thought five degrees below zero feels. No amount of wind-chill factor will make it feel any different. And if I want to go out in my bathing suit, please don't tell me I'll catch cold. I never pay any attention to that kind of advice because I'm one of those kids whose mother always told him, "Be careful, dear."

HOT AND COLD

The weatherman on the radio this morning was saying how many degree-days there have been. He seemed to think it was quite remarkable so I tried to be impressed, but because I've never been clear about what a "degree-day" is, it wasn't easy. I don't even know for sure whether the windchill factor influences degree-days or not.

Because the thought of warm weather is so appealing when it's cold and the thought of cold weather so nice when it's hot, it's difficult to decide which is preferable. Most people prefer warm to cold but there's a lot to be said on both sides. I've made four lists:

Ten Good Things About Hot Weather:

1. No neckties for men, no stockings for women.
2. A jump in the lake.
3. Starting the car easily in the morning.
4. A cold drink with ice tinkling in the glass.
5. An air-conditioned car.
6. Going barefoot.
7. Leaving the kitchen door open.
8. Not spending money on fuel for the furnace.
9. A hammock and a good book.
10. Vacation.

Ten Bad Things About Hot Weather:

1. Clothes and sweat.
2. Getting into a car that's been parked and locked with the windows closed while you were in the supermarket.
3. Inertia.
4. Dripping ice-cream cones.
5. Panting dogs you feel sorry for.
6. A wet bathing suit.
7. Trying to sleep upstairs.
8. Flies and mosquitoes.
9. Air-conditioning electric bills that are higher than the ones in the winter when you had the lights on for Christmas.
10. Cooking.

Ten Good Things About Cold Weather:

1. A warm bed with a warm person next to you.
2. Working.
3. A hot shower in the morning.
4. The sounds of walking or skiing on country snow.
5. A wood-burning fireplace.
6. Being home after work and knowing you don't have to go out in it again until tomorrow.
7. A cold drink with ice tinkling in the glass.
8. Knowing the oil bill is paid.
9. Down jackets.
10. Shoveling a little snow.

Ten Bad Things About Cold Weather:

1. Getting out of a warm bed and a hot shower.
2. Zippers.
3. Putting on boots.
4. Starting the car and driving ten miles before the heater starts working.
5. The oil bill.
6. Postcards from people in Florida, California and Arizona.
7. Drafty windows.
8. Funny weathermen.
9. Feeling sorry for cattle out in the cold.

10. Having to pick up the kids at school be-
     cause they can't walk home in this.

Take your pick. I'll take cold over hot any day.

GARDENERS

There are things I hate about a beautiful spring day. Mostly I hate looking out the kitchen window and noticing how much work needs to be done on the lawn and in the garden.

I don't garden. I like the garden to look nice but I do not move a finger toward achieving that end. There are hard jobs I enjoy, but gardening isn't one of them. Ask me to carry the fertilizer from the back of the car to the side of the house and ask me to fix the broken handle of the rake, but do not ask me to garden. Gardening is for people with more patience and a better perspective on life than I have. When I do some work, I want to see results. I'm not interested in sitting back and waiting for something to grow. Growing is *its* problem.

We had our first great spring day early in April and I had a fine time. I went out early and picked up the newspaper in the driveway, sucked in the spring air, agreed with a passing jogger that it was a beautiful day and then returned to the house. I had another cup of coffee, read the paper and then did one of the things I like to do most on a beautiful day. I went down to the dark, dungeonlike basement. I took with me three pairs of shoes and a leather briefcase and spent an hour slathering them with a creamy leather conditioner and preservative.

Preserving leather in the basement is one of the many things I'd rather do than garden on a nice spring day.

People who like to garden have a superior attitude. I don't dislike gardeners but I'd be just as pleased with them if they didn't go around trying to make me feel as if I hated nature. I don't hate it. I just don't like to grovel in the dirt.

Gardeners make a big thing of loving nature but I notice they tear up as many plants as they encourage. They're awfully set in their ways about what's a weed and what isn't. Weeds, after all, are just plants that gardeners have given a bad name. Weeds spring from the same source of eternal goodness that gardeners worship. Why are gardeners so vicious with weeds? Have you ever seen a gardener attack a patch of weeds with the sharp part of a hoe? Gardeners like nature, but only if it's arranged according to their idea of how it should look. Give a gardener time enough and he or she will have everything looking as though it were made of wax.

I noticed one weekend that the crocuses were coming up all over town. There's nothing more attractive than those first flowers that poke their heads above the ground with very little help from gardeners. Once they're down there, they just keep coming up, spring after spring. They emerge unbidden, unraked, unfertilized.

The best-looking flowers are the ones growing untended along the sides of the road, in the fields or in the woods. Every time I see a field of wild flowers, I think of all the weekend waterers. They drag out their hoses with their expensive sprinkler attachments and spend hours soaking the ground around a small patch of growing things that they've spoiled rotten.

Flowers at their worst are those in a florist's refrigerator. They're as out of their natural element as animals in a zoo. I should think being a florist, unless you hate flowers, would be the most depressing job on earth. In a hospital, a doctor's charges usually get well and leave to live a normal life. Once a flower gets into a florist's refrigerator, its days are numbered. If I were a florist, I'd lie in bed nights thinking of all those unsold, dying flowers back at the shop.

Please understand I do not dislike gardeners. Some of my best friends are gardeners. Gardeners are admirable people just so long as they go about their business and let me go about mine . . . down in the basement, out of the sun.

GRASS ATTACK

It is the end of March, the grass is just sitting there, looking benign with the residue of dead branches and junk that was left on it when the snow melted. It looks so innocent, but already I can tell it's got something on its mind. It's going to start growing, that's what it's going to do.

Already there are splotches of dark green showing. A novice might think they were a good sign. A seasoned homeowner knows they're the first indication of the dreaded onion grass. The dandelions will come next. Everyone will say how cute they are, but to anyone intimately connected with the lawn, they aren't cute. They're a weed that should be wiped out just as certainly as the common cold.

After the grass starts to grow, some bleeding hearts will say it looks hungry. They'll say you have to go to the garden center and spend a lot of money on grass food. There are tens of thousands of people starving in the world and we're all getting ready to feed our lawns. I hate the very name *lawn*. *Lawn* is a weak and sneaky, namby-pamby word.

I'm not going to feed the lawn myself this year. I'm going to pay someone to come and feed it for me. It's a wonder people don't call the Red Cross.

These lawn experts come with big cans of chemicals and plastic tubes and give the lawn an intravenous shot in the roots. There are several places where the grass in our lawn always dies. I wouldn't be surprised if these people come up with an idea for a root transplant or an artificial root for our grass.

Any sensible person with a home would pay

grass not to grow if it would take the money, but instead most of us encourage it to get longer. Just when it reaches a nice height, we cut it off so it looks like a Marine drill sergeant's haircut.

This year I'd like to pass the word among my neighbors that I'm one of those nutty nature persons who thinks it's a crime against plantkind to cut grass. Or maybe I'll tell them I've taken up a new religion from the Far East and my religion teaches that it's a sin to cut grass. I'll kneel and pray in the high grass every morning. If my neighbors complain, I'll take my case to the highest court in the land, claiming that if they make me cut my grass, they're infringing on my religious freedom. If God had meant grass to be an inch tall, He would have had it grow to that height and stop.

I don't know how we got so caught up with grass and what our lawns look like. Grass is nice but it isn't that nice, and it's a lot more trouble than sidewalks, trees or bushes. If everyone in America decided not to take care of his grass for one year—not to feed it, not to cut it, not to rake and pamper it—we could start to pay off the national debt with the money we'd save.

The only place that grass grows easily around our house is in the driveway where we don't want it and in between the cracks in the patio. There's something perverse about grass. It wants to grow where no one wants it and it hates being where we plant it. If there's a flower garden near the lawn, grass loves to grow there.

Grass is a lot smarter than it looks, too. For instance, it knows when you go away for a vacation in the summer. It hates having you go away, too, and shows it. To get back at you for leaving, your grass lets everyone know the house is empty. You could put a neon sign on your front lawn saying NOBODY HOME FOR TWO WEEKS and it wouldn't be any more obvious that you were away than just the way the grass looks. Even if you get one of the neighbor kids to cut it, grass has a special way of looking when people are away from home.

I look out the window at that brown mass starting to turn green and it's as if I could see an iceberg coming down the street.

TO KILL A MAPLE TREE

Last Saturday morning I was making the coffee when I heard that terrible sound of the chain saw across the land. Someone was at a tree.

It was a neighbor across the street cutting down a one-hundred-year-old maple on the corner of his lot nearest us. Our house was built in 1886 and there are five trees like it on our property, so I suppose the tree was originally on land that went with our house.

This wasn't a good year for maple trees. The leaves on two of ours began looking dried and yellow during late August. I called the tree man and asked him to come and look at them. He said he would but he didn't. I didn't call him again. I figure that if the trees have survived one hundred years, they've been through all the droughts and floods and had most of the diseases that would have killed them by now. I like my trees a lot.

I liked the tree our neighbor cut down, too, even though it wasn't really mine. I say "really mine" because I think of old trees in a neighborhood as common assets that are not so much owned by anyone but shared by all.

The neighbor who cut the tree, with the help of another man who knew how, seems like a good fellow. I don't know him except to say hello to, but he has two nice little kids, an attractive wife and he keeps his place looking neat and clean.

The neighbor's house was built in what is really the side yard of another, older house. The two houses are much too close together because several years ago some real-estate sharper split the lot. We don't have zoning regulations that amount to much and when the zoning board makes a decision, it always seems as though there must be foxes guarding the chicken coop. It didn't seem possible that anyone would build a house on that lot but there it is, without a tree now.

At first I wasn't sure whether they were cutting down the tree or just trimming off some dead limbs. After breakfast I wandered out into our driveway, walked a little way up the street and tentatively approached the scene of the slaughter. It was apparent now that they were cutting down the tree.

"That tree's been there a long time," I said, trying not to sound unfriendly.

"It's in bad shape," the neighbor said.

"Are you sure?" I asked.

"I didn't want to take any chances," he said.

I saw the house he lives in being built several years before he bought it, and it's my opinion that his house is more likely to fall down in a high wind than that maple tree was.

By noon the trunk of the tree had been severed at its base. It was thirty inches in diameter. I looked at the wood, and obviously the tree had been eating that morning, sucking sustenance through its xylem and phloem. It was wet with sap and solid as a rock.

Just as soon as a tree is cut, I begin thinking of it as lumber. I like lumber almost as much as I like trees. It's the same dilemma I face as an animal lover who enjoys steak.

The man with the chain saw was cutting this beautiful wood, not into lumber but into fireplace logs.

It seemed like a little tragedy to me. I don't know why there are any trees at all left in populated areas. In a tree's lifetime there must be dozens of occasions when someone thinks about cutting it down for one inconsequential reason or another. It takes so little time to kill a tree by cutting it off at its base and it takes so long for a tree to grow to thirty inches in diameter. It ought to be necessary to get a permit to cut down a tree more than fifty years old.

The neighbor who cut the tree won't stay in the house for long. It isn't the kind of house you love and cherish. It's the kind you move away from when you have the money.

The people who follow my neighbor in that house will never know about the tree, but the house will always be just a little less because it's gone.

III

COUNTRY LIFE

NO ELECTRICITY

We lost our electricity late yesterday afternoon and didn't get it back until almost midnight. The lights often go out in the little town where we live in the summer. I don't know if it's our weather or our power company that's so bad, but when we have a storm, we invariably lose our electricity.

Last night, we got out the candles and the flashlights and started thinking about how we could cook dinner. It was cold and damp and pouring rain, so I lit a fire in the fireplace.

So far, so good. It was an adventure.

I'd been in my workshop all day and had sawdust in my hair and in various recesses of my clothing, so I started upstairs to clean up.

"Don't flush the toilet," Margie said. "And you can't take a shower, you know."

Our water comes from a well 350 feet down in the ground. Two years ago, we had a disaster when there was a brownout, not a blackout, and the motor at the bottom of the well burned out. That was an expensive summer. The first thing we do now with any electrical interruption is throw the switch on the pump so it won't burn out again.

I walked into the bedroom and, as an automatic reflex, hit the light switch. Nothing, of course. I changed my clothes in the dark and went back downstairs dirty.

"We might as well have a drink," I said.

"You'd better not open the refrigerator door," Margie said. "We've got a lot of things in the freezer we don't want to lose."

The only way to get ice cubes is to open the refrigerator door. The blackout was beginning to seem less like a camping trip and more like a flat tire.

Among the more boring people in the world are those who keep telling you how things used to be. I have old friends who can't stop talking about World War II or how steak dinners used to cost $1.75.

In spite of knowing the danger, I can't keep from remembering what it used to be like as a kid living in a house without electricity. My parents had a cottage on a lake, and during my early years there we had neither a telephone nor electricity.

We used kerosene lamps and candles. I'd still rather watch a candle burn than watch most of the shows on television, but for a kid, the fragile glass chimneys on the lamps were a terrible hazard.

The chimneys were stable enough sitting on a table, but as soon as you picked one up and started to walk somewhere with it, it began to wobble. I'd learned from sad experience that they were too hot to touch, so, when one started to fall, there was no way to stop it. I was always being bawled out for breaking a chimney that cost thirty-five cents. My mother said it wasn't the money, she just didn't like me being that careless. I think it was the money, though.

Every winter, Duane Irish, who ran the little local store, cut thousands of huge chunks of ice from the lake and stored them under a thick protective cover of sawdust in his icehouse. Three times a week in the summer, he came in his truck and put a block of it in our icebox.

Ice cut from a clean lake has great beauty compared to the little cubes produced in a refrigerator.

Last night, I decided to open the refrigerator door quickly and get a few ice cubes. We sat and had a drink by candlelight and wondered what we were missing on television. Margie filled in a few holes in the crossword puzzle.

For a while we considered cooking in the fireplace, but when we got to thinking of the complications, we gave up.

I called the pizza place in the next town. (I'm always surprised that the phone works when the electricity's out.) They said they still had power, so we went over there, used the plumbing facilities and had a pizza with a soggy crust and a bottle of bad red wine.

Not having electricity isn't as much fun as it was when I was a kid.

THE $371.49 ZUCCHINI

There are few things in life more satisfying than saving money by growing your own vegetables in a little garden. Last night, we had three small zucchini for dinner that were grown within fifty feet of our back door. I estimate they cost somewhere in the neighborhood of $371.49 each. There may be more before the summer's over. Zucchini are relentless once they start coming.

I'm just an observer when it comes to the garden. Except on the infrequent occasions that I'm pushed into service to carry some heavy bag of something from the car to the garden, I don't have anything to do with it. I look at it once in a while and say things like, "Your garden looks good," to encourage Margie, but except for helping to consume its bountiful harvest, like the three zucchini, I'm aloof from the whole thing. The store has everything I want and they put it in bags.

To estimate the true cost of the vegetables from the garden, you have to go back a few years and figure in labor and capital investment.

For the first few years after the garden was established, we got almost nothing from it. We had several late and wet springs, so it wasn't planted until early June. Everything was just beginning to come one year when the temperature went to twenty-nine in late September; that was the end of our vision of fresh garden vegetables that season.

The following year Margie decided that the garden, which is about fifty feet long and twenty feet wide, should be plowed by a farmer who lives within a few miles of us. He agreed to do it for the bargain price of twenty-five dollars. It took him only a few minutes to plow, but it must have taken him more than an hour to drive the tractor to our house and back over small, local roads.

The farmer said that the soil was too heavy and needed a load of sand tilled into it along with some good, organic fertilizer like cow manure.

Sand doesn't cost much if you have a sand bank handy and cow manure is a drug on the market if you own cows, but we don't have a sand bank handy and we don't own cows. The load of sand and the trucking cost seventy-five dollars. Unfortunately, the farmer couldn't come back to plow it in.

As for the cow manure, Margie found another farmer who would give us all we wanted but we had to bring our own containers. I'd rather not talk a lot more about this episode.

By the late 1970s the garden began to show promise. One problem still remaining was the little grove of trees that kept the sun from hitting it in the afternoon, so we paid a man with the proper equipment to cut down several of the less attractive trees. This operation ran us in the neighborhood of $150.

In the early years of the 1980s, Margie found a

good but expensive nursery within half a tank of gas of our house and she started buying plants instead of seed. She figured it would give the garden the head start it needed. I noticed that already she was edging closer to the supermarket.

It was 1981 when she had what looked like her first really good year. The weather was just right and the vegetables and the weeds were thriving, side by side. (I don't do any weeding because of my inability to tell one from the other in their infancy.)

We often went out to the garden in the evening, and to encourage her I would admire it. It looked as if we might have to get migrant workers to help with the picking.

That was a sad but wisening year. It turned out that the local woodchucks, rabbits and deer were also waiting. They apparently don't like their vegetables as ripe as we do because a few days before the vegetables would have been ready for us, the woodchucks, the rabbits and the deer moved in and had a banquet.

The answer, of course, was a fence. The fence is in place now. I don't know why banks don't give mortgages on gardens.

So, that's the garden report. If the weather holds up, we should have a tomato later this year.

KNOCK IT OFF, GEORGE

An open letter to my friend, George R. Cooley:

Dear George,
  You have probably been waiting for me to thank you for the twelve zucchini you left on our back porch last Saturday while I was in town getting the newspaper.
  Let me lay it on the line, George. I greatly admire the good things you have done with your money since you retired with a bundle from the investment business thirty years ago. You have made major contributions to the college we both attended and you have been one of the principal supporters of that fine organization, the Nature Conservancy. I don't know anyone who has done more of everything after he was sixty-five than you have. You're a person who could give rich people a good name. Because I do admire you and because I haven't wanted to jeopardize our friendship, it has taken me a long while to get up the courage to say this to you: George, we do not want any more of your damn zucchini.
  When we first met, I was just one of the boys who dated your daughter, Barbara. If we spoke at all, I called you "Mr. Cooley" with great deference and respect. After you retired, we all admired you for going back to college

to get your doctorate in botany. Some people even call you "Dr. Cooley." I don't but I am just as respectful though less deferential now. Please knock it off with the zucchini, George.

Your garden is the envy of all the weekend gardeners. There's no doubt you're good at growing things but you have an inflated idea of the desirability of your zucchini. I don't understand how someone who made so much money in the stock market by being alert to every little trend could be so unaware of the fact that zucchini are a glut on the market at this time of year. Does it have to show up on a chart in *The Wall Street Journal* before you realize that? A person doesn't need a doctorate in botany, George, to grow zucchini. We have more zucchini than we can eat in our own garden without having you leave yours on our back porch while we're out. As a botanist, why don't you come up with a weed killer that would inhibit the growth of zucchini?

Several times during the summer, you have put eight or ten zucchini that got away from you on the little table in front of the library down in the village. When it comes to zucchini, George, bigger is not better. I hate to be the one to tell you this, but when those giant zucchini disappear from in front of the library, you probably feel some needy family is enjoying them for dinner. Nonsense, George. No family in town is so needy that they'll eat a zucchini the size of a watermelon. What happens is that someone who doesn't want your feelings hurt takes them and puts them in the garbage where they belong.

Last week I met you at the post office and you were telling me what Barbara says in her zucchini cookbook about how to make soup.

"Cook the zucchini until it's soft," you said, "and then put it in the blender. Then heat it with chicken soup, milk and a few tablespoons of margarine."

Is this the kind of inaccurate advice you gave people when you were in the investment business? I looked up zucchini soup in Barbara's book and, just as I thought, she uses cream and butter, not "milk and margarine." If you were telling me how to live to be eighty-nine, that's one thing, but if you were telling me how to make good soup, you shouldn't have rewritten Barbara's book. I'd also like to point out to both you and Barbara that if you put cream, butter and chicken stock in anything, it'll taste good.

I know that you're a Republican and a strong supporter of the free-enterprise system, so it seems unlikely that you approve of government price supports for farmers, but I'm trying to raise some private capital in the community so that next year we will be able to pay you not to grow zucchini.

Sincerely,
Andy

UP ON THE ROOF

If I were writing a postcard to you while I'm on vacation, it would read, "Having a fine time up on the roof I fell off last year when I broke my ribs. Wish you were here—to hold the ladder."

It's true. Last July 29 was a day that shall live in infamy in my personal memory book. That was the day I fell off the roof of the small pentagon-shaped building I'm constructing behind the garage. I abandoned the project last summer because I couldn't swing a hammer without hurting and never got back at it until now. The building weathered the winter with just tar paper covering the roof.

I never roofed a building before and I'm never going to roof one again. Roofing is dangerous, dirty work. If I hadn't been covered with sticky tar, I might have slipped off the roof again this morning.

The problem is ladders. It isn't the fault of the people who make ladders. We ask too much of ladders. Ladder makers must get sued a lot because they paste little warnings all over a new one. I bought one this week to replace the old wooden one that broke under my weight last summer, and if I read all the warnings on it, I'd never climb up on any ladder again.

Most professional people use wooden ladders because they eliminate the danger involved with electricity, but a sixteen-foot wooden extension ladder is so heavy and cumbersome for one person to handle that I bought an aluminum one.

A tool is seldom just right for the job, and there's no ladder made for what I want to do. The roof is sharply angled, so I can't stand on it and work. If I put the ladder upright against the side of the building, it rests on the overhang of the roof and I can only reach a small part of it. What I have to do is lay the ladder flat against the roof and extend it, at an extreme angle, to the ground. Then I lie flat on the roof with my feet braced on one rung of the ladder. I depend on the feet of the ladder being dug in so they won't slip out from under me.

This morning, I was tippy-toe on the top rung, my body flat against the roof, wrestling a heavy piece of roofing paper into position when I heard a noise behind me on the ground. I had the hammer in one hand, a bucket of roofing tar in the other, the cutting shears in my left pocket and my mouth was full of nails. The noise I heard was Margie asking me a question.

"What should I do with this?" she wanted to know.

Fortunately for our marriage, I couldn't answer because of the mouthful of nails and couldn't turn to see what she was holding.

What I need is a full-time gofer when I'm working on a job. I don't mind being up on the ladder or doing a lot of heavy lifting, but I hate it when I get up on the roof and discover I left the hammer on the ground or find I need more nails. I need someone to go for them.

Laying roofing is easy enough until you come to the corners or the peak of the roof. On this five-sided building, there are five roof sections and five ridges, so there are five places where I have to stop and make some kind of joint. I can't seem to figure out how to do this. I gaze in wondrous admiration at every roof I pass these days.

I planned it as a little office for myself where I'd write and nap. I've ordered the telephone, I already had a little air-conditioning unit installed and last week I hung the door. Up until then, I had the opening boarded up with plywood. Hanging doors is safer, but not a lot easier than roofing. I never thought of so simple a question as whether it should swing in or out. It's a serious decision. My building is only eight feet long on each of its five sides, so the door will swing out.

I'm going to finish this building if it's the last thing I do and if I fall off the ladder again, it could well be the last thing I do.

I'd pay a carpenter to come and finish it for me, except I hate to be laughed at.

COMPLETED . . . ALMOST

When I started my vacation in 1983, I decided to spend a week or ten days building that little place out back of our summer house so I could be alone and write.

I am pleased to announce that just a little more than two years and several broken ribs later, that ten-day job is completed . . . well, almost completed. For electricity, I still have a fifty-foot extension cord running to it from my shop.

With the exception of World War II, putting up this building has been the learning experience of my life. I'd always taken buildings for granted. They had floors, roofs, walls, windows and doors, but it never occurred to me exactly how one was built.

Like almost everything else I've ever done in my life, I started without a definite plan. For some reason that is no longer clear to me, I decided to build a five-sided building, a small pentagon. The length of each side was governed by the fact that I could conveniently get eight-foot boards of heavy, treated timber for the base of the building in the back of my station wagon.

Problems began to arise almost immediately. I placed five heavy stones on the ground for the timbers to rest on and then started trying to figure the angle at which I should cut the timbers to make them fit together at the corners.

There are all kinds of devices that help a carpenter cut a 45-degree angle, but with five sides, all the miter angles in this building were 72 degrees. This is not a right angle, it is a wrong angle. I know now why most buildings have only square corners in them.

Don't ever take a door for granted if it opens and closes easily. My door is made of oak and it swings on two huge old brass icebox-door hinges I bought at a junk shop. Everything about it is great except it doesn't fit very well into the frame I made for it. I don't even know whether you make the door or the frame first. Whichever is right, I did it wrong.

Yesterday, with the construction finished, I went into town to buy some cheap carpet with which to cover the ugly plywood floor.

"How big an area are you covering?" the woman behind the desk at the carpet store asked. "How many square feet?"

"I don't really know," I said. "None of the feet in this building are square ones."

"What are the dimensions?" she asked. "Perhaps I can figure it out for you."

"It's a little less than eight feet on a side," I said. "About ninety-three inches, but it has five sides."

"Five sides! Oh, goodness. All the men are out on a job. I'm just answering the phone here. I fill in once in a while. Maybe if you come back tomorrow one of them can help you."

I ended up buying a few remnants of green carpet and they're under my chair now, but there are a lot of bare areas.

When I left the place last fall, there was a lot of work to be done, but the door was on and I thought the place was tight.

When I opened up last week, there was evidence of animal life everywhere. I took the cover off my typewriter and there were hickory nuts down between the keys where the chipmunks had stored them. There was the beginning of a bee-hive in the corner of one of the triangular windows overhead. There were mice droppings on the floor and three kinds of ant parading across my reference books. Obviously, a vast assortment of animal life thought I'd erected the building as winter headquarters for them. They'd all moved in. My family may laugh at this place but the animals love it.

It rained yesterday and you'll probably think highly of me when you hear that the roof only leaks in two small places. As long as I keep things out from under the drips until I fix them, they will bother me hardly at all.

I just hope you'll understand if some of these pages are a little damp and have tiny footprints on them.

SUMMER WITHOUT WALLY

What do I care that I won't be having as much fun this summer because Wally moved away? Fun is a waste of time, anyway. I've had plenty of fun. This summer I'll be doing something better with my time than just having fun with Wally.

Wally never said a word to me about moving. I had to hear it from the other kids on the street.

"Did you hear Wally's moving?" they said to me. I said I knew he was because I didn't want them to think Wally hadn't told me.

In the winter Wally lives in Washington, D.C., to be near the fellows he plays bridge and gin rummy with at his club, but every summer he moved to the same small town in upstate New York that we go to.

If Wally needed the money he got selling his house there, he should have told me. I doubt it, though, because he spent about an hour on the telephone every day talking to his stockbroker. I think he got free phone calls, too, because he used to be vice president of the telephone company.

We only met six years ago, but we've spent many hours together ever since, trying to solve the problems we each run into as amateur furniture makers. Wally says he's eighty-four but it wouldn't surprise me if he's lying about his age. Moving away like that without telling me is more like something someone eighty-five would do.

It was good to have Wally around when you were handling wood because he's about six feet, seven inches tall and still strong as an ox. There was no project he wouldn't tackle, either. Last summer he made a four-poster bed and a Queen Anne armchair with ball-and-claw feet.

When either of us had a question or when we were bored being alone, we'd stop by the other's house. Wally knew I couldn't help him, but he always flattered me by asking highly technical questions.

"What do you think they mean here?" he'd say, pointing to a sentence in his cabinetmakers book.

"Make the reeding template," the book would say in the section on four-poster beds, "by band-sawing two pieces of three-eighth stock to a contour that matches the cross section of your turning."

I didn't have the slightest idea what it meant but it never mattered. We'd usually decide to quit working for a while and go off through the pleasant, hilly countryside looking for small lumber-yards that might have some pieces of cherry, walnut or figured maple. We each have more good wood than we ever have the time or ability to make anything out of, but that never stopped us from going out to look for more.

We'd drive twenty-five miles to a lumber mill or to the backyard of a farmer with a saw powered by a belt that ran off the wheel of an old truck. We'd laugh, telling stories all the way there and back. It was worth the trip even when we never found anything we wanted but companionship.

That's all over, though. A thing of the past. Good riddance, I say. If Wally wants to move without telling me that's his business. Who cares? If I want a good laugh, I'll buy a joke book or watch television.

I've got plenty of friends. I'm not saying I have a friend just like Wally, but I'll make out. I like being alone anyway. What do I need Wally for just because he was good to talk to?

I expect I'll be getting a lot more done this summer without Wally wasting my time every day. I won't have to pick up his newspaper over at Bryant's either.

Last weekend was the first time I've been up to the country since Wally moved. I didn't even glance at his house when I drove past it. After all, it's just another house.

I'll see Wally again some day when he comes back to visit our little village. I'll be just as nice as pie. I'll even call him by his real first name.

"Hello, Wellington," I'll say to him. "How good of you to drop by. I gotta leave now. I'm going over to Sawmill Joe's. Have a nice day."

Then I'll climb in my car, drive off and disappear over the hill all alone.

POLICE REPORT

When the music and the news on the radio begin to get repetitive and I want some friendly noise in my workshop, I turn on a shortwave scanner that picks up police, fire and aircraft frequencies.

I listen most to a police frequency emanating from state police headquarters. People listening would have to be impressed, if they didn't already know, with how many problems there are all around us.

All I hear on the shortwave radio is the voice of the person at police headquarters talking to the officers out on patrol. My radio isn't strong enough to pick up the weaker signals from the mobile radios in the police cars.

The area is primarily rural. The voice from police headquarters giving information or direction to the officers in the field often has difficulty identifying the location of a trouble spot, because there are no street numbers on the country roads. Often it's "the brown-and-white house three houses on the left after you cross a small wooden bridge" or "up a small dirt road just after you pass the red barn on the left two miles west of the village."

Here's a sampling of the kind of trouble America is in:

—"There's a family dispute at the white house with red shutters just off Route 10. Subject left the house after a fight. Residents request to talk to a trooper."

—"Please proceed to the Great Escape Amusement Park in regard to a hit-and-run accident in the parking lot there. Accident occurred to a stationary vehicle. There were no injuries."

—"Trooper Walker, can you go to One Twenty-four Lincoln Street in Whitesville in regard to the larceny of a bicycle."

Five minutes later, the voice from headquarters returned to the case of the bicycle.

"Trooper Walker, disregard the larceny of that bicycle. Subject's brother has returned the bicycle to the backyard."

So much for crime on Lincoln Street.

—"Residents at Fifty-eight Morris Avenue request the presence of a trooper in regard to loud music from the house next door."

Loud music from a neighbor's house is one of a trooper's most persistent problems. I sense a generation-gap problem here.

There are many mysteries. In one sense it's more entertaining than a television drama, but in another it's less satisfying because you never hear the solution.

—"Occupants of disabled red Mercury report aqua-blue 1977 Ford pulled up next to them and displayed a handgun and drove off."

Why did the occupants of the aqua-blue Ford display a gun? Did they demand anything from the people in the disabled red Mercury? What happened?

—"There's a dead horse in front of a green house on Route 10 a quarter mile off the main highway. The horse is covered with plastic and cardboard. Please check. Complainant does not wish to be identified."

A lot of complainants don't wish to be identified. I suppose if your next-door neighbor had a dead horse out in front of his house and you called the police, you'd be reluctant to let the neighbor know you'd complained to the police, too.

—"Bud's Bar and Grill would like the presence of a trooper. An irate customer has just left there, but is returning with a baseball bat, possibly to do bodily harm."

The broadcaster dispensing information from police headquarters is usually a woman. She's faultlessly calm, cool and collected. She never changes the tone or volume of her voice. A barking dog gets the same emphasis as a body found in the bushes.

The language used by the police broadcaster is always wonderfully pseudolegal. There are "perpetrators" and "subjects." Perpetrators are not caught, they are "apprehended."

Most of the problems to be solved call for the state troopers to have the combination of the qualities of the pope, the president and 007.

For me, it's a great comfort to listen to so many problems I don't have.

LADY

It's the beginning of August, and about the end of my vacation. Next week I'll be back at work where I can relax and get some rest.

The animals around here will miss me, I'll bet. The mice who creep into the kitchen after the lights are out are going to find it slim pickings with no more crumbs on the floor.

There's a chipmunk at work just outside the door of this homemade "office" of mine. He's doing a better job of making himself a place than

I did. I've been watching him all month and he never stops what he's doing to go to the store to buy another tool or a piece of hardware. He keeps on working with what he has.

He must have built himself an underground apartment complex for the winter in the side of the small hill outside my door because he's dug half a dozen holes for entry and exit and then cleverly concealed each hole by pulling a few stones or some greenery over it.

I wish I could ask him some questions about his family and his lifestyle but you can't get much information out of these animals. As George Bernard Shaw said, "No matter how loud a dog barks, he can't tell you that his parents were poor but honest."

There are gray squirrels around but they're more nervous about people than chipmunks are. This chippie doesn't seem to mind if I stand five feet away and watch him. Occasionally he'll stop and look at me out of the corner of his eye but then he'll go back to work as though I weren't there. I like animals who trust people.

I don't mind mice although I don't share Walt Disney's enthusiasm for them. Why do they choose to live in my house? Why don't they build their own houses like the chipmunks do?

Squirrels are pretty to watch as they jump through the trees but they seem mean and I have the feeling they aren't nice to each other.

Yesterday Bob showed up to do a little job for me—Bob knows how to do things—and when he was finished he asked me to come over to his house in his truck to see something. Naturally, I went without asking what it was he wanted me to see because that's the way he put it to me.

We drove up behind his house and then walked up the hill into the woods behind it. Bob started calling, "Lady! Lady! Come here, Lady!"

I began to think that Lady, whoever she was, would fail to appear, but pretty soon there was movement in the brush and out came a brown-and-white fawn no more than eighteen inches tall. This was Bambi in person.

The baby deer came right to Bob and rubbed up against his legs. He reached down to pet her, then pointed to me.

"Go see him, Lady."

The tiny deer came to me on her spindly little legs. I'd never had more than a fleeting look at a deer. I reached down and rubbed her neck. She wasn't unfriendly but she returned to Bob.

We started back to the house with Lady following along behind us.

"This would be illegal if I had her in a pen or something," Bob said. "I wouldn't do that. She lives alone by herself in the woods. Someone from New York City killed her mother right after Lady was born, but she lived." (There was no way Bob could have known the deer was killed by "someone from New York City." It's a phrase people here use for anyone who's bad.)

Whoever killed the mother had left a pail of water and some hay for the infant deer. It was a strange gesture of compassion but Bob snorted at it.

"Lady couldn't eat anything but milk. She would have died."

I'm leaving the animals now. The raccoons will have to find someone else's garbage pail to tip over. The squirrels and the chipmunks can pick up the nuts from our hickory trees without worrying about the back door slamming. The woodchucks can have what's left in the garden. The bees can rebuild the hives I've knocked down under the eaves. I'm sure Bob will take good care of Lady until she's old enough to take care of herself.

I'm going back to New York City where the animals can talk.

WOOD

It was almost dark when I got to the country last weekend but I couldn't keep from going up to my woodwork shop and turning on the lights for a look around before I unpacked the car.

The sliding barn-type door rumbled on its wheels as I pushed it open wide enough to walk in. Even before I hit the light switch, I loved it. The blend of the fragrance of a dozen kinds of wood went down into my lungs with my first breath of the air inside. The smell had been intensified by the whirling saw blade as I'd shoved the wood through it the previous Saturday. The teeth had turned the kerf into tiny sawdust chips, and those thousands of exposed pores had been exuding the wood's fragrance while I'd been gone all week.

My shop is equipped with good tools but there is nothing merely good about my wood. The wood is magnificent. I've owned some of it for twenty years and will, in all probability, never have the heart to cut into a few of the best pieces.

I sat for a minute on a little stool in front of my workbench. It suddenly struck me as death-sad that in two weeks, three at the most, we'd close up the house for the winter and I'd have to lock up and leave my wood. It would lie there alone all winter, the great smell that emanates from it gradually dissipating into thin air without ever being smelled by a human being. Such a waste.

I looked at my favorite piece of walnut, the one taken from the crotch of a hundred-year-old tree.

"What are you going to make out of that?" people ask me when I show it to them.

Make out of it? They don't understand. It already has been made into one of the most beautiful things in the world, a wooden board.

Look at it! Its grain and the pattern of growth are as distinctive as a fingerprint and ten thousand times prettier. Its colors are so complex they do not even have names. Brown, you say? Are there a thousand colors named brown?

My production of tables, chests, chairs and beds has been severely limited over the years because of my reluctance to cut a piece of my wood into smaller pieces. I have nine cherry planks twenty-five inches wide, fourteen feet long and an inch thick. There are any number of things I could make out of them but I like them better as boards than I would as furniture. To me, they're already works of art that exceed anything I might make out of them.

I wish there were an American Society for the Prevention of Cruelty to Trees. Too many people are using wood to heat their homes. I hate to see an oak or maple log sawed into eighteen-inch lengths and then split for firewood.

A piece of oak or maple, walnut, cherry, even simple pine is more beautiful to me than any painting. From time to time, I've suggested we might replace some of the paintings in our living room with pieces of wood from my collection. I've had no luck with the idea.

It would be relatively easy to attach little eye screws to the backs of boards so they could be hung like pictures from the living room walls. I wouldn't trade my cherry boards for Whistler's Mother.

When I first began to like wood, I was attracted to exotic species. Wherever I could find them I bought teak, rosewood, padauk and a wide variety of mahogany. My taste in wood has become more sophisticated now, though, and I find those exotic woods to be out of place in America, so far from where they grew. Now I look for good pieces of native American hardwood.

A good piece of wood is beautiful and strong and it does what you wish to do with it. Do you wish to make a chair? A table? Perhaps you are skilled enough to make a violin. Maybe you want to build a house, a seesaw, a boat or a fence.

I turned out the light in the shop, filled the cart with the junk in the car and went down to the house. It's going to be hard to leave my wood for the winter.

IV

WORLDLY GOODS

THE GOD OF DINGS, DENTS AND SCRATCHES

The Greeks had a god for almost everything. Each one of their gods controlled one of the elements or some phase of life. Apollo was the god of poetry; Ares was the god of war; Poseidon was god of the sea; Athena, the goddess of wisdom.

I don't know whether the Greeks had one or not, but there must be a god who controls the dings and the little scratches, spots and dents that always show up within a few days on anything new I buy. Where else would they come from? Who else but an all-powerful master of imperfections could possibly put all these little marks on new things?

Last week I bought a new pair of shoes. Never mind how much they cost, I bought a new pair of shoes. On the second day I had them, I was climbing up on a small step stool to take down the electric clock in the kitchen to reset it. Somehow, as I stepped up, my left foot caught the underside of the bottom step on the ladder, and as I pulled it back quickly, it caught on a sharp piece of exposed aluminum. It made a cut in the leather of my new shoe that looked as if it was done by a razor blade. I've put polish on the shoes several times since then and the rip doesn't show much, but I know it's there and the shoes will never be new again. They lost their newness the second day.

I've never bought a new car that didn't pick up some little scratch or dent in the first few weeks. Everyone in the family says they don't know how it happened. It never happened when any of them had the car, they say. Obviously, it is the work of this god of dings.

My new neckties always get spots on them on one of the first occasions that I wear them. I recently caught the pocket of a new raincoat on the door of the car and it ripped about two inches of the pocket away from the coat.

"It'll be as good as new," the tailor told me.

Well, it will not be as good as new even if he does a good job. When the god of dings, dents and scratches gets through with something, it's never as good as new again. It's used merchandise no matter how minor the job he does on it may be.

It couldn't have been more than three weeks after I got my new watch that the ding god put a scratch in the crystal. It's not much, mind you, just enough to remind me that I no longer have a brand-new watch.

When anyone goes out to play a game of golf or tennis with a new ball, something beyond the power of man is at work. If there's a damp place on the tennis court with the tiniest puddle of water back in one corner, the ding god will draw the ball there as if it were magnetized. New golf

114

balls that are not hit squarely are marked for the rest of their lives by the ding god.

In our house, we must have several dozen plates, glasses, platters and things like gravy boats that were chipped when they were young. Whenever I go to the cabinet that holds the glasses, the ones with little chips out of their rims always seem to have worked their way to the front where it's easiest to choose them. We must have six whole glasses for every one with a chipped rim but when you reach for a glass quickly in the cabinet, chances are that the ding god will lead your fingers to the one with a nasty imperfection in it.

Once you have chipped or cracked a glass or plate, you can often go for as long as twenty-five years using it constantly without ever hitting it on anything again. The great god of dings likes to do his work early in the useful life of anything. That way he can chortle for years over what he's done and, at the same time, devote all his energy to chipping new glasses bought by other people down the block.

Today I'm wearing a new pair of gray slacks. I hardly dare move in them and I certainly don't dare have lunch. I feel if I can get past these first few days without having them ruined by the ding god, I have a fair chance of having them last for many years.

A WORLD-CLASS SAVER

There is a pair of crutches leaning against the wall opposite the oil burner in our basement. I'm not sure who ever used them. They've been there as long as I can remember. I suppose one of the kids broke something once or maybe we bought them for my mother the year she broke her hip.

No one ever used the crutches much, I know that. I was looking at the rubber tips last weekend and they're almost new. I suppose I've kept them because, in the back of my mind, I know someone's going to break something again some-day . . . me, maybe. They're an unpleasant re-minder of that possibility every time I see them, though, and I think I may throw them out. If anyone breaks a bone, we'll just start fresh with a new pair. Crutches cost about twenty dollars. It would be worth coming up with that when we need them rather than having these crutches star-ing me in the face every time I go downstairs. On the other hand, maybe I'd better keep them just in case.

It's this kind of thinking that makes me realize I lack the executive's decision-making ability. I hem and haw, never quite making up my mind whether to keep something or throw it out.

For example, I finally got at going through about five big cardboard boxes of scripts I wrote for a radio show with Garry Moore and Durward

Kirby. The show was on five days a week for ten minutes each day. I wrote it for five years, so you can imagine the stacks of paper involved. The scripts I have even include the commercials.

For twenty years I've saved these scripts with the five boxes taking up valuable space.

What am I saving them for? I thought to myself. In a hard-headed moment, I dragged a major plastic trash can down to the cellar from the garage and started dumping the scripts in it.

I needed help carrying the can upstairs, and when I finally got it out in the driveway for the trash pickup, I started idly looking through some of them.

Gee, I thought to myself, some of these are pretty good. Like most writers, I'm not my own harshest critic. Ten minutes later, I was taking the scripts out of the trash container and putting them back in the boxes.

This is no way to clean up.

Margie saves clay flowerpots. I hate clay flowerpots and, if I think I can get away with it, I throw them out.

She hates the coffee cans, old broken dishes, odd lengths of wood and the assorted junk I save, and she throws out any of them she thinks I won't notice. Sometimes there's been an undeclared war between us. If I find she's thrown out some of my treasured junk, I retaliate with her flowerpots.

The boxes of scripts are back down in the basement now, right where they were before. Saving them was part sentiment, part the practical thought that I might find a use for them someday, but it was neither of those that brought me to the point of putting them back in the boxes. What did that was something different altogether.

It occurred to me that for twenty years I'd kept them; for twenty years they'd taken up space; for twenty years they were part of my life. If I threw them out then, all the space they've taken and all the thoughts I'd had about them in those twenty years would have been for nothing. In that case, I might as well have thrown them out the day I wrote them. This is the kind of thinking that makes a saver. A good saver can always think of a reason not to throw something out.

Being, as I am, a world-class saver, don't look for those crutches in my trash can anytime soon, either.

PRORATING THE REFRIGERATOR

Just by chance, I hit on the solution to the problem of house clutter. It's a foolproof system for deciding what to throw out and what to keep. Here's the idea:

First, figure out how much your house or apartment costs you a year. If you own the house, include your mortgage, taxes, electricity, heat and repair bills. If you rent the house or apartment, add everything to your basic rent. Say your house costs you $7,500 a year.

Now figure out how many square feet you're paying for. It's easy enough. The simplest way is to multiply the length by the width of your house, and if you have two floors, double that. Say you have 1,500 square feet in your house.

To decide how much each square foot costs you, divide the money by the feet. In this case, it would mean each square foot of space costs you five dollars a year: $7,500 divided by 1,500.

Next, you estimate how much space is taken up by various items in your house.

The trick is to decide whether the rent for the space they're taking up is worth it. I first looked at the refrigerator as a test case. It probably occupies six square feet of floor space. (I'm not figuring cubic feet.) If it does, I should charge it six times five dollars, or thirty dollars rent a year. For the refrigerator, it's worth it. I don't throw out the refrigerator.

There are other items that I determine can go, in the cold light of these space-rental figures. For instance, there's an expensive little love seat over at one side of the living room. I've always hated it and no one ever sits on it. I guess that it takes up more floor space than the refrigerator. Prorating the cost of housing that couch compared to the pleasure it has ever given anyone sitting in it would certainly make the dump its destiny.

Many years ago, when the children were young and loved bad music, I bought a stereo outfit

119

complete with record player, quarter-inch tape player and AM-FM radio.

This stereo outfit, which looks classy enough, was never very good but it must occupy five square feet of space. In the past five years, it's been used ten times that I know of. On five successive Christmases, I've put a set of eight Christmas records on it early in the morning and played them through breakfast and opening ceremonies. The sixth time I've used it was once during the half-time of a Monday night football game when I got curious about whether the record "Hats Off to Larry" was as funny as I used to think it was when the kids played it.

I have assigned a yearly rental space of twenty-five dollars to the stereo player. Six years at that price is $150. It's been costing me about nine dollars a minute in rent to listen to a little music. I'm giving the stereo outfit to a charitable organization.

We've allotted more space to books we don't read than to anything else in the house, but books are not negotiable and they only take shelf space. You can't put a price on the pleasure books give you. I have books I know I'll never read again but wouldn't think of parting with. A big book like a dictionary takes up about one square foot of space. I'm willing to rent that much space in the house for five dollars a year for most of the books I have.

In my closet, I have at least four pairs of shoes that are perfectly good in all respects except they hurt too much to wear. They're on the floor in the back of the closet, which I concede is the low-rent district in the house. Nonetheless, they've been there for as long as ten years and must have accumulated at least fifteen dollars in unpaid rent. Figuring it this way, it's going to hurt less to throw them out.

Systematically, I'm going to assign a rental amount for everything taking up space in the house or in the garage.

I may get rid of that Flexible Flyer yet.

DECISIONS, DECISIONS

Dressing in the morning isn't one of my favorite things to do. I don't mind the process of pulling clothes on my body, but making the decision about what to wear is difficult. It isn't that I have a big choice because I buy so many new clothes. I don't buy many new ones but I never throw away any of the old ones.

There is a whole list of considerations you have to think about when you're dressing. It's work for a computer:

—What's the temperature going to be?

—Is it going to rain or snow?

—Are you going to be seeing anyone important for whom you'd like to look well-dressed?

—Do the clothes you'd like to wear still fit?

—Are there any holes, spots or missing buttons on the article of clothing you've chosen?

Sometime in the future every closet will probably be equipped with a little computer. You'll type in all the day's variables like temperature and who you'll be seeing. The computer will come up with what you should wear.

There are things to be taken into consideration when you're choosing what to wear that are hard to put in a list. For no reason that you can express in words, a coat, a pair of pants, a sweater or a pair of shoes is either comfortable or it's not. You have the feeling that you look better in some pieces of clothing than in others. It doesn't matter whether you really do or not. If you feel that way, it gives you a definite bias for or against those clothes. One of the worst things that can happen is for someone to comment when you first wear something, "That looks good on you."

That's a piece of clothing you're never going to get rid of. The person may have been lying to make you feel good but it doesn't matter. For the rest of its days, that's a special piece of clothing.

The reverse is true, too. All someone has to say is, "That makes you look as though you've put on weight," and it's the end of that suit or dress. American closets are filled with once-worn clothes that got a bad review from a friend on their first appearance.

I'm often biased for or against a jacket or pair of pants for some very small reasons. For instance, while I believe that zippers are an amazing invention, I prefer buttons to zippers every time. Completing the process of turning a button into the buttonhole with your thumb and forefinger is a simple, satisfying process. Zipping something gives me an angst. There's always the fear it will get snagged. I suppose they'll have battery-operated zippers in pants before long but I'm going to hold out against those, too. It would be just my luck to get caught with run-down zipper batteries.

While I change my shirt, socks and underwear every day, I'm shameless about wearing clothes that get ripped, torn or otherwise debilitated. Once I get a piece of clothing I like I keep it no matter what condition it's in. I don't throw away a glove if I've lost the mate, either. I know I'll never find the other one but I can't bring myself to discard a perfectly good glove. There ought to be an international one-glove exchange where people who have lost one could go to to find a mate for it.

No one would guess from looking at me but I spend a minute or two choosing a necktie every day. I have a clear idea of which tie goes with which shirt and jacket. It's not a random process at all. That's true with most people. They think they have some kind of a matching ensemble on but most of the time no one else notices.

Shoes used to be easier to choose when I was younger because I owned fewer pairs. In choosing what shoes to wear, it's essential to balance comfort against appearance. A lot of shoes that look terrible feel good on your feet. You have to decide either that you don't care what you look like today or that you're going to wear shoes that hurt your feet.

I don't know what the rest of the world does about shoes but I don't think I've ever discarded a single pair.

Who knows, I might find the perfect day to wear them.

IRONING

This morning I ironed a shirt. If you don't think that's worth mentioning, it's either because you've never ironed one yourself or because you're a lot better at it than I am.

There are jobs to be done in life that I'll never master, and ironing is one of them. I enjoy the idea of pressing something to make it look better but as soon as I start, I remember all over again how impossible ironing is for me.

They've never made a shirt that doesn't need ironing, no matter what it's made of. All "permanent press" clothing needs pressing. "Permanent press" is as inaccurate as "one size fits all" or "no-stick frying pans." One size doesn't fit anybody, and when I cook in a no-stick Teflon pan and spray it with no-stick Pam, things still stick.

It doesn't have to be a shirt, though. I remember trying to iron a bedsheet once. Here's this perfectly flat piece of cloth, free of pleats, buttons or irregularities of any kind, and I could not get the wrinkles out of it without ironing in more wrinkles than I was removing.

Ironing pants is even harder than ironing shirts. If I make a mess of a shirt, I can always put a jacket on and cover most of my mistakes. Pants are right out there in the open where everyone can see them.

The only really major change in men's clothing in my lifetime has been the elimination of cuffs on pants. It doesn't seem like much. But if the time ever comes when the fashion people decide it would look good for men to wear pants with two creases up the front of each trouser leg, I'll have several pairs of very fashionable pants. When I iron my pants, I almost always end up with two creases, the old one and the new one. I just can't hit that old crease with my iron.

I'm not at all satisfied with irons in many respects. We have one that is supposed to emit steam from little holes in the bottom, but at least once while I'm ironing, it gets some water it doesn't like and spits it out all over my clothes.

And who decided what shape an iron should be? I don't notice the dry cleaners using anything like they sell us to use at home. I can do the left side of the front of my shirts with the iron. It's when I get to the right front side, the side with the buttons, that I get into trouble. How do you get in between buttons three inches apart with an iron five inches wide? The pointy nose doesn't help at all. The only part of a shirt I can really do a good job on is the shirttail—and no one sees that.

The shape of an ironing board isn't any better than the shape of an iron. Most of what you're trying to press hangs over the sides and pulls wrinkles into the cloth you're trying to smooth out. Our ironing board is too small to lay a pair of pants flat and too big for me to be able to slip the pantleg over the end.

If I was a spy who got caught and my captors wanted to make me talk, the most effective thing they could do is put me in a small room with a pile of shirts to iron. Before the day was over, I'd crack and tell them everything they wanted to know.

DRESS SNEAKERS

Women have made progress in recent years in emancipating themselves from the silly, high-heeled, pointy-toed shoes with the paper-thin soles but they still have a way to go. Yesterday I went to a dressy business party in New York City and after it was over I came out the front door of the building in which it was held.

Don and Marilyn were standing there. Marilyn looked helpless. Don looked for a cab.

"I can't walk ten feet in these," Marilyn said, looking down at her high-heeled, black leather pumps. "My feet aren't too good anyway."

"So why are you wearing those shoes?" I asked.

"Every once in a while I have to dress like a lady," Marilyn said, smiling through the pain in her toes.

You are normally a particularly bright, sensible person, Marilyn, and I hate to be the one to tell you this, but that's a dumb statement. If you put on an item of clothing that hurts just because you have an idea it looks better or conforms to what other people are wearing, it's dumb.

I know that the farther a shoe gets from the actual shape of the foot it was designed to cover, the more fashionable it's considered to be, but does this make any sense?

Why is it that most shoes for men and women bear only the vaguest resemblance to the shape of the human foot? The more comfortable a shoe is, the more it looks like the foot it covers. That's why old shoes are the most comfortable. After it's been worn a few months, a shoe reluctantly gives up trying to stay in the shape it was built and starts to assume the shape of the foot that is jammed into it every day. By the time they're ready to be thrown away, most shoes are thoroughly comfortable.

About three times in my life I've seen a market for a product so obvious that I couldn't understand why some entrepreneur wasn't making it. If I were a businessman, there's a business I'd go into tomorrow. There is a great market available to the first company that produces a women's dress shoe built like a sneaker or athletic shoe. It would have the same comfortable, cushy rubber sole that athletic shoes now have. The only change would be in the uppers. They'd be the same shape but instead of finishing the canvas in bright colors with stripes and the name of the maker emblazoned on them, the sneakers would be fashioned instead of some material that women find acceptable to wear on their feet to a party.

All the makers of athletic shoes would have to do is substitute black silk for canvas or use some flower-patterned material for the upper parts of their sneakers so women wearing them would feel as comfortable in their minds as in their feet.

Cybill Shepherd was reported to have worn athletic shoes with a long evening gown to an Emmy Awards party. If her shoes hadn't been made with the gaudy stripes they use on sports footwear and if they hadn't had the name of the maker printed all over them, no one would have noticed. Hooray for Cybill Shepherd, I say.

Everyone has a wild urge to wear crazy clothing once in a while. We all have things in our closets that are different from what we usually wear. A dress, a pair of pants, a shirt or a hat can be anything that amuses the wearer. They can be too big, too small, too long, too short. So you look a little funny in them. Shoes are different. We shouldn't play with shoes.

Shoes should not be an item of fashion any more than the chair you use in your living room. No one should have to sit in a smart, decorator-designed chair that looks good but feels terrible, and no one should have to wear a pair of shoes that makes it impossible for the wearer to walk from here to there.

TYPEWRITERS

Buying a new typewriter used to be easy if you had the money. You went to a store that sold them, hit some of the keys to see which machine you liked best and then chose either the Underwood, the Royal, the Smith-Corona or the Remington.

Typewriters were invented to help people transfer information or ideas from their brains to paper. Those thoughts then appear in a neat and readable form and can be reread, sent to someone else or stored.

Royal started the modern typewriter revolution when it came up with its Magic Margin. By the 1950s everyone was using an electric typewriter they couldn't lift and typed faster than they could think of anything to say on it.

The advertising always suggests the new typewriters will help you write. No machine can help anyone write. The best a machine can do is stay out of the way. When I'm writing, I don't want to think about how wonderful the machinery is. Just put the letters I hit on the paper, that's all I ask. When a typewriter does anything more than that, it's intruding.

Electric typewriters are already a thing of the

past. Expensive old IBMs are collecting dust on top of filing cabinets in offices across the country. They cost too much to throw away.

The new typewriters aren't electric, they're electronic, and they begin to get dated the day you buy one. They have a brain all their own. They hardly want you around at all. I can't wait to read the first novel written by an electronic typewriter or a word processor without the help of a human. All the owner would have to do is press a key that says "novel."

Yesterday I spent several hours shopping for a typewriter.

"This one has a lot of good features," the salesman said to me. "Look. It tells you how to spell."

"I know how to spell and so does Margie," I said to him. "There are only two words I use that I can't spell and I'll look them up."

"Which words?" he asked. "Spell them."

"If I knew how to spell them, what do I need the machine for?" I said.

"Just start them," he said.

I could tell he wouldn't quit, so I gave him a word I always have trouble with, *occasion.*

"O–C–C–A–I–S," I began.

"That's enough," he said, and he entered it but nothing happened.

"You must have misspelled it," he said. "'Just give me the first three letters."

"O–C–C," I said. He entered those, punched

130

the "spell" key and up came "O–C–C–A–S–I–O–N."

"How did it know enough to do that?" I asked, impressed. "Why didn't it spell O–C–C–U–L–T, for instance?"

"*Occasion* comes first," he said. "Give me the other word you can't spell."

"*Surprise*," I told him. "I always forget whether it's with an *s* or a *z*."

He typed in the letters S–U–R and hit the "spell" key again.

The word *surcease* appeared on the little screen. He hit the key again and got the word *surcharge* and then, in rapid succession, *surcingle, sure, surely, surety, surf, surface*. It was more than fifty words later before it got to *surprise*.

"See," the salesman said proudly, "there it is: S–U–R–P–R–I–S–E."

"I could have looked it up in my dictionary a lot quicker," I said.

I didn't buy the electronic typewriter that spelled but when I got back to the office, I looked up *surprise*.

"*Surprise* or sometimes *surprize*," the dictionary said.

So much for timesaving typewriters.

I did eventually buy an electronic machine with a small memory, a lift-off erase feature and something called "word-wrap," which I believe means you don't have to hit the "return" key when you come to the end of a line. It may be an electronic marvel but it's cheaply made of tin and plastic. It wasn't for me anyway.

The trusty Underwood No. 5, on which I write at this moment, is sixty-five years old. If the new electronic typewriter lives a tenth that long, I'll be surpised/surprized.

TOOLS THAT ARE BETTER THAN WE ARE

Ever since the cavemen scratched pictures on their walls with sharp rocks, people have been inventing better tools to write with. I'm constantly puzzled by the fact that, while the tools are always being improved, the things people write don't get any better. The writing may even be getting worse. (Someone recently surveyed teachers to assemble a long list of books every educated person should have read. Not one of the books on the list was written in the last thirty years.)

The typewriter is fast becoming a thing of the past. Newspaper reporters, lawyers, students and office workers of every kind are using either word processors or electronic typewriters. I'm not even sure you call it "typing" anymore.

The basic difference between these new implements and typewriters is that the new ones don't operate on the principle of a key with a letter on it striking the paper through an inked ribbon. What you write comes up in lights on a little screen. If you want it on paper, you have to press another button to have it printed.

People tend to do the work that is easiest for them whether that's the work that most needs to be done or not. When I get up Saturday mornings, I'm usually faced with a dozen household jobs that seriously need doing. I invariably take the job that pleases me most, not the one that needs doing most urgently. It's apparent that inventors do the same thing. They don't invent the things we need the most. They invent things that amuse them.

There are dozens of new products that no one needs that have come on the market in the last few years. Most people would rather buy a new piece of kitchen equipment than learn how to use the basic ones they have properly. They buy elaborate kitchen gadgets to do the jobs that would be more simply done with a sharp knife. They don't bother to sharpen their knives or learn how to use them. Nine kitchens out of ten in this country have more modern equipment than a good restaurant in France.

Camera technology has gone far beyond the average picture taker's skill or need, too. Photographers are always buying new equipment that's better than they are. If they took a few days to study lighting, it would improve their pictures more than any lens they'll ever buy, but you can't stop them from buying it.

The new emphasis in cameras is on how easy

they are to operate. They cost hundreds of dollars because they're equipped with devices that allow people to take fair pictures without knowing a thing about photography.

I'm stunned by the advertisements I see for hi-fi equipment. You can spend several hundred dollars for just the speakers and thousands for the woofers and the tweeters. The rock music I hear doesn't seem to need any highly sophisticated receivers for anyone to hear the delicate nuances of its tonal quality. I mean, it's like piercing, man.

I can't help believing that modern audio equipment is better than the music people are listening to on it.

People are constantly buying sports equipment that's better than they are at the game. Last winter, I invested in a very good, expensive tennis racket. It hasn't done any more for my tennis than a word processor would do for my writing.

STARTING ANEW

I'd like to have new everything. I'm tired of this old stuff I've got. There's something wrong with all of it.

This morning while I was dressing, I realized my socks are a disaster. I must have thirty or forty socks. Not *pairs* of socks, just socks. There are only four or five real pairs left and some of them have holes in the toes. I think to myself,

"They're good enough for Saturdays," but I should get rid of all my socks and buy four or five new pairs that I could keep together.

My shoes are in worse shape than my socks, although I've kept them in pairs. It takes strength of mind to throw out shoes that look terrible but feel good. I'd love to dump every shoe, every sneaker and every old moccasin in my closet and go out and buy three new pairs of shoes, two pairs of sneakers and several pairs of loafers or slippers. It would sure give my closet a lot of class it doesn't have now.

I'm tired of the lamps in the house. The switch on one is broken so you have to twist the bulb to turn it on and off. The shades on several of the lamps were once yellow or white, but they're brown now from years of heat from the bulbs. I'd dump every one except the student lamp with the green glass shade. It would be a delight to go to a good store and pick out about twenty new lamps.

Last night in the kitchen, I noticed some of our dishes have seen better days. They used to be in sets of twelve, but down through the years three or four of each set have been broken and others are chipped and faded. I'd like to start over with new crockery.

There are books in my office and at home I ought to ditch. I see so many good new books I'd like to buy but don't have room for. I should throw out my old dictionary and get a new one. Yesterday, I looked for *polyurethane* in my old *Webster's New Collegiate*. The word isn't in it because it's a 1936 edition. *Zucchini* isn't even in it.

Some of the furniture in the house ought to be thrown out. Half of the chairs are either broken, uncomfortable or worn out, and if we threw away every one of them and bought new furniture, the house would look better and be more comfortable to sit in. I'm never going to glue those rungs in the dining-room chairs and it would cost more to reupholster the red-velvet chair in the living room than it's worth.

I'd like to start new with all the keys and locks I own. There are six mystery keys in my dresser drawer. I have no idea what they unlock but I don't dare throw them away. I'd like to get a fresh start with locks and keys.

My little telephone book could go. There are at least six names in there of people who have died and a dozen more who no longer speak to me, so I won't be calling them. A fresh start with a new telephone book would be good for me.

In my workshop, there must be twenty cans, jars and old cigar boxes with odds and ends of nuts, bolts, screws and nails. I can never find the size I need and none of the nuts seems to fit any of the bolts. I'd like to discard the whole batch and get neatly packaged new ones, all sorted according to size and purpose.

On my desk sits an old, cracked cup filled with pencils and pens. Many of the pencils are broken and their erasers are hard with age. The ink in some of the pens has dried up. I ought to dump all those shorty pencils and dead pens in the wastebasket. And while I'm at it, it wouldn't do any harm if I threw out the wastebasket and got a clean, new one.

With many of these items, I'm torn between practicality and sentimentality. Would throwing out all this stuff and buying replacements cost a lot of money? I suppose I'm tired of money, too. I've got hundreds of pennies in drawers and little boxes, and I know it's wasteful, but I'd feel better if I could throw all that change out and start all over with new dollar bills.

MENDING MOLEHILLS

You can buy a new one but you can't get the old one fixed. That's the crisis in America.

If your car needs a new engine, they'll do that for you, but if the window on the passenger's side is sticking, forget it.

You can get a plumber to install a new sink but don't ask one to come to stop a leaky faucet. You can stand a lot of dripping for the price a plumber gets for a cameo appearance.

If you want your old kitchen torn out and done over, there are contractors who'll do that, but don't spend any time trying to have the broken toaster fixed.

Every time I want to turn the light on or off in the lamp on the big table behind the chair I sit in to read or watch television, I have to crawl around behind the chair and fish up under the lamp for the switch. At night, when it's time to go to bed, I reverse the process and feel my way to the door in the dark. I should have an electrician put a switch by the door but it's too small a job to bother with. As a result, I've been inconvenienced by that light for thirty years.

The whole world is looking for help with the little things and can't get it. We need someone who specializes in fixing things that are too small to bother with.

We have a two-car garage and one of the two garage doors is hard to lift because the track the door rollers fit into is slightly out of line. Maybe it was banged with something. Is there someone who realigns garage-door tracks? Maybe, but it's easier to buy a new door or live with the reluctant one we have.

If I could find a tailor who'd sew on a button or take a few stitches in a jacket with a rip under the arm, I'd go to him several times a month but you don't bother a good tailor with things like that. Like everyone else, tailors are busy with something more important.

For quite a few years, we paid a man to cut our lawn. He used to do everything. If he saw a beer can in the bushes, he'd pick it up and throw it away. If a low branch on a tree needed trimming, he'd trim it. No longer. He doesn't do the little jobs anymore. In fact, he doesn't even cut the grass. He's hired a crew to work for him and they do it. They sweep in once a week, unload their machinery from the truck, give the grass a quick trim and they're out in fifteen minutes. Meanwhile, the hedge needs clipping, there are leaves that need to be raked and that beer can stays over in the bushes until Saturday when I get out there, see it and pick it up.

No one does small jobs anymore. The catch on my briefcase is broken; the pin in one of the hinges on the washing-machine lid dropped out; the decorative strip along the side of my old Ford wagon is loose and flapping; the upstairs toilet keeps running if you don't jiggle the handle; the pane in one of the cellar windows is cracked; the "s" on my typewriter is sticking; some of the grout has fallen out of the cracks between the tiles in the shower; the linoleum on the kitchen floor is loose over by the refrigerator. There are enough little jobs to be done that would keep every unemployed person in the world busy for life, but we don't seem to know how to get the jobs that need to be done together with the people who need work.

We can't even get anyone to repair the minor things wrong with our bodies. You can find a doctor to do a heart-bypass operation but if you have a bad cold or a flu virus and a 101-degree fever, learn to live with it. What we need is a group of doctors who specialize in ordinary illnesses. We could call them "general practitioners."

We have to do one of two things in this country. We've got to make things that can be fixed or start making them good enough in the first place so they don't always need fixing.

A QUARTER
FOR YOUR THOUGHTS

It seems to me I'm getting more nickels and dimes and fewer quarters these days, and the penny shortage is certainly over because at the end of the day I have more pennies in my pocket than I know what to do with. My dresser drawers look as though they got caught under the payoff spout of a penny slot machine. There are pennies everywhere.

We ought to face the fact that pennies are a thing of the past. It's gotten so I hate pennies. I've become increasingly impatient with small change of any kind. It isn't because I'm making more money than I used to. It's because there's nothing to buy with pennies. No one wants them. We ought to start rounding off prices to the nearest nickel. Even poor people don't want pennies. If a bum came up on the street asking for money and you gave him pennies, he'd probably throw them at you.

There was a time when a penny bought something, but these days pennies are just a weight in your pocket. They're the odd change produced by an eight-percent local tax and the custom of many stores to charge $3.99 or $19.99 for an article. In the company cafeteria I eat in, they're still saying there's a penny shortage and they ask us to help, but then they charge seventy-five cents for toast and coffee plus six cents tax, which comes to eighty-one cents. They end up having to give me four pennies in change on a pricing system that's their own. Why don't they help me with my penny problem? They could charge seventy-four cents plus six cents tax.

It's difficult to figure out a purchase so that you don't end up with a lot of pennies. At the gas pumps, the thing to do is buy gas by the dollar amount, not by the gallon, but there aren't many things you can buy that way.

I think the increase in the number of dimes I get and the decrease in the number of quarters have to do with the fact that New York Telephone raised the coin-box rate to a quarter. That alone makes a great difference in the number of dimes and quarters available in the area. A telephone coin box holds a lot of money, so much, in fact, that since they raised the price of a call, vandalism and theft of phone boxes have increased dramatically. Ten thousand phone boxes storing hundreds of quarters each for a week or more take a lot of coins out of circulation.

I called a man at the Treasury Department to find out exactly how many pennies there are in circulation. I have a lot of pennies around the house and office, and I thought if they were still scarce I'd dig them out and put them in circulation. I don't have to worry.

There are 50 billion pennies in circulation and they're making 14 billion new ones every year. There are a total of 90 billion coins out worth $7,750,000,000.

According to the Treasury there are 8 billion nickels, worth $400,000,000, and 16 billion dimes, whose worth you ought to be able to figure out yourself.

"Quarters are the workhorse of our coin system," the official at the Treasury Department told me. "There are 13 billion quarters out, worth $3,250,000,000. The games and the machines take a lot of quarters," he said.

There are so few fifty-cent pieces and dollar coins out that the Treasury Department doesn't even try to keep track of them. I don't know why that is. Few things are more satisfying than to have a fifty-cent piece in your pocket. It feels real and important, as though it was worth something. I'd certainly rather have two fifty-cent pieces than one paper dollar.

It's a good feeling to have a little money in your pocket. At best, it's a mixture of bills and coins. If I have three ones, a five-dollar bill, a ten, two twenties and the weight provided by $2.50 in coins, I feel ready for anything.

If I reach in my pocket to pay for something and pull out a handful of change that turns out to be mostly pennies, I get discouraged about life.

OUTBOARD AND OVERBOARD

Just when I begin to think I'm making a nice, comfortable amount of money, the National Boat Show comes to New York. I go to it. I look at the forty-foot sailboats and the yachts with two luxurious staterooms, a hot-water shower, two bathrooms, known in nautical talk as "heads," and an ice maker, and I realize that, compared to the people who buy these toys, I should be applying for food stamps.

At every display in the boat show, there is literature describing the boat or nautical equipment in great detail. The only brochure I've never seen is one describing how you get the money to pay for one of these boats.

The "Super Sport" is forty-four feet long and sells for a special boat-show price of only $318,000. That's with air-conditioning, of course. You wouldn't want a cheap boat that wasn't air-conditioned, would you, sailor?

I'm always surprised to see a boat that's air-conditioned because I thought the point of a boat was to get out into the open air.

The "Ericson 38" is a "sloop-rigged performance cruiser with a suggested list price of $91,200." How does that suggestion grab you, sailor?

143

Our family spends a lot of time on a lake in New York State in the summer. We own two wooden canoes, a Sunfish and a clinker-built twenty-foot Lyman inboard. The Lyman, a nice, wide wooden boat that can go about twenty miles an hour, was made in 1959.

Last summer the Lyman sprung a serious leak and when we had it pulled out, the boatyard people said we'd probably get through the summer with it but that the mahogany planking was soft and spongy, and the bottom should be replaced. It's an expensive job and I had it in mind when I went to the boat show.

I finally spotted one fiberglass runabout that looked practical. You can't buy a wooden boat anymore so I've conceded that if I ever buy a new boat it will have to be fiberglass or plastic.

The boat I was checking out had somewhat the same lines as the Lyman, no cabin or anything like that, just an open cockpit with seating for six or seven. It was simple and practical-looking.

"How much does this go for?" I asked the man tending the display.

"Beauty, isn't she?" the man said. "The special boat-show price is twenty-seven."

I don't know how much I expected the boat to cost but I was slowly comprehending and I stopped myself at the last instant from saying, "Twenty-seven what?"

He meant $27,000, of course.

I realized at that moment that I was only a window-shopper at the boat show.

The one thing that caught my attention more than any other this year wasn't the Formula or Cigarette boats that cruise at one hundred miles an hour and sell for something like $120,000 or the two-engined Donzi, which may be able to pass either one, for all I know. The eye-catcher was Evinrude's six-hundred-pound, three-hundred-horsepower V-8 outboard motor.

I stood, entranced. The memory of my first four-horsepower Johnson outboard came flooding back to me. I used to clamp it on the back of our rowboat and travel all over the lake with it, except on the days that my grandfather wanted to use the rowboat for fishing.

In those days you started all outboards by wrapping a rope with a wooden handle around the flywheel and pulling as fast as your strength allowed.

My first outboard accounted for one of the saddest days in my life. I clamped it on the back of the rowboat too hurriedly one day. Out on the lake I made a sharp turn, the engine kicked up, the clamps pulled loose from the transom and the joy of my young life plummeted thirty feet to the bottom of the lake. I envisioned this six-hundred-pound monster plummeting to the bottom of some lake or the ocean floor when its clamps came loose.

I like boats but all but a very few people tire quickly of boats as toys. It accounts for why many of those grand boats at the boat show will spend most of their lives motionless, empty and moored to a dock, some with their air-conditioning on.

RECREATIONAL SHOPPING

The other day one of those newspaper columns that gives advice on how to lose weight, make money and live happily ever after gave some suggestions on how to stay within a budget when we're shopping.

The suggestions were to shop alone, stick to a list and not to shop for food when we're hungry.

The only part I accept is the advice to shop alone. I like to shop alone because I don't want to move through a store at anyone else's pace. If an aisle doesn't interest me, I cruise through it with my shopping cart at the speed limit. I don't want to stand around staring at detergents with someone who's turned on by detergents. Shopping alone is the only way to go.

The person who wrote the column suggesting we buy only what is on our lists doesn't understand that shopping is recreation in America. Recreational shopping is more popular than television or the movies. Anyone who thinks we go to the store for the single purpose of getting food enough to keep from starving to death doesn't understand us.

Some of the easiest, cheapest fun I have is shopping. Often I don't even buy anything and I can spend as little or as much time as I wish. I can shop for twenty minutes or three hours.

On Saturdays I often do some chores around the house for as long as I can stand it and then I announce that "I have to go out."

"Where are you going?"

"I have to go to the store."

Well, I don't "have to" at all, of course. It's just that I'm tired of what I'm doing and want to take a break and get out where the action is. If this house in which I sit writing were suddenly transplanted to a remote wilderness area, we could survive in it for months with what we have in the refrigerator and on the shelves.

Last weekend I "went to the store" five different times. If I hadn't gone at all it wouldn't have mattered. I went twice to the supermarket, twice to the hardware store and once to a big clothing store.

On the first trip to the supermarket, I did have a list of seven items and I went to the hardware store specifically to get one type of screw. I went to the clothing store because I'd convinced myself I needed new socks.

Let me try to recall what I bought. The following items were strictly recreational purchases, acquired more for pleasure of acquisition than for need.

At the supermarket I bought a bag of walnuts, a pint of sour cream, a half-pound of dried apricots and a bottle of imported olive oil. Hardly items critical to survival.

As much as I enjoy shopping for food, it doesn't compare with the pleasure I get from going to the hardware store. My shop is filled with things I've bought just for fun over the years. I have tricky tools and gadgets lying around everywhere. It may sound as though I'm a spoiled kid with too much money but I spend less and get more pleasure out of a little recreational shopping than most women spend on cosmetics or some men spend on golf, a boat or bowling.

The biggest kick I get out of my hardware collection is looking at what I paid for the items last year and the year before compared to what they cost today. Saturday I came across one of those three-prong adapters I'd bought two years ago for an electrical outlet. It was still in the bag and was marked fifteen cents. Later that day I went to the same hardware store and they'd packaged two of those adapters in plastic and marked them $2.50. It made me feel all over pleased for having bought the one I didn't need several years ago. This is my idea of a good time.

At the clothing store I forgot to buy the socks I went there for but I came home with a new waterproof nylon jacket, a leather belt and two sports shirts.

I wonder what fun the lady has who wrote the column giving advice on how to avoid buying things.

ANTIQUES

Either antique shops aren't as antique as they used to be or I'm more antique. The other day I stopped in several places along a quiet country road and I was surprised to see what the owners considered old enough to qualify as antique. If you can still buy whatever it is now, it isn't old enough.

One place had a collection of glass milk bottles they were calling antiques. Now, I realize paper cartons replaced glass milk bottles about the time they started homogenizing milk, but are glass milk bottles antiques? I think they're more a sign of the times. Replacing glass with something you can't see through is a great advantage to anyone selling a product they'd rather you didn't see until you got it home.

Next to the milk bottles were six or eight little green Coke bottles. I'm reluctant to tell you I bought two of them for seventy-five cents each. For most of its life, Coca-Cola was sold either at the soda fountain or in one of those little bottles. There were no cans and no bigger bottles. I bought those two because I always liked them and they're collector's items. The decline of the Coca-Cola Company in relation to Pepsi can be dated, in my mind anyway, to the day Coke abandoned them.

I'm sympathetic to antique dealers who are trying to make a living. You can't expect them to have only fine old Early American chests of drawers or Chippendale dining chairs made in the late 1700s, but when they start passing off items as antiques that were made after I was old enough to vote, I object.

There's a fine line between an antique shop and a junk shop. I like junk shops as long as they don't have pretensions about being antique. Old, empty Prince Albert tobacco cans belong in a junk shop, as do wooden cigar boxes that date from the 1950s. In the same genre are the empty tin candy boxes that some candy makers used to sell their chocolate in. You often see that lavender Louis Sherry box for sale as an antique but the fact is, Louis Sherry still sells its candy in the same box. That disqualifies it as an antique.

The other item often featured in the junk shop posing as an antique is a box of old 78 RPM phonograph records. They're a sign of their times, but are they antiques? I know Guy Lombardo and His Royal Canadians are a thing of the past but I can't imagine anyone wanting to save any of their scratched old recordings.

Anyone more than forty years old has one dominating thought when he or she goes into one of these places and starts looking at the prices they're getting for old toys, Ball jars, hula hoops, Flexible Flyers or Parker Duofold fountain pens: Why in the world didn't I save mine? I had about six of those and they're worth a fortune now.

There are two kinds of antiques, real and junk. The best reason for revering something old is that it was well made and reveals something about the people of the age in which it was produced. Junk antiques are mostly interesting for their curiosity value. Junk antiques reveal something about an age, too, but it is an age many people still remember. A real antique is good to have around the house because it reminds us of another age and of our own mortality.

WASTE

We waste more in the United States than the people of most other countries have.

Driving through the streets of any major city on the day the trash collectors come—or are supposed to come—is an experience the citizens of a hundred less prosperous nations would find difficult to believe. This very morning I must have passed enough furniture being cast out to equip a four-bedroom house. There were couches, chairs, parts of several beds, refrigerators and air conditioners.

It seems wrong. Yesterday in New York I passed one of those huge dumpsters they park outside buildings they're gutting. It was heaped high with doors, plumbing fixtures, mattresses and pieces of metal I couldn't identify. Perhaps they were parts to a defunct elevator. The contents of that dumpster must have cost someone hundreds of thousands of dollars when it was first bought and installed. Now it was costing someone another thousand dollars or so to cart away. Much of New York's refuse is towed out into the Atlantic and dumped. That's civilization's way of ruining the earth from which the materials were taken and the ocean into which they are dumped a few years or centuries later.

The pathetic bag ladies wander the streets of the city, often with old shopping carts laden with bits and pieces of junk they've rescued from a pile of trash by the curb as it waited for the collectors to come. I know how the bag ladies feel. At heart I'm a bag lady myself. When I see something good being thrown out, I often have the urge to stop and throw it in the back of my car.

In the office area where I work, there is an efficient young woman who takes care of all sorts of logistical and housekeeping problems for about twenty-five people. She is a ruthless disposer of goods. She never agonizes over throwing something out. Often as I leave for the night, she will have assembled a pile of miscellaneous office items by the elevator door. They're to be picked up by the night crew who clean up.

Last night, as I pressed the elevator button, I saw a note pinned to a somewhat battered IBM electric typewriter. "Please throw out," the note from the efficient office manager said curtly.

This is the mark of an executive who doesn't want to waste a lot of time. She knew, better than I, that to get that old machine repaired and back in use would have taken more time and money than it was worth. It was an old model that no one liked to type on and she wanted no part of it. I've argued with her before about the things she throws out. In all likelihood she's right from the point of business efficiency but I can't reconcile myself to that kind of waste. If it cost twice as much to fix the old typewriter as it would to buy a new one, I think I'd choose to fix the old one. That's why I'm not president of a successful company or even an office manager.

In many cities of the Middle East and Far East, there are shantytown suburbs constructed of materials the residents have salvaged from waste heaps. If they had our waste heaps and trash containers from which to choose their shantytown building materials, they'd have shanty palaces to live in. When demolition experts move in on one of our buildings, they have no mercy, no sentiment. They tear it down, break it up and throw it away. They don't much care what they're breaking up or throwing out. It costs more to sort it out and save it than they can get for it.

If I took that IBM typewriter home, I wonder if I could fix it. I hate electric typewriters but not as much as I hate to see one being thrown away.

WORLDLY GOODS

I was there when they auctioned off the residue of Arthur Godfrey's possessions. They were what was left when family, friends and loyal employees took what they wanted to remember him by.

I went to the gallery—they called it a gallery but it was just a big room—where the auction was held, and looked over hundreds of items. I was very sad.

For five good years I wrote for Godfrey. He was never a close friend, but he was an important part of my life. No one who knew him will ever forget him.

At the gallery I was torn between laughter and tears. Here were literally hundreds of trophies, plaques, inscribed statues, silver plates, boxes and framed testimonials proclaiming Arthur's great virtues to himself. I stared at them and wondered, for what purpose?

Why did the student body of the University of Oklahoma give him a plaque on "Karl Keller Day" in 1966? Did Arthur ever look at it again after they handed it to him?

What would the chamber of commerce from a small town in Kansas hope to get in return for a paperweight proclaiming him an honorary citizen entitled to a "Key to the City"?

I carried the gallery's catalog with me.

No. 186—Box of pajamas.

No. 129—Three awards from the National Sheriff's Association.

No. 149—Antelope head.

No. 522—Steinway piano.

The piano was solid ebony. A young man sat down at Arthur's beloved piano and started to play. I thought perhaps he worked for the gallery, but after a few minutes, he stood up and put his coat on.

"Is it good?" I asked.

"I'm a pianist. It's the most magnificent instrument I ever played," the man said. "I wish I could buy it." If Arthur had been standing there, he might have given it to him.

Downstairs in my own workshop, I keep a few choice tools that I want to protect in a beautifully made wooden box. I love the box and I always think of Arthur Godfrey when I use it.

I remember the first day I saw it. The package was addressed to Arthur and came wrapped in layers of protective cardboard. When one of the five young women Arthur employed to open his mail in 1953 lifted the top of the box, she revealed a magnificent, handmade model sailboat, full-rigged. The box had been made by the same craftsman to protect the boat.

Someone brought the sailboat into Arthur's private office, but I got the box it came in. At the auction gallery, I kept looking for the model sailboat. I never saw it again after that first day it arrived and never knew whether Arthur kept it or gave it away. He was overwhelmed with gifts during the years of his great popularity.

I never found the sailboat at the auction. I wish I knew who made it; I'd write and tell him that while the boat may never have hit its mark, I've enjoyed the box for years.

I did bid on a silver desk box that had been

given to Arthur by the members of Archie Bleyer's orchestra. Each had inscribed his name on the top of the box. I didn't get it, though.

No. 56—Eleven volumes, leather-bound, Shakespeare.

No. 24—Box of erotic books. That's more like Arthur.

No. 140—Framed Presidential Appointment signed by Richard Nixon.

"I collect autographs," the man standing next to me said as we looked at that. "That's done by machine. It isn't really Nixon's autograph."

The ancient pharaohs of Egypt may have had the right idea when they ordered that all their worldly possessions be buried with them.

V

THE QUEST FOR
AN HONEST
POLITICIAN

THE QUEST FOR AN HONEST POLITICIAN

Any good politician could tell us what he thinks and where he stands on every public issue in ten minutes if he or she boiled it down to brief answers.

Here are some tough questions I'd like to ask the people running for office. I don't want any runaround.

—What's the worst thing about you?

—Tell me five books you've read and liked.

—Do you think the defense budget should be bigger or smaller?

—What time do you get up Sundays?

—Are you for or against killing murderers?

—Do you think the government should do more or less for the people who can't or don't do things for themselves?

—Abortion, yes or no?

—If you were supposed to meet your wife in an hour and you were driving on a long, straight, deserted highway, seventy miles from where she was in Cheyenne, Wyoming, and there were no cops around, would you be on time?

—Do you believe in religious freedom?

—Do you believe a person has the right not to be religious?

—What's your favorite kind of dog?

—Do you make the toast or does your wife?

—At what age do you think people should be allowed to drink alcohol in public?

—Would you try to help or hinder the building of more nuclear energy plants?

—Do you take astrology seriously?

—Would you go to a chiropractor or an orthopedist if you had a back problem?

—Is it okay for men's clubs to keep women out? Just yes or no, please.

—Are you for or against gun control?

—Would you open up or further close down the public's access to government information through the press?

—If the most able and experienced man for the job was homosexual, would you appoint him?

—Busing, yes or no?

—Affirmative action?

—Whom do you like better, rich people or poor people?

—Have you ever smoked marijuana?

—Are you for or against farm subsidies?

—What about tobacco? Do you feel the same about taxpayers subsidizing farmers who grow tobacco?

—Do you carry a fountain pen?

—Which do you like better, chocolate or vanilla ice cream?

—How do you take your coffee?

If I could get the candidates to answer these questions honestly and briefly with no double-talk, I'd know how to vote. Of course, if they gave honest answers, we all might decide not to vote for any of them.

PRESIDENTIAL DEBATES

One of the most depressing thoughts of my life came to me when I was thirty-eight. I realized that I'd never be anything but what I was. I'd never be more, never less.

Before that thought came to me, I'd always imagined that by trying harder, studying and gaining experience, I'd be able to improve myself and become more than I had ever been before. Over the years, I've been so persistently myself, for better or for worse, that the dream I'd had of being more than that faded and I became reconciled to being only what I am. It isn't bad but it isn't good enough, either.

That's what I think about during Presidential debates. These two men are as trapped with who they are as the rest of us. They have only their own personalities, their own intelligence or lack of it, their own virtues and their own defects. No amount of makeup or preparation can conceal their true selves from us. We see through all their attempts to convince us that they're more than they are. It isn't bad but it isn't good enough, either.

More than for most of us, it's necessary for politicians to try to convince people that they're

161

better than they are. In order to get elected, they have to make believe they're smarter and more capable than we are. Voters don't want ordinary people, flawed people like themselves, as their leaders. We need to be convinced the people we vote for are extraordinary even when they're not.

One of the ways politicians try to convince us that they're better than they are is by giving speeches that have been written by someone else. It's the most common form of political deception. (When I hear a political speech, I think occasionally of John Hylan, the mayor of New York many years ago, when he was giving a speech that had been written for him but which he hadn't had time to read in advance. The writer had put a joke in the speech and the mayor saw the punch line coming and started laughing so hard before he read it aloud to the audience that it was minutes before he could continue.)

We all know that the candidates' speeches are written by someone else and yet when one of them stands before us and gives it, we are fooled. We temporarily accept it as his or her own.

It seems wrong for anyone to say things in public that have been written by someone else. There ought to be a law that every speech should have a byline attached to it. ("The President's speech tonight was written by . . .")

A speech by a potential or actual President shouldn't be a lot of words or ideas cleverly strung together by a professional writer. A speech that pretends to be the actual words and thoughts of a candidate should be exactly that.

The written speech may account for why so many Americans are disappointed with their candidates, no matter which ones they are, in Presidential debates. None of them measures up in their ad-lib answers to questions, to the way we are used to hearing them in their written speeches. Where are those quotable phrases? Where is the clear, progressive logic and the smooth transition from one subject to the next?

The debates are a good thing because the candidates are revealed to us only as big or as good or as equal or unequal to the challenge as they really are. On the occasions, during the debates, when they remember bits and pieces of previously written word arrangements, they sound like just that.

In the debates, there is no hiding place. The candidates are out from behind their written speeches where all of us can see them. We can see, for instance, that like us, they are mortal men . . . and mortal women.

They don't dare let us know, of course, but I suspect that, like the rest of us, they wish they could be more than they are.

THE WHITE HOUSE?
NO, THANK YOU

I'm always pleased but surprised that anyone will take the job of being President of the United States. Of all the jobs in the world, it's the one I'd least like to have. I know you get a big house to live in for free, a salary of $200,000, a helicopter, an airplane, your own doctor and a big staff but I still don't want the job. Don't even ask me because I won't take it.

The President doesn't even have a White House psychiatrist, which is probably the doctor he needs most.

It's always been a mystery to me why anyone would want to be President. Anyone who'd want to be President has to be some kind of nut who loves misery and criticism. If I were President, I'd call my personal physician and say, "What's wrong with me, anyhow?"

As President, any decision you make affects millions of people. You put thousands of people out of work every time you say, "Cut that." How do you sleep nights or in a Cabinet meeting knowing someone couldn't feed his family tonight because of some policy of yours that cost someone a job?

A President can't go down to the basement of the White House on a Saturday morning and putter around. He can't decide to climb up on the roof and straighten the television antenna. He never gets the satisfaction of taking a load of trash to the dump. Considering he's probably the most powerful man in the world, he's almost powerless to do anything he wants to do. If he does do something he wants to do, some newspaper or television reporter will see him doing it and claim he's wasting the taxpayers' money.

It's nice to have someone concerned about your welfare if it's a friend but I certainly wouldn't want a lot of guys running alongside my car every time I started down the street to make sure I didn't get shot. Furthermore, I'd want to drive my own car. I don't like to be driven anywhere by anyone. I like to go where I want to go the way I want to get there. The President can't do that.

You can bet there have been nights when the President sat down after a hard day's work dealing with world affairs and wanted nothing more than to go to a good movie. Presidents of the United States can see any movie they want right in the White House but that isn't what "going to the movies" means. "Going to the movies" is getting dressed to go out, driving to the theater, finding a parking place, standing in line to buy the tickets, buying the popcorn and then groping your way down the aisle to find a seat. A President can't go to the movies. Can you imagine the complaints he'd get if he took the First Lady to one of those dirty, R-rated movies?

There are a thousand things I can do the President can't. I can go to any restaurant I want to eat dinner or I can stay home and eat leftovers. He can't do either of those things.

I can wander down a street and window-shop, eat an ice-cream cone or lie down and take a nap and not do anything at all if I feel like it. Why would I want to be President?

For all the power he has to change the world with a snap of his fingers the President can't decide to turn over and go to sleep in the morning. He can't even make a plan for a week from Saturday. His calendar is full for the next four years . . . not just the days, but the hours.

I hope you have a happy and successful time in office, Mr. President, but frankly, you can have it.

TIME TO GOOF OFF

It's not anyone's business but his own and I hope he'll excuse me for thinking about it, but I often wonder when the President has time to do any of the ordinary things the rest of us do in the course of an average day.

He probably has a battery-operated watch so he doesn't have to wind it, but what about his television set? Does he have to get up out of his chair when he switches channels or does he have one of those remote-control gadgets? Is he any good at fixing things or is he the typical American male klutz?

I don't care how much help people try to give you, there are times when you have to do things for yourself. Often you'd *prefer* doing them yourself. Does the President ever get to park a car in a tight space, change a light bulb, lick a stamp, light a candle, pull down a garage door, fry an egg, turn up the heat, erase a mistake or put new laces in his shoes?

There are so many demands on a President's time that often he doesn't even have time to read a speech that's been written for him before he gives it. Everyone is trying to get his attention, asking him for a decision or wanting to have a picture taken with him. The normal reaction most of us would have is, "Hey, get off my back, will ya?"

The President has so many important decisions to make that he must spend more time than most of us acquiring the information with which to make them. His staff prepares a news summary for him, but do they include the juicy items? If not, when does he read all the good stuff? When does he take time to read the sports pages or the fluff in the gossip columns? Does he read the columnists, the stock-market tables, the social notes, the obituaries and the comic strips? He's missing a lot if he doesn't, but if he does, when does he have time?

What I'd miss most if I were President is free time. Most of us don't like being programmed.

One of the best parts of the day is the time we waste. Wasting time is a wonderful way to spend some of it, but if the President wastes ten minutes where anyone can see him, the press complains that he's not doing his job.

Every day the White House issues a bulletin with the President's calendar. It's all business. The President's press secretary ought to have the courage to lay it on the line once in a while. Somewhere down on the minute-to-minute list of the President's activities for the day should be some of the same breaks we all take.

2:00 P.M.–2:45 P.M. President Goofs Off
5:15 P.M.–6:30 P.M. NOYDB*

The way a President's schedule is now, it's so full he doesn't even have any time to think. Is he supposed to do all his heavy thinking after he goes to bed or in the shower in the morning? The President ought to have quite a bit of thinking time set aside every day along with his goof-off and NOYDB time.

The President is supposed to do everything on his Things-to-Do-Today list every day. I'd find this terribly depressing. For one thing, if I did everything I planned to do, I'd be making a lot of mistakes. A great many of the things most of us plan to do when we get up in the morning never get done and it's probably a good thing, too. The

*None of Your Damn Business

President, on the other hand, makes a lot of mistakes because we're always pressing him to do what he said he was going to do. He does it and sometimes it turns out to be wrong.

I want our President to have a more relaxed schedule. Some reporters say he already takes time out for an occasional nap but I'd like to see more free time written into his schedule. It would include time for napping, sitting and staring at the wall, reading junk not worth reading, worrying about dying, arguing with his wife, cutting his fingernails, making a tuna fish sandwich for lunch.

SPECIAL SALE TODAY: NEW YORK

The Senate recently voted to require a balanced federal budget by 1991. It sounds good but it's going to be difficult, and how do we get rid of the present national debt? I propose that we pay off the two-trillion-dollar national debt by selling one of the fifty states.

The only question that remains is, which state would most Americans prefer to sell if we had to sell one?

A while ago a survey was taken for me at Disney World's Epcot Center.

The question was this:

"If you had to sell one of the fifty states to pay off the national debt, which state would you sell?"

Disney World asked the question of 2,781 adults. That's a huge number by professional sampling standards.

Here are the ten states Americans would most like to sell, and the number and percentage of the votes each state got.

New York	361	13 percent
California	247	9 percent
New Jersey	194	7 percent
Texas	165	6 percent
New Mexico	104	4 percent
North Dakota	78	3 percent
Mississippi	75	3 percent
Georgia	64	2 percent
Kansas	60	2 percent
Alaska	57	2 percent

Very few of those polled wanted to sell Connecticut, Delaware, Minnesota, Missouri, New Hampshire, North or South Carolina, Tennessee, Vermont, Virginia or Wisconsin. Only one person voted to sell Colorado. It must have been some kid who got thrown out of college there.

It's a silly idea, of course, but it's interesting as a popularity contest. We weren't surprised at New York and New Jersey being high on the unpopularity list but we were surprised to see California come in second and astonished to find Kansas in the top ten.

Why would anyone want to sell such an all-

American state as Kansas? It has all those great rolling plains, and Kansas City may be the most underrated big town in America.

In some cases, people voted for places like Alaska, Hawaii and North Dakota, not because they disliked anything about those states, but because they felt we could afford to do without them. One woman told me she voted to sell Hawaii because it's a luxury we can do without.

A majority of people from the South voted to sell New York. That figures, but apparently people from the Northeast didn't reciprocate. A majority of people from the Northeast voted to sell New Jersey, one of their own.

California got almost ten percent of the votes. It has apparently lost its reputation as the sunny frontier where any American can go and make his or her fortune working two hours a day and playing the rest of the time.

The biggest number of voters with college degrees voted to sell New Jersey. In recent years New Jersey has replaced its reputation as the home of truck gardens, heavy industry and much of the country's pharmaceutical business with an unsavory identification with gambling and toxic waste.

A majority of those polled at Disney World who were between fifty and sixty-four years old voted to sell Texas. For some mysterious reason, those over sixty-five would have put New Mexico on the market. Can anyone explain that? What do

Social Security recipients have against New Mexico?

The most interesting statistic of all was the vote by the people with graduate degrees. The biggest number of them voted to sell Mississippi. I suppose that's because Mississippi ranked near the bottom of the amount spent on education by states.

I didn't vote and wouldn't tell you which state I'd most like to get rid of if I had. I'm prejudiced against a couple of states but I don't like to go out of my way to make enemies.

ANNEXING THE MOON

What I want to know is, why are we ignoring the moon? Pretty soon we're going to hear that the Russians are setting up a space station on the moon and then we'll get excited about it. Meanwhile, what are we doing about the moon? Nothing, that's what.

Was our brief exploration of the moon a bitter disappointment to scientists and space experts? How come they've dropped it like a cold potato?

It's been seventeen years since Neil Armstrong and Edwin Aldrin landed on it and Armstrong said, "That's one small step for man, one giant leap for mankind."

That was a historic statement all right but we haven't taken even a teensy-weensy step up there since the Apollo program ended in 1972.

be no smarter, and probably even dumber,
urs. This isn't easy sometimes.

question the wisdom of spending several mil-
dollars on these new paint jobs. To tell you
ruth, I question the value of camouflage
ether. Early in World War II, the Air Force
ed that painting a bomber did nothing for it
add hundreds of pounds of weight, so they
ed painting their airplanes. This was good
king.

the Army wants its vehicles to blend into the
ground, it ought to think about painting its
s and trucks in the same variety of colors that
roit paints its automobiles. We'd have red,
n, black, yellow and silver tanks. They might
out in a forest or on the desert but on a city
et, where wars are so often fought, they'd be
noticeable. Nothing stands out more than a
g line of olive drab or camouflage-painted vehi-
s moving down a road, bumper to bumper.
ey are very like the Secret Service operatives
o protect our government officials. Secret Ser-
e men try to dress in ordinary, unobtrusive
ts. When you see a group of ordinary, un-
trusive men standing around somewhere in
ashington, you know the President's coming.
ese men are so average they stick out like a
mouflaged tank.

It has been my experience that when a soldier
oks out across a field at an enemy vehicle, he
entifies it as either "a tank" or "a camouflaged

176

Armstrong and Aldrin spent twenty-one hours
there kicking dirt and stones around, then they
packed up pounds of the stuff, loaded it on the
spaceship and came home. They said at the time
that it would take scientists several months to
analyze the material brought back from the moon
but I don't recall hearing anything much about
their analysis. Isn't it good for anything?

Who knows what great minerals lie buried beneath the moon's surface? Maybe it's pure gold
beginning just a few feet down. Maybe it's coal or
solid diamond. Whatever it is, we ought to find
out. I suspect the American public would be more
interested in the idea of using the moon for some
practical purpose than the public is in Star Wars
expenditures. I should think the moon would even
make a perfect military base.

If I were planning a Star Wars defense system
for the United States, the moon is the first place
I'd start putting things. It's about a third the size
of earth, so there's plenty of room. You have to
figure the Russians aren't going to develop a
weapon that will knock down the moon. Where
would they knock it down to? We don't want
warheads in space, either. Space, like Switzerland,
should be neutral.

Scientists talk about Mars, and those new solar
systems billions of light years away. Here's a good
solid object only 239,000 miles from us. The question is this: Why is the moon a second-class celestial object?

If we're going to take the moon seriously as

173

something other than a word that rhymes with *tune, spoon* and *soon* in love songs, perhaps the first step toward giving it more stature in our space plans would be to stop using the word *honeymoon* and then make the moon the fifty-first state.

If the moon had representation in Congress, it would be getting some of that easy money Congress is always voting for its members' constituencies. We'd have federal highways, bridges, dams and public-works programs of all kinds on the moon.

At first people might be just as reluctant to go to the moon as they were to settle in Alaska years ago. All they'd have to do is find one valuable element in the ground of the moon and people would line up to get there. First thing you know they'd be having lotteries and welfare programs on the moon. One of the National Football League franchises would probably move there. Before you know it, we could have air pollution, hazardous waste dumps and crime on the moon. Finally, it would be accepted as just another state.

There are some things that would have to be done to the moon to make it habitable. I'd love to be on the planning commission. We'd import a few little white clouds to float around overhead on the moon but no big dark ones. We'd then extract water from the atmosphere. Everyone who lived there would have a little creek in the backyard of his home. No two homes would look alike.

The state holiday on the moon would be a day

off for everyone. They would
the moon moved between eart
blacked out all the people li
fifty. It would be known as Ec
tradition would be simply to lau
silly people in the dark back on

out t
than
I q
lion
the
altog
realiz
exce
stop
thin

CAMOUFLAGIN
BUDGET

The Army is dissatisfied with the p
its camouflaged equipment and l
repaint everything. This includes a
and the Army doesn't take them to
have them done, either. So far, i
three hundred dollars for each vehicl
the Army, that's pronounced "ve-HI

The new camouflage paint will t
three colors instead of the four they'v
Experts think the three colors will be
tive in concealing things like tanks,
jeeps. The new color scheme was d
experts in the German army, and our
it so much they're going to copy it.

The German army has always seeme
I'd like to point out to our Army that t
army lost two wars that I know of.
German forces may seem smart, they

If
back
tank
Det
gree
stick
stre
less
lon
cles
Th
wh
vic
su
ob
W
T
ca
lo
id

out to be no smarter, and probably even dumber, than ours. This isn't easy sometimes.

I question the wisdom of spending several million dollars on these new paint jobs. To tell you the truth, I question the value of camouflage altogether. Early in World War II, the Air Force realized that painting a bomber did nothing for it except add hundreds of pounds of weight, so they stopped painting their airplanes. This was good thinking.

If the Army wants its vehicles to blend into the background, it ought to think about painting its tanks and trucks in the same variety of colors that Detroit paints its automobiles. We'd have red, green, black, yellow and silver tanks. They might stick out in a forest or on the desert but on a city street, where wars are so often fought, they'd be less noticeable. Nothing stands out more than a long line of olive drab or camouflage-painted vehicles moving down a road, bumper to bumper. They are very like the Secret Service operatives who protect our government officials. Secret Service men try to dress in ordinary, unobtrusive suits. When you see a group of ordinary, unobtrusive men standing around somewhere in Washington, you know the President's coming. These men are so average they stick out like a camouflaged tank.

It has been my experience that when a soldier looks out across a field at an enemy vehicle, he identifies it as either "a tank" or "a camouflaged

176

off for everyone. They would celebrate the day the moon moved between earth and the sun and blacked out all the people living on the lower fifty. It would be known as Eclipse Day and the tradition would be simply to laugh all day at those silly people in the dark back on earth.

CAMOUFLAGING THE BUDGET

The Army is dissatisfied with the paint jobs on all its camouflaged equipment and has decided to repaint everything. This includes a lot of vehicles, and the Army doesn't take them to Earl Scheib to have them done, either. So far, it's cost about three hundred dollars for each vehicle painted. (In the Army, that's pronounced "ve-HICK-le.")

The new camouflage paint will be applied in three colors instead of the four they've been using. Experts think the three colors will be more effective in concealing things like tanks, trucks and jeeps. The new color scheme was developed by experts in the German army, and our people like it so much they're going to copy it.

The German army has always seemed smart but I'd like to point out to our Army that the German army lost two wars that I know of. While the German forces may seem smart, they often turn something other than a word that rhymes with *tune*, *spoon* and *soon* in love songs, perhaps the first step toward giving it more stature in our space plans would be to stop using the word *honeymoon* and then make the moon the fifty-first state.

If the moon had representation in Congress, it would be getting some of that easy money Congress is always voting for its members' constituencies. We'd have federal highways, bridges, dams and public-works programs of all kinds on the moon.

At first people might be just as reluctant to go to the moon as they were to settle in Alaska years ago. All they'd have to do is find one valuable element in the ground of the moon and people would line up to get there. First thing you know they'd be having lotteries and welfare programs on the moon. One of the National Football League franchises would probably move there. Before you know it, we could have air pollution, hazardous waste dumps and crime on the moon. Finally, it would be accepted as just another state.

There are some things that would have to be done to the moon to make it habitable. I'd love to be on the planning commission. We'd import a few little white clouds to float around overhead on the moon but no big dark ones. We'd then extract water from the atmosphere. Everyone who lived there would have a little creek in the backyard of his home. No two homes would look alike.

The state holiday on the moon would be a day

Armstrong and Aldrin spent twenty-one hours there kicking dirt and stones around, then they packed up pounds of the stuff, loaded it on the spaceship and came home. They said at the time that it would take scientists several months to analyze the material brought back from the moon but I don't recall hearing anything much about their analysis. Isn't it good for anything?

Who knows what great minerals lie buried beneath the moon's surface? Maybe it's pure gold beginning just a few feet down. Maybe it's coal or solid diamond. Whatever it is, we ought to find out. I suspect the American public would be more interested in the idea of using the moon for some practical purpose than the public is in Star Wars expenditures. I should think the moon would even make a perfect military base.

If I were planning a Star Wars defense system for the United States, the moon is the first place I'd start putting things. It's about a third the size of earth, so there's plenty of room. You have to figure the Russians aren't going to develop a weapon that will knock down the moon. Where would they knock it down to? We don't want warheads in space, either. Space, like Switzerland, should be neutral.

Scientists talk about Mars, and those new solar systems billions of light years away. Here's a good solid object only 239,000 miles from us. The question is this: Why is the moon a second-class celestial object?

If we're going to take the moon seriously as

tank." One is no more difficult to see than the other.

If the people who design camouflage colors could dictate the terrain over which a war was fought, they might be able to paint things so they'd be difficult to see. They can't do that, though. When a tank painted to be difficult to see against a forest background is seen by the enemy as it crosses a snow-covered field, it isn't camouflaged at all. If they could design a paint called "chameleon," which would change depending on the color of the vehicle's surroundings, camouflage might work.

Forty years ago, we fought in the Hürtgen Forest. To help make the tanks and trucks invisible from the ground or the air, they should all have been painted white. There isn't time to paint a tank in the heat of battle, so the green-and-brown-and-black tanks trundled out onto the snow-covered fields, standing out like bull's-eyes.

One of the strangest fashion trends of the past thirty years has been the vogue for camouflage fatigue clothes. At first, kids started buying them at Army-Navy surplus stores. Then the Paris fashion designers picked up on it and started designing brand-new clothes made out of the camouflage material. None of the young people I ever saw wearing them looked as if they wanted to look inconspicuous. They wore them because, in those clothes, they stood out from the crowd.

If we're looking for a place to start cutting

down on the military budget, I have thousands of three-hundred-dollar suggestions.

SPY DUST

Some American officials have accused the Soviet Union of using a chemical powder to trace the movement of our . . . well, spies, in Moscow.

The material the Russians are accused of using is dusted on any object they know our people will touch. They might put it on the steering wheels of Americans' cars, for example, or the doorknobs of Americans' apartments. For days after that, anything those U.S. operatives put their hands on will light up under ultraviolet rays.

At the present time, the only product the Russians make that many Americans think is worth buying is their vodka, Stolichnaya. If they want to expand their trade with us, they should open up the spy-dust market and get it into the big department stores here so it would be available to everyone. I would certainly be one of their first customers. I'd love to have a bag of spy dust.

There are so many uses for spy dust that I can think of. I would determine, for example, who put the keys to my car in those old corduroy pants hanging in my closet. I admit that I was the last one to use the car but I can't believe I put keys in those pants. Someone must have sneaked them in there, and if I'd had a little spy dust sprinkled on my car keys, I'd know who it was.

If spy dust wasn't expensive, I'd even use it on my own hands. I could locate important papers I'd mislaid just by turning out the lights in my office and turning on the special ultraviolet light that makes the spy dust luminous.

A little spy dust on my hands would be a great help in my workshop. I'm always forgetting where I put the tool I just had in my hands, but if the handle could be made to glow once I'd touched it, it would be harder to misplace.

Spy dust sprinkled on the hands of family members would help. It would resolve, once and for all, who left the iron on. It would point the finger at the person who finished the last bottle of beer or who ate the last cookie. To determine who ate the last cookie, it would only be necessary to fish the empty box out of the wastebasket and put it under the special spy dust–revealing light.

I see no reason why some further refinement in spy-dust technology couldn't produce a safe, radioactive dust whose presence could be detected from a distance with a Geiger counter even when it wasn't visible. None of us even seems to know for sure where our money goes. With a spy dust that activated a beeper, we could dust our money with this chemical powder and trace it to the stores and other places of business where we divested ourselves of it.

Trying to track down spies with spy dust would

be one of its least practical uses. The Russians ought to know better. No American spy worth his salt would make his way into the secret chambers of the Kremlin, for instance, and leave his fingerprints all over the door of the safe with the Soviet Union's greatest secrets in it.

Even the most secret organizations in both our governments seem to take their ideas about spies from the movies. You'd think they'd know better, inasmuch as they're the ones who actually do it. The Russians must know that their spies would never get caught red-handed with spy dust on their fingers. They ought to know ours wouldn't either. Spy dust would obviously be a better product for domestic than international use.

Take, for example, so intelligent, urbane and gentlemanly a diplomat as the Soviet ambassador to the United States, Anatoliy Dobrynin. If the CIA found a way to get spy dust on his hands, it would do them no good at all. At the end of a week it could probably be proved that he went to twenty-six Washington cocktail parties, shook hands with nineteen congressmen and ate in some of the best restaurants in town, getting spy dust all over their silverware in the process.

THE ONE-MAN, ONE-GUN CONFERENCE

Sooner or later the world will have to return to the good old days when we fought wars and killed people the old-fashioned way, one at a time.

Killing people by the hundreds of thousands and planning to kill them by the millions, as we are now, is simply too costly. It's a luxury we can't afford.

In 1985, the United States alone spent $305 billion on weapons. The fact is, this country is now spending $180 billion more than it takes in, much of it on weapons.

In those good old days, wars were fought with slingshots, bows and arrows, spears, swords and single-shot muskets. Progress in weapons should have stopped there, when we could still afford to pay for them.

It's apparent that scientists today can invent things so expensive that we can't afford to make them. It doesn't seem right but it's true.

Wars cost too much now because weapons are automatic, recessed, stainless, streamlined and they go faster than sound. It's silly. There's no need to kill someone with a laser beam that travels at the speed of light when a bow and arrow would do the same thing.

The Russians and the Americans are balking at

the details of reducing each country's ability to destroy the other fifty times over with nuclear weapons, to the point where we can only destroy each other ten times over. Maybe both countries would be willing to talk about going back to the musket or rifle. It might be called The One-Man, One-Gun Conference. No one could make a weapon that would kill more than one person at a time.

This concept would not only mean fewer people would be killed, but it would have a profoundly beneficial impact on our national budget. You know how it is when you see troops or guerrilla forces in Central America or the Middle East shooting their weapons. They don't aim at anyone. They see the man coming with the television camera behind him and they start spraying bullets at an imaginary enemy. I don't suppose one bullet in a million hits anyone. This is terribly wasteful.

When I was drafted during World War II, they issued me a Springfield rifle. It was shortly to be replaced by the M1, but if our Army was still armed with that Springfield, and the Russians were armed with their equivalent of it, war would be a lot more affordable and we wouldn't have to be so worried about having one.

The Springfield carried a clip that held six bullets. You put the rifle to your shoulder, shot the bolt to put the round in the chamber, aimed the Springfield at something, pulled the trigger and sent one lethal metal missile toward its target.

It often hit what it was directed at and, of course, there were no television cameras.

Now our infantrymen are equipped with the M16 rifle. Even that is about to be replaced in part by a faster-firing gun called the "SAW" or Squad Automatic Weapon.

In case you don't think the savings would be significant if we returned to the Springfield rifle, keep in mind, as you look at these figures I got from some cooperative people in the Pentagon, that one bullet for an M16 costs about fifty cents.

Last year the Defense Department bought 613,700,000 rounds of M16 ammunition. That included blanks and belted rounds.

This year the Defense Department has ordered 705,000,000 bullets, which they prefer to call rounds of ammunition.

It seems as though they must have shot up the 600,000,000 they bought last year or they wouldn't be ordering all these new ones. Together, in just two years, that's 1,300,000,000 shots our soldiers have taken. Remember, that's without being at war. At half a dollar each shot, it comes to $650,000,000 we've spent in bullets alone, not to kill anyone.

Next time you see someone shooting a rifle, think of it in terms of fifty cents a shot. It's the sort of thing that could end war.

THE PERFECT WEAPON

It seems as though, with all the world's technical know-how, someone could invent the perfect weapon. What the world needs is a weapon that could lead one country to a military victory over another without killing or hurting anyone.

I've been thinking about the problem, and while my suggestions may not be worth anything, they're at least in the right direction. Here are ten ideas for new weapons. All they need is a little work:

1. A new bomb that, when dropped, would give everyone for miles around a bad cold. No country could mount an offensive if they all had to call in sick.

2. Drop money. If we bought or printed as much money as a nuclear weapon costs us and dropped the cash in small bills all over the Soviet Union, you know darn well it would take the Russian citizens' minds off fighting us. They'd all rush to the stores to find something to spend it on.

3. The argument against money might be that a lot of our potential enemies don't have anything to spend money on. Okay, then. Drop them the real thing from parachutes. Drop packages of gourmet food, drop cameras with little parachutes to float

them gently to the ground. Divert the enemy. Take their little red minds off war and get them concentrating on the material things of life the way we do. We might even drop electrical appliances that don't work and drive them crazy.

4. Drop video tape recorders with reruns of *Bill Cosby* on them to keep them happy.

5. A concussion bomb that wouldn't break anything but glass. It would break all the glass for miles around. If it were dropped on Moscow, there would be no windows left in the Kremlin, no windshields in Russian cars and any Russian leader who wore glasses wouldn't be able to see until he got a new pair. In Russia the war could be over by that time.

6. Have half a dozen of the best newspapers in the United States translated and printed in Russian. Drop them in bundles on Russia every day so the Russian people could find out what's really going on in the world. Drop some Rupert Murdoch papers, too, just to confuse them.

7. Bombard enemy cities with Wonder Bread.

8. Broadcast live debates from Congress and feed them by satellite into Russia. No Russian soldier watching what happens on the floor of the House of Representatives or in the Senate would take this country seriously.

9. Sneak large amounts of bubble gum, designer jeans and Michael Jackson records into Russia.

10. My last suggestion would be a device to use only as a last resort in the event none of the others worked. It's cruel and probably would have been outlawed by the Geneva Convention if they'd thought of it, but there are times when you have to take extreme measures. It's almost too horrible to mention, but I'd do this: Send all the presidential candidates in an election year to the Soviet Union for a six-month speech-making tour and bore the Russians to death.

None of these may be the answer but there must be a better way to fight a war than by killing people with bullets, bombs, chemical weapons or nuclear explosions. For the money we're spending on figuring out ways to kill people, we ought to be able to figure a way to win a painless war.

NONE OF OUR BUSINESS

I was walking along Eighteenth Street about eight o'clock last Thursday night when I saw a man and a woman ahead of me having a violent argument.

Suddenly the woman slapped the man in the

face. He grabbed her and they started wrestling and punching. I was getting closer.

I don't know how you judge these things, but I judged they were husband and wife and that they'd had the same argument before. It was a terrible moment of decision for me. Do I interfere? Do I ask her if she wants help? What kind of help do I give her?

I crossed the street and walked on. I looked back and saw her break and run in the opposite direction. I was relieved.

I wasn't comfortable, though. Did I do the right thing? I wondered. If the woman had wanted help, I guess she'd have yelled. But would she? And . . . where did she run to? Did he catch her? What did he do then? The following day I leafed through the paper, nervously expecting to find a small notice of a murder on Eighteenth Street. Did he have a gun? A knife? Was I obliged to intervene no matter what the consequences in physical damage to me might have been?

The same questions come to my mind in relation to America's foreign policy. When something is wrong in another country, what should we do? Is it any of our business, or is doing the right thing always our business?

The day following the incident on Eighteenth Street I went to the Lebanese consulate to get a visa for a trip I'd planned to Beirut.

The consulate is in an important-looking stone townhouse on an expensive street in New York.

The windows were dirty and curtainless, and even from the street it has a seen-better-days look.

Inside, a pregnant woman sat at a small desk with a telephone switchboard. The floor was bare wood, worn and water-stained.

I was impressed with the informality of the place. I had half-expected to be frisked for weapons or explosives but when I asked for the visa office, the woman politely indicated I should just walk through the double doors in front of me.

It must have been a grand drawing room at one time but it looked dreary and sad now. It had five battered old desks in it and a nondescript collection of chairs. Over what had been a working fireplace was a framed picture of Amin Gemayel. It hung alone on a stained and dirty yellow wall. Gemayel looked like a young foreign student at Cornell. Under the picture was that tired cliché of a slogan that began with "I ♥ New York." It read, "I ♥ Lebanon."

The man at the desk on the right as I came in had papers spread out over his desk and several passports. Having dealt with passport people before, I acted a lot sweeter to him than I would have with the average Lebanese stranger.

He took my papers, looked them over with that skeptical air passport people have and started writing and stamping.

"You want a multiple, don't you?" he said.

He sounded as though he expected me to say yes, and although I had no idea what a multiple meant I said, "Oh, yes. Please."

It turned out a multiple meant that I can return to Beirut as often as I want to in the next six months. That's as lucky as a person can get, isn't it? I was sure glad I'd said yes.

While the man worked on my visa, I struck up a conversation with a woman working on an IBM typewriter with Arabic script on it. She thought she recognized me from *20/20*.

"The bad news must be depressing for you," I said.

"It's been bad for nine years," the woman said. "You get used to it."

I left the Lebanese consulate with my visa, and found myself idly thinking what a terrible coincidence it would be if she was the same woman I'd seen running from the man on Eighteenth Street.

EXPLAINING IT ALL FOR YOU

Not today, but soon perhaps, I'll be explaining the war between Iraq and Iran to you. I'll tell you how the war started, what the war is about, who is fighting whom and why. I think by the time I finish my explanation, it will make a lot more sense to you than it does now. First, of course, I'll have to find out myself.

I haven't quite decided how, but I'll probably start by explaining the difference between the two

189

countries. One of them is predominantly Moslem and I think the other may be, too. If not, it's something else. I'll make all that clear for you.

One of the big troubles with that war for most Americans is that the names of the two countries are so much alike. It isn't as though they were called France and Germany. Calling two countries France and Germany makes it a lot easier to tell them apart than calling them Iran and Iraq. Don't worry about it for now, though. Just as soon as I find out what it's all about, I'll let you know.

While I'm at it, I might as well explain what's going on in India for you.

In 1984, hundreds of Indians were killed when the Indian Army attacked the Golden Temple in Amritsar. The Golden Temple is headquarters for the Sikhs. (I'll be explaining who the Sikhs are.)

Amritsar, according to the newspapers, is in the Punjab, so naturally, I'll be telling you where and what "the Punjab" is, too. As I understand it now, it is not a religion. The Punjab is a geographical area of India.

India, by the way, is no longer to be confused with Pakistan, although the food is a lot alike. I'll go into a detailed explanation of why Pakistan is no longer part of India and how the Sikhs in the Punjab differ from the Hindus.

If I have the time, I'll probably explain how the Hindus differ from the Sikhs, the Moslems, the Buddhists, the Baptists, the Seventh-Day Adventists, Jehovah's Witnesses, Methodists,

Jews, Shintoists, Catholics and Confucians. Most of the world's wars have begun over religious differences between people who honestly believe their religion is the only right one, so I think it's important that you understand how the religions differ from each other. A detailed explanation will be forthcoming from me very, very soon, probably.

Nor do I wish to exclude Central America. There are still a few people in the United States who don't completely understand why Nicaragua is constantly having trouble with its neighbor, Honduras. I'll be making that clear so you'll all better understand our problems there. Likewise, I'll be telling you the difference between San Salvador and El Salvador. Unless I'm very much mistaken, one of them is a city and the other a country. When I finish, there won't be any doubt in your mind.

Because there's also some doubt about which are the good guys and which are the bad guys in the guerrilla war in either El, or San, Salvador, I'll find out and let you know once and for all about that, too.

Everyone hates war, everyone says. If we're going to do something about stopping wars, we ought to do what we do with any problem. We study it and write a report. That's why I'm going to do this public service, explaining all the wars of history, just as soon as I get some free time. I'll be explaining not only the differences that brought on the war between Iran and Iraq, but I'll also be telling you the details of the Punic Wars, the Napoleonic Wars, the Crimean Wars and the Peloponnesian War. I'll refresh your memory about the Crusades and what the Crusaders were crusading for and why they killed so many people doing it. I'll tell you whether Attila the Hun was really all that bad a guy or not.

On a separate occasion, I'll tell you why we got into the war in Vietnam.

I won't leave one war unexplained . . . if there is an explanation for one.

VI

PLAIN SPEAKING

"AMATEUR" ATHLETICS

When the local hardware store in our little community put up the money for the uniforms for one of the teams in my son's Little League more than fifteen years ago, I should have known that was the beginning of the end of amateur athletics in America.

If there's money in sports, you can bet business organizations are going to get into it. I don't know how high schools and colleges have kept advertisers off the backs of the shirts their teams wear but you can be sure that's coming.

I find it disgusting and objectionable to see the name of a cigarette company as sponsor for a major tennis tournament. Cigarette makers have no business associating their product with anything as good as tennis. They ought to be thrown out.

There's nothing wrong with professional sports, although it strikes most of us who don't do it for a living as funny that anyone would be working when he's playing.

What is wrong is when athletes pretend they're amateurs when they're not. That's the kind of dishonesty that's prevalent in so-called amateur sport these days. College football and basketball are filled with closet professionals who exchange their services for something of value. It happens in any sport where there's much money involved. A lot of sports organizations have invented ways of getting around the rules so that the athlete doesn't lose his amateur status. I don't understand why they don't just admit some college sports are played, not by students, but by professionals.

One of the sports that went honest not so long ago was tennis. For many years the biggest tennis tournaments were billed as amateur. The people who played in them did nothing else but play tennis all year long and some of them arrived at the courts in Rolls-Royces, but they called themselves amateurs.

Tennis did the sensible thing in 1968. It admitted players were doing it for money. Now even our Davis Cup team is composed of professionals. That seems wrong, but at least it's honest.

Every year, I go to the granddaddy of all indoor track meets, the Millrose Games. It was run for many years with impeccably high amateur standards by an old Philadelphia department store, Wanamaker's. Little by little, each year, those standards have become increasingly peccable. Now, at the Millrose Games, many of the events are named after some product or corporation that, presumably, chipped in some of the money that went to the amateur competitors.

I often see Herb Schmertz, the public-relations genius for the Mobil Oil Corporation, across the arena from me. The name Schmertz has been important to the Millrose Games over the years, and I thought to myself, Herb's not such a bad guy after all, he's a track fan like the rest of his family.

A few pages further along in my program I was disillusioned. The event in my program was called "The Mobil 5000." Now I don't know whether Herb was there because he loves track or Mobil.

Amateur track-and-field athletes and the people who run the meets have found a new and interesting way to maintain the athletes' amateur status. The big-name runners and jumpers who bring the crowds in and sell tickets (at twenty-five dollars a seat) set up trust funds for themselves. These trust funds are handled for them by the governing body of amateur track-and-field athletes, called The Athletics Congress, with offices in Indianapolis.

The trust-fund system is simple. If a meet organizer wants a star miler to compete and help fill the hall, he pays perhaps $7,500 into the athlete's trust fund. An outstanding amateur track star can put as much as $100,000 into his trust kitty in a good year.

While the trust fund is technically held by The Athletics Congress, the athlete can draw from it for travel, training and living expenses. He can even buy himself a car.

So what else is there? That's what I do with my salary.

A FAN'S NOTES

We all like sports and we're all agreed something's wrong. We want sports that put more emphasis on the action and less on the money. We want sports to go back to the basics.

I have some suggestions about how to bring several professional sports back down to earth.

Start with tennis.

First, make John McEnroe and all the other professional tennis players chase their own balls. Stop pampering them. Eliminate the ball boys. No one would be carefully bouncing balls at the players as if they were three-year-olds sitting on the living-room floor.

A big part of playing tennis is finding the balls you lose and going to get the ones you've hit into some remote corner of the court. It's all part of the game, and the pros ought to be made to play it the way the rest of us do. If McEnroe had to go get his own balls, it might make him more careful of where he bangs them in anger after losing a point.

It would be good fun for spectators, too. Most of them are tennis players themselves. Getting a loose ball back to an opponent so he can serve it is an art. Some players do it better than others. It would be interesting to see how the experts do it.

The way a player picks up a ball instead of bending over for it is part of the game, too. Some hit it with their racket to get it bouncing; others catch it between the instep of one foot and the head of their racket and flip it up so they can catch it. Women often store an extra ball under the elastic of their underpants. Fans want to see the real game, not an antiseptic version of it as played by our current professionals.

Next, we've got to make losing less profitable. The winner of the tournament in Forest Hills, New York, gets $100,000 from the sponsor, and the second-place finisher gets $40,000. This is ridiculous. Giving $40,000 to the loser could make losing popular. The winner should get everything. Give the losers carfare home. We all know John McEnroe can beat Jimmy Connors now.

Baseball players are pampered, too. Let's put baseball back where it belongs. Some of the big-league games ought to be played in empty lots where the grass isn't like a putting green. The umpire shouldn't always be feeding the pitcher a new ball, either. The rule ought to be that a baseball game has to be finished with the same ball it was started with. If the original ball is lost, everyone would have to go home and help his mother.

Any kid who played much baseball knows that after a few Saturdays in the vacant lot, the cover starts coming off a baseball. You don't always have a rich kid whose father can afford to buy him a new one, so you wrap the old one with black tape. I'd like to see how many no-hitters Nolan Ryan could pitch with a baseball wrapped with friction tape. I'd like to know how many home runs Darryl Strawberry could knock with a ball twice as heavy as its original weight because of the tape that holds it together.

Hockey players wouldn't get a new stick every time they cracked one. It would make a dirty player more careful about who he hit over the head with the one he was playing with. Hockey sticks, like baseballs, should always be heavy with tape toward the end of the season.

I'd insist that in pro football the same players be in the game on both offense and defense, the way it used to be. I'd like to see whether a runner like Tony Dorsett can make a tackle and whether a tackler like Lawrence Taylor can run with the ball. If football players are going to be paid all that money, they ought to have to work full-time, not half-time.

The American sports fan has a list of demands. Someday he's going to become unionized and get what he wants or strike.

PLACE YOUR BETS

In recent years several officials—including the governor of New York State, Mario Cuomo—have proposed that betting on sports be legalized.

I'm very suspicious of any politician who thinks it's a good idea to try to subsidize government by taking money away from the citizens who can least afford it by offering them false hope they're going to get rich. (You can't convince me that it isn't the poorest and the dumbest who usually buy the state lottery tickets.) State lotteries are like legalizing theft from the poor in order to pay for their welfare checks.

There are certain things that come naturally to us. The urge to gamble is one. Governments have usually protected their citizens from this urge by making it illegal, thus removing it as a temptation to law-abiding people.

In recent years lotteries and numbers games have been started in a dozen states. It's a mystery to me why it's illegal for a private citizen to go into the betting business if it's okay for the government. Either it's right or wrong. Which is it? If it's right, there shouldn't be restrictions on anyone's right to gamble or take bets. If it's wrong, no government should be in the business.

Proponents say people are going to gamble anyway, so it might as well be legalized. What about prostitution? Where there's gambling, there's usually sex for sale. If New York State approves sports betting, will the state be opening adjacent whorehouses to help finance education? You aren't against education, are you?

If gambling is as good a way to raise money for government as people are saying it is, maybe gambling's the answer to a lot of our problems.

Politicians need money to finance their election campaigns. Why not have betting on elections? Whatever the odds, politics would make a very attractive thing to bet on. If a government ran political betting parlors and took twenty cents out of every dollar the way they do on most games they run, politicians would all have plenty of money for their campaigns. Politics would appeal to people who wouldn't bet on a sports event, too.

In Las Vegas, the gambling tables are open twenty-four hours a day. In New York City, they have horse races all winter so the state and city can collect the betting money. If we ever have betting on elections, I suppose we can expect to have politicians running all year long because they need the money.

There's no reason, if you consider the proponents' arguments reason, for us not to have betting on the Olympics, too. Instead of those games being limited to a competition among athletes of the world, they'd be a huge, international fund-raising gamble.

Every country would be interested in betting on its team or its individual athletes. Every red-blooded American would put up dollars against the kopecks put down by blue-blooded Reds betting on the Soviet team members.

Each country's government would get a proportionate share of the take from this giant international gamble. The vast amounts of money a country would make on sports could be used to build up its military forces or its nuclear-weapons systems.

At the other end of our governmental structure, perhaps local governments in small towns could bring in added revenues by putting in pari-mutuel machines at local sandlots so proud parents could put down a few dollars on their own Little League teams.

I suspect voters will be smart enough to continue to reject governmental sports-betting proposals.

Anyone wanna bet?

NAILING THE BANK

New York police were faced with a crime that might have been committed by any one of a million people.

Someone broke windows in twenty-four branches of the Chemical Bank, setting off burglar alarms at each location. Police suspect that the person breaking the windows was an angry customer. This does not narrow the number of suspects much.

If the police start looking into people who, at one time or another, have been angry with the service they get from Chemical or any other New York bank, they're going to have to grill every customer the bank has ever had. I'm going to be plenty nervous myself. As a Chemical customer, I'd be a prime suspect and it wouldn't be hard for the police to establish a motive. If the police want a lineup of possible perpetrators of this crime, all they'd have to do is go to any one of the eighty-

203

five branches of the bank any day of the week and look over the people standing ten-deep for twenty minutes in front of the tellers' windows waiting to put in or take out some of their money. The police aren't going to find many customers in the lineup who haven't thought of throwing a rock at a bank window once in a while.

The man or woman who's been breaking all these windows has used something called a high-powered nail gun. It's a tool used by builders instead of a hammer. It shoots a heavy nail into wood with great force at the press of its trigger. This makes it an ingenious weapon for anyone bent on destruction because it apparently is as efficient at breaking a window at fifty feet as it is at driving nails close up. If anyone were apprehended by the police with one of these tools in his or her car, he could not be charged with possessing a gun.

As angry as I've often been with my bank, I've never left it, because all banks are substantially the same. From time to time one may offer some service or an interest margin the other doesn't, but sooner or later they all even out.

Sue is the other reason I haven't thrown a rock at a window or left my branch of the bank. Sue is a lower-level executive at the bank who has actually helped me through several sticky banking situations. Her phone extension at the bank has changed thirty-seven times in the nine years I've known her but she's the one banker who actually thinks of me as a person and not a number.

Sue is the only banker I've ever called by a first name and she's exactly what banks need more of if they're ever going to improve their public image and eliminate the kind of attitude in their customers that leads to window-breaking rage.

I suppose we expect too much of our banks. We'd like to think of banks as quasi-government institutions with all the benevolent qualities of the Red Cross, when all each of them is, is a business like the candy store down the street.

Banks were on the leading edge of a strange revolution in wages that has taken place in America. For most of our history, white-collar office workers were routinely paid higher salaries than manual laborers. In many cases this is no longer true, and bank tellers are near the bottom of the pay scale. In large cities, they make half as much as the garbage collectors. It accounts for the rapid turnover of help at most banks and for the lack of personal contact between customers and bank employees. I've been with my bank longer than anyone who works there. That doesn't make for much continuity in our relationship.

In banks in the smaller towns and cities, the relationship between banks and customers is often better, but not always great, either. The people in the rural Minnesota community in which a young man shot and killed two bankers who had come to look at his family's farmhouse, which they had repossessed, were reported to have been more sympathetic to the murderer than to the bankers.

I don't envy the New York police their job of finding out who broke my bank's windows.

SAVINGS

How much of your income do you spend and how much do you save for later?

Some of those people who are always announcing things in Washington announced that Americans saved less of what they made last year than they have in all history. The savings figure the Commerce Department gave was 1.9 percent of income after taxes. That means people saved just $19 out of every $1,000.

The experts have a lot of theories, naturally, on why people aren't saving. They say, for instance, that car prices were low and good deals on loans were available so people bought cars instead of saving.

To use a word that was popular among my classmates in high school, "Baloney!" People aren't saving money because when they do, they get taken and end up having less than they started with. The trouble is, there is no longer a good way to save money. It used to be that people put it under their mattresses, in the sugar bowl or in savings banks, but none of these makes any sense now. Neither the mattress nor the sugar bowl pays interest and the banks don't pay much more. Not only that, people have learned that by the time they want to use the dollars they've saved, their money is going to be worth less than when they stashed it away.

Banks are smarter about money than people are. People have learned that and they're bank-shy. Even though people aren't saving much money, savings banks and other savings businesses are going to make $5 billion in profit this year. That's because of all that mortgage money they loaned out a few years ago at figures like 14 percent. The savings banks are paying something like 5 percent in interest to the people with savings accounts whose money the banks are loaning out now.

A lot of us have had to relearn what our fathers, mothers and Ben Franklin taught us about thrift. We all grew up on phrases like "A penny saved is a penny earned," "Waste not, want not" and "Prepare today for the wants of tomorrow." Savings these days, we've discovered, are better for the bank than they are for us.

When I made money delivering newspapers, my mother got me to open a savings account. Every once in a while I'd put an amount like $1.70 in the bank, and at Christmas I'd add the twenty-five dollars Uncle Bill gave me. My mother said I'd need it to help pay for my college education. Over a period of years I saved $189. The bank gave me $6.25 in interest. The trouble was, by the time I got ready to go to college, tuition, room and board were $2,000 and I realized I might as well have spent my newspaper money on the expensive Duncan yo-yo and the pogo stick I always wanted.

That's what people are doing now. They aren't saving money, they're buying yo-yos with it because they know it's too hard to save.

How do you save? There are thousands of savings institutions keeping a total of $826 billion of Americans' money, but you can bet not many of the executives of those banks keep their money in a low-interest savings account.

I liked the idea of a savings bank. I liked it when I put that $1.70 away with some confidence that I was doing the right and the smart thing. Fortunately for savings banks, they still have $826 billion of our dollars that they can loan out at 10 percent and pay interest on at 5 percent. This is dumb money the banks have, and they have it because it's relatively safe and because a lot of people put it there from habit or because they don't know what else to do.

Many young people today who never had a newspaper route or a piggy bank just say the hell with it. They admit they don't know how they should handle their money so they spend it.

Our whole economy is based on spending and borrowing. You just know in your bones that it's wrong. Someone has to figure a way for us to go back to the honest pleasure of saving for our own futures.

A KIND KING

One of the great mysteries of life is why we always make the worst choices when we're picking things to save money on. People do it and so do governments. When the mayor decides to cut back, he starts with the schools, the museums, the parks and the libraries.

A high-powered research organization in Washington recommended that the government cut back on Social Security payments. That fits in with my theory. Will everyone who's living luxuriously on Social Security please stand up?

Reducing Social Security payments is the last economic measure the government should take. Social Security is one of the most civilized institutions in the civilized world . . . which is not usually as civilized as it ought to be. What happened before we had Social Security? What in the world did elderly people do with no income and no savings? When I was growing up, there was always a place called "The Poor House." I suppose, before Social Security, people went there.

If people save money during their working lives, retire and supplement Social Security with their savings, they can live quite comfortably. If they have nothing but Social Security, they can, at least, live. President Reagan attended what they call an "economic summit meeting," and I imagine the delegates thought up some international ways to save money, comparable to closing the libraries on Mondays and Wednesdays.

I read some of the stories about the economic summit, more because I thought I ought to than because they interested me. I'd have preferred to hear less theory about the danger of rising U.S. interest rates on the world economy and more about how we can get the world economy to produce a better life for more people. I'm not that interested in interest rates, oil prices or trends in the stock market. The economists attending the meeting ought to be finding some economic advantage for countries to spend money on services and facilities that are good for all of us.

Here in the United States, for example, we've got plenty of television sets, cameras, cars, dishwashers and air conditioners, but our schools, our libraries, our parks and our museums are in bad shape. I'd also like the economists to figure out a way to pay for better garbage disposal, more efficient airports, bumpless highways, rebuilt railroads and a brand-new, improved criminal-justice system. Paying for these is the real economic problem.

Every once in a while, I sneak the wish that we had a dictatorship or a monarchy in the United States. If I were the king of America, I'd take these economic measures:

—Decree that everyone pay ten percent of his or her income as tax regardless of how much or how little it was. This would hit the rich loopholers hardest and make the poor aware that they have some responsibility, too.

—Move the unemployed workers in one city to another city where they're needed.

—When unemployment was high, my royal government would hire people to do all kinds of good things. When there was no unemployment, I'd drop the people from the royal payroll.

—Make everyone save fifteen percent of everything they earned and put it in a savings account.

—Let people who need money borrow from the savings accounts of the others at a firm interest rate of 7 percent for the next fifty years so everyone could depend on it.

—Eliminate the national debt by suspending all weapons manufacture for one year.

I'd be a kind king. I'd be one-third dictator, one-third socialist, one-third hard-core free-enterprise businessman. I'd protect business from government and use the government to protect the people from business.

If someone said, "Your Highness, some people in Arizona and Florida have money of their own and are also drawing Social Security," I'd wait until the reporters were around and then I'd say, "Fine. Let them eat cake."

THE QUALITY OF MERCY

When a man came and knocked on our back door and asked for something to eat, my mother always fried him two eggs and made him toast and coffee but, no matter how cold it was, she made him eat it outside. Her quality of mercy was tempered with caution.

This was during the Depression in the late 1930s when I was growing up in Albany, New York. There was seldom any question that the man was anything but hungry. He was not looking for money with which to buy whiskey. All the man ever wanted was food. I remember asking Mother why no women ever came begging for food. She didn't know.

All this came flooding back to me last evening when I was standing in line at Grand Central Station to buy a train ticket. There were five or six people in front of me and the line was moving slowly. I contemplated switching to another line, but experience has taught me this is usually a mistake so I started reading my newspaper.

In the middle of a paragraph, I sensed someone standing next to me. I looked up and into the eyes of a small young woman wearing a belted trench coat that wasn't very clean. She had straggly, dark blond hair and, while she was not unattractive, she appeared to be no cleaner than her coat.

"Could you spare a quarter?" she asked.

She said it perfunctorily, in a manner that suggested she'd said it thousands of times before. "No," I said, without malice. I looked into her eyes but didn't get any feeling I was seeing her. There was a curtain behind the cornea so I turned back to my newspaper. I wasn't reading it anymore, though.

"No" had not been exactly the right answer, I thought to myself. Of course, I could have spared a quarter. I must have had nearly fifty dollars in my pocket, three of them in change.

Why hadn't I given this poor soul something? Or is she a poor soul?

Where did she come from? I wondered. What are her parents like? What did her classmates in school think of her? Does she have friends? When did she eat last? Where did she sleep?

If it was peace of mind I was looking for, it would have been easier to give her the quarter. I can't get her out of my mind and yet the people who drop change in cups and hats anger me. It seems like cheap gratification that does more for the psyche of the giver than the receiver. I don't like their smug assumption that they are compassionate people.

I pretended to be reading the paper for thirty seconds more and then looked up to see where the young woman had gone. She was standing a short way off, on the heartless marble floor of the station, doing nothing. I thought how close to barefoot she looked in her thin, old leather shoes.

Most beggars in New York City are either con

213

artists or alcoholics. She didn't seem to be a con artist or an alcoholic, and I don't know what someone looks like who's on drugs or smoking marijuana. You can't make enough begging to be a drug addict, anyway. Drug addicts steal. She didn't look like a thief.

There aren't a lot of beggars in New York but there are all kinds, and every passerby has a decision to make. The black kids stand at the clogged entrance to the bridges and tunnels and slop soapy water on your windshield with a dirty sponge. If you give them a quarter, they clean it off. If you don't, they don't. I'm torn between compassion and anger at times like this. It's blackmail but it's better than stealing and I laugh and give.

The ordinary street beggar will not be helped by what anyone gives him, though. And, anyway, I have the feeling the saddest cases and the ones who need money most desperately don't beg for it.

Everyone in New York is approached at least once a month. You have to have a policy. Mine is simple. To beggars on the street, I give nothing. I wish I was certain I'm right, I keep thinking of the young woman in Grand Central and the two fried eggs.

WHOSE FAULT?

Television news broadcasts have shown us a lot of pictures of homeless and hungry people lately.

Those of us who have a comfortable place to live and plenty to eat should be reminded that there are people in America who do not. The thing that bothers me about these broadcasts is the suggestion that it is my fault.

I'm not speaking here of people who are poor and hungry because, through no fault of their own, they have become unemployed or because they are sick or elderly. I am speaking of people who have never tried to contribute anything to the society in which they live.

Television doesn't usually say so in so many words but the news broadcasts usually leave me with the feeling that it's my fault, your fault, the city's fault, the state's fault, the federal government's fault or the fault of some anonymous monster known as The System.

I don't want you to think I'm cold, cruel and heartless but sometimes, as I watch these people on television, I can't help thinking it's their own fault. Should I be drummed out of the human race for thinking that?

Recently on *60 Minutes*, Ed Bradley interviewed a woman living under terrible circumstances in a New York City hotel room. Various government agencies were paying the hotel owners $2,000 a month for her filthy, roach-infested room. Ed's story was about the inefficiency of government and the greed of the welfare-hotel owners. It was a good story but there were some questions I'd like to have asked the woman that Ed didn't.

First: "Madam, why do you keep having children when you have no husband and can't take care of the children you already have?"

Second question: "Wouldn't this room be a better place for your children to live if you spent ten minutes a day cleaning it, no matter how evil the management may be?"

Third question: "Could you give us exact details of what you spent your last welfare check on?"

The last question would be to myself. It's one I've never been able to answer satisfactorily: "Is a person who isn't very smart and can't take charge of his or her own life any more or less deserving of happiness than people who are capable?"

It seems as though the right answer would be "Yes, they have the same right to be happy," but that leads to another question: "Does the person who steals or cheats have as much right to be happy as the person who is honest?"

Now I'm in over my head and I quit asking questions.

It seems obvious that we have to take care of people who can't or won't take care of themselves no matter who or what they are. I don't know why we do but we do. It comes with being civilized.

People, no matter how poor or screwed up, ought to be made aware that they are responsible for themselves, too. If they can't take care of themselves, we help them. If they won't take care of themselves, we still help them but we don't have to like it.

No one knows where society's obligation stops and starts but it seems as if more effort has to be put into making irresponsible people feel responsible for themselves. None of us minds helping to feed or house genuinely poor people, but when it is apparent that they're never going to be any better off or any happier no matter how much help they get, I feel ill at ease. I don't like anyone being less happy than I am, but if they're less happy because it's their own fault, the best way to help them is to make them understand their problem.

Most of us don't resent welfare or charity because we pay for it. We resent it because it doesn't seem to do any good. People who give to charity and taxpayers who see their money go to welfare want some personal satisfaction. We want to know that what we gave wasn't wasted. We want to know that it helped make someone's life less desperate, less unhappy. That doesn't make it our fault.

A CONSPIRACY AGAINST SILENCE

There's a conspiracy against silence in the world. We seem to prefer a shout to a whisper.

Everywhere you go, someone is making noise. They aren't making sounds, they're making noise. People who make noise for their own amusement intrude on the privacy of silence to which the rest of us are entitled.

Silence is the natural state. Any noise is a deviation from the norm. A lion doesn't roar for more than a few minutes out of twenty-four hours, and while I don't know any lions personally, I'll bet there are days lions choose not to roar at all. How often do you hear thunder, the eruption of a volcano or the rumble of an earthquake? These natural sounds are special and they only break the earth's silence on rare occasions.

I don't understand why some people insist on filling the air with noise. They can't stand to be in a car without having the radio on. They can't stand being anywhere with nothing but the natural sounds of earth in their ears.

The most loathsome telephone practice instituted since Alexander Graham Bell asked Watson if he was there is the hold button that automatically feeds music into the waiting caller's ear. In many offices, when you call and are put on hold, the company apparently feels the need to amuse, entertain or distract you, so it feeds music into the line. If I have to wait for someone on the phone, I don't want the thought of what I wish to say crowded out of my head by some inane bit of music.

Many airlines pipe music into the passenger section upon landing. I'm trying to gather my wits and remember which overhead bin I put my coat in and they're playing soothing music. Soothing music irritates me more than music that isn't soothing. Soothing music sets my nerves on edge.

I can stand the sound of a neighbor mowing his lawn because it is not a noise made merely for the sake of noisemaking. The machine making the noise is performing a necessary function and I accept it.

It's the gratuitous noise that irritates me most. When a driver stops in front of a house in the neighborhood and blows the horn to attract the attention of someone inside, it's thoughtless and rude. We're all conditioned to the sound of a horn. Why should ten people have to bother to look out the windows of ten houses to find out the horn means nothing for them? As a matter of fact, I don't think there are more than ten times in a whole year of driving when it's necessary for someone behind the wheel to blow the horn.

I question the frequency of use of ambulance sirens. If the ambulance people use the siren, they ought to mean it. There ought to be a genuine medical emergency, not just a cowboy at the wheel.

In New York City there are 12,000 licensed taxis. Half the drivers are tuned to both a commercial radio station and the cab company's short-wave frequency, which advises them of pickups. The drivers play both radios simultaneously and keep turning up the volume on each to override the other until they can hear neither. The paying passenger, besieged in both ears, is helpless.

I realize now that when I was a kid, some of the boys I played with were constant screamers. They always made more noise by yelling louder than the rest of us. It's a trait some people carry with them through life. They do everything louder than everyone else.

Most people don't mind the normal and necessary sounds. If I'm writing, I can ignore a vacuum cleaner, a lawn mower or a conversation in another room, but when a kid goes past the house with his car windows open and rock music blaring from his radio, I forget what I'm doing. It's those unnecessary noises, deliberately made, that call themselves to our attention and get on our nerves.

We have a day to celebrate almost everything else. I propose A Day of Silence.

BALLET

When they announced that Darci Kistler would be replaced by someone else and 4,999 people in the audience muttered their disapproval in a sound that grew into a low growl, I knew I didn't belong. I was the 5,000th person in the audience at the ballet performance. I didn't disapprove because I'd never heard of Darci Kistler or the dancer who was replacing her.

The people who love ballet make the people who love Madonna, Prince, the Chicago Cubs or bullfighting seem pale by comparison.

All of us tend to dislike things we don't understand. Every year, on our annual cultural trip to Saratoga, I am uneasy about not understanding ballet and, therefore, not liking it very much. The event in Saratoga takes place in a spectacular open shed that you get to by walking down a long, sloping hill. On the lawn above the roof line, people spread blankets and beach chairs. These are the cheap seats, but the people sitting on the lawn seem sublimely happy and at peace with the world.

If you had to pick a crowd of people most different from the rioting hockey or soccer fans, you'd pick this group of ballet nuts. Even the people at the ticket gates are courteous and helpful. As I stood by the gate, a man came up to the ticket taker and said he was part of a group that had come by bus from a nearby city. They were to have had dinner in a restaurant on the grounds and then to go to the ballet. This man had been separated from his group and didn't have his ticket. The employee at the gate went into the gatehouse, picked up the telephone and was trying to help this ballet fan when I left. Try that at a baseball park or a rock concert.

When I watch a football game on television, I often turn down the sound to eliminate hearing the announcers tell me things I can see and understand for myself. At the ballet, I feel the need to have a balletomane equivalent of Frank Gifford sitting next to me to explain the moves. I am impressed with the great athleticism of many of the men and women onstage but I do not understand what it is they're trying to convey.

Ballet is the most muscular of the performing arts. The performers build some of the same muscles as gymnasts. Because of the jumps, the whirling moves and the contortions the dancers' bodies have to make, ballet produces almost perfect physical specimens. The men seem to make out better than the women in this regard. Heavy thigh and calf muscles do more for the appearance of the men than for the women.

It's interesting that anything so physical has such an intellectual appeal for so many smart people. Fans wouldn't admit it, I don't think, but it's a very sexy art. The bodies of both men and women are clearly revealed and the men are always taking hold of the women in socially unacceptable places, turning them upside down and generally handling them a lot.

It strikes me as funny, too, that it is the men in form-fitting tights and not the women in tutus who enhance their parts the most with padded underwear. Some of the women may wear padded brassieres but all the male dancers wear what athletes like hockey goalies call a cup, which fits into the pouch of a jockstrap.

In the case of the ballet dancer, the plastic cup produces a protuberance in the area of the crotch that, for a man who knows what's really down there, is comic. I don't know whether this is a cause or a result of the fact that the audience ratio was four-to-one female.

You won't find me laughing much at ballet, though. It isn't my dish but in a world of war, terrorism and savagery, there is something reassuring about a group of 5,000 people getting together to have a good time watching the animated movements to music of skilled and handsome performers on a beautiful stage on a pleasant summer evening.

BACK TO BASICS

When the teachers and administrators of our schools start deciding what and how to teach, I hope they decide to start from the beginning.

Before a kid learns how to use a computer that can solve mathematical problems, he or she should know how to do arithmetic without a computer.

Before getting a word processor equipped with a program that corrects spelling, a child should learn how to spell without it.

For the last three weeks I've been living in a house supplied with well water and equipped with a septic tank. Every American child should live for a while in a house with a limited supply of water and a fragile sanitation system. There's nothing that keeps you in touch with supply and demand and the sensitive balance of our earth better than knowing firsthand that there's a limit to how much you can take out and how much you can dump back into it.

Kids should learn that the world did not come equipped with toilets and endless amounts of water available at the twist of a faucet handle. They should understand early in life that everything they wish to get rid of—garbage, human waste and junk of every kind—doesn't disappear from the earth just because they flush a toilet or throw the potato peels in a garbage can.

When our well was dug many years ago, we were told it had a flow of four gallons a minute. If all we needed was drinking water, that would be a great deal, but on weekends, when we often have guests or other family members in the house, it's not much. If the dishwasher is turned on while someone is doing a load of laundry and someone else is upstairs taking a shower, four gallons a minute doesn't go far.

The pump at the bottom of our well cuts off automatically when the water level gets very low and it takes half an hour to get it started again. Being without water for half an hour is a learning experience. Being in a house where the septic tank overflows provides a college education in sanitation. Both are bitter experiences everyone should have. The world would be much more careful of both water and waste if it had been through the experience of being temporarily without those facilities.

A lot of education starts too far into the subject. Take such a nonacademic subject as driver education. Before learning how to drive a car, people ought to know something about what makes it go. I don't think we have to be mechanics but we should have some basic knowledge about the problems that can develop in a car.

There's nothing onerous about starting at the beginning. People like to get back to basics. That's why it's fun to leave the comforts of home and rough it on a camping trip. That's why so many people love to have a little flower or vegetable garden. The whole process of doing it yourself is not only educational, it's satisfying. It makes people more appreciative of the things we get the easy way, by buying them in a store.

It would be harder for manufacturers to sell us shoddy products if we all knew more about how things ought to be made. If you know how to make a loaf of bread, you're more aware of how bad the average commercial loaf is.

The opposite is true, too. If you've tried, without much success, to make or grow something yourself, you're much more appreciative of the product when it's been done well by a professional.

When I'm working, my shirts go to the laundry. On vacation, I often try to iron a few myself. It sure makes me appreciate laundries and dry cleaners.

When it comes to educating all of us about the most basic things in life, it seems to me we need more kindergartens and fewer graduate schools.

SCHOOL PRAYER

In Poland, it isn't prayer in the schools they're arguing about, it's the crucifix. Devout Catholics want the symbolic crosses restored to the public schools from which they were removed by Communist officials.

There must be some non-Communist Poles who oppose the display of the crucifix. They're probably having as difficult a time as religious Americans have with their opposition to prayer in public schools.

In this country, those opposed to school prayer have to explain, before they say anything else, that they are not opposed to religion. In Poland, the independent minority that opposes the display of the crucifix must have to explain first that it is not Communist.

The U.S. Senate defeated the proposal for government-sanctioned school prayer, but only after a bitter debate.

I wondered, reading about the crucifix debate in Poland, how many Americans who approved of school prayer would be in favor of the compulsory display of the crucifix? Most of the arguments in favor of school prayer could just as well be used in favor of displaying the cross.

The objection to it is easier to argue than the case against school prayer. The crucifix is used as a symbol by just one religion, Christianity. Prayer, on the other hand, is endorsed by all religions.

While Christianity is the choice of most Americans, the number of Buddhists, Hindus and Moslems in the world far exceeds the total number of Christians. In the United States, Jews are a substantial minority. Even militant Christians are reluctant to force their convictions or their symbols on people of other religions.

The objection to prayer is the same as the objection to the crucifix. We don't all believe the same thing. Many of us don't know what we believe. People say they're Baptists, Seventh-Day Adventists or Episcopalians, but if they're Baptists, don't ask them how they differ from the Methodists around the corner.

There is obviously a great human need for religion because life seems to be such a mystery.

227

Why were we born? Why must we die? Is there a meaning to life or is our civilization just a felicitous accident in an otherwise totally disorganized universe? Our brains have come to expect an explanation for everything. We assume there is always a logical reason for what happens, and when we can't find a reason, we need a substitute.

The people in any country eventually believe what their government wants them to believe. Unfortunately, propaganda works. The U.S.S.R. is officially godless, and while there are still millions of worshipers in Russia, they are a diminishing number because the government discourages religion.

It is wrong for any government to be anything but neutral in regard to religion. Religion is none of the government's business. I'm as offended by the Soviet Union's official policy of discouraging it as I am by our government trying to encourage it.

Faith, or the lack of it, is up to the individual and is subject to as many variations as there are people on earth. If an individual finds others who seem to believe as he or she believes, and wishes to pray with them, under a crucifix or a Star of David or kneeling facing Mecca, this is a private decision.

It's discouraging, though, to see how many people who talk about the Bible take so little of its advice. The book of Matthew says this was Jesus' advice on the place for prayer:

"When you pray, you must not be like hypocrites, for they love to stand and pray at the streetcorners that they may be seen by men. Truly, I say to you, they have received their reward. But when you pray, go to your room and shut the door and pray to your Father who is unseen. Your Father, who sees in secret, will reward you."

A HUNG JURY

Opinionated people who are sure of what they think about everything are usually more interesting than people who can't decide. I like to be opinionated and there are a lot of things in life I'm sure of, even if I'm wrong. I wish there weren't so many major public issues I can't make up my mind about.

The other morning, I read three stories in the paper about which my mind is a hung jury.

—The first was a story about a white fireman who was suing the town in which he worked because he had been passed over for a promotion in favor of a black fireman who had scored lower than he had on the examination promotions were based on. The promotion was given to the black fireman on the basis of the affirmative-action policy in effect in that town.

No one questions that black Americans got a bad start in America when they were brought here as slaves or that they have been treated as second-class citizens for much of the time since then. The rest of us owe blacks something. We not only owe them something but it's going to make a better life for all of us if black Americans are helped out of the social, financial and educational ghetto in which so many of them live.

Black Americans dominate city crime in percentages far in excess of their numbers, and that statistic won't change until they become mainstream Americans. Affirmative action is a program designed to help blacks toward that goal.

I realize this and I'm all for affirmative action but . . . do you promote a black policeman or a black fireman over a white one who is better at the job just because one man is black and the other white?

Don't ask me to decide. I can understand the anger on either side.

—In New York City, they've opened up a high school for homosexuals. The justification offered by the Board of Education is that these sexually disoriented young boys and girls were subject to so much harassment and even violence at the regular high schools that many of them didn't dare go to school.

Is a separate school for homosexuals in a big city right or wrong? If a boy is born with some feminine characteristics, can he be blamed? Doesn't this homosexual boy have the right, just as any handicapped person, to an education?

Or wait a minute. Won't this special school be like an official stamp of approval for homosexuality? Won't it suggest that homosexuality is a normal and acceptable way of life and so tend to promote more of it? Won't it exacerbate the problem by encouraging homosexuality in young people who could go either way?

Don't look to me for an answer.

—The most popular cause among bright, well-meaning college students this year is the campaign against the racial separatist policies of the South African government.

Many colleges in the United States have millions of dollars in endowments that are invested in places where they will produce the most money. When it comes to money, colleges, like everyone else, set aside ethical considerations, and many of the endowment funds have bought stock in companies that do business in South Africa. Students want their colleges to sell that stock.

That seems right, doesn't it? Why should American colleges support inequality in any part of the world? Perhaps cutting off South Africa's economic lifeline will make the government there change its apartheid policy . . . but wait a minute. Many South Africans, like Alan Paton, author of *Cry, the Beloved Country,* who violently oppose apartheid, also oppose the American student movement to get U.S. business out of South Africa. They make the point that the people who will be hurt the most are the poor black South Africans they're trying to help. Who's right?

May I have the envelope, please!

STRANGERS ON A TRAIN

This morning the commuter train I take to work was crowded. I get on far enough up the line so I always get a seat, but by the time the train reached Stamford, the last stop before Grand Central Station, many people in the crowd waiting to board couldn't find seats for the forty-five minute trip into the city.

From an aisle seat in the middle of the car, I watched as a very pleasant-looking black woman in her late thirties got on. She held onto a small child with one hand and with the other she clutched her suitcase, her pocketbook and a small brown paper bag. She glanced hopefully up and down the aisle, but after a moment it became apparent to her that all the seats were taken. She put down her suitcase, resigned to standing for the long trip to New York. There were a dozen men seated within a few feet of her.

Men don't give up their seats to women the way they used to, I thought to myself.

Should I walk up the aisle past all those people and offer her my seat?

That would be sort of a grandstand move.

If that was Gloria Steinem standing there and I offered Gloria my seat because she's a woman, would she take it? I don't think she would.

Would Gloria just smile and say, "No, thank you," or would she yell at me for being a male chauvinist pig, for being condescending and suggesting she was less capable of standing for forty-five minutes than I was?

As these thoughts went through my mind, a distinguished-looking gentleman seated near the woman got up and quietly offered her his seat.

I was elated.

I already knew the woman was not Gloria Steinem so it didn't surprise me when she smiled gratefully and sat down with the small child on her lap.

How good, I thought to myself. The man looked like the president of a bank or, at the very least, a $150,000-a-year advertising-agency executive. He was reading *The Wall Street Journal* and I judged from looking at him that he made several trips a year to Europe, owned two expensive cars and voted for Ronald Reagan.

The woman was reading nothing. She was neatly and cleanly dressed and had an exceptionally pleasant face, but from the condition of her suitcase and her general appearance, I judged that she was near-poor. Perhaps, I thought, my own prejudices at work, her husband had left her and she was bringing the child to New York to leave him with her mother so she could look for work.

She stared straight ahead, looking content and relieved to be sitting down. The man folded his *Wall Street Journal* so he could hold it with one hand while he held onto the pole with the other.

The man's simple and generous gesture made me feel great to be alive.

Most of the people in the world are good and decent if you give them a chance to be, I thought. I found myself wishing that some of the black activists like Jesse Jackson could have seen what I just saw.

This man in his pin-striped suit didn't care whether the woman was black or white, rich or poor, I thought to myself. She was simply a person who needed a seat more than he did and he gave it to her. That's all there was to it. I was practically glowing with a feeling of warmth and fellowship with the people around me on the train.

At this point I became aware that the man in the seat across the aisle from me had also watched this little vignette.

I looked at him and smiled. He scowled back, and in a disgusted half-whisper said, "I don't know why people like that don't take a train later in the day."

I turned from him, my euphoria gone, and picked up the newspaper.

17 BLACKS KILLED BY SOUTH AFRICAN POLICE, the headline read. So much for goodness and decency.

REPORTERS

The public and quite a few politicians don't know what they're talking about when they criticize news organizations. The trouble with most news organizations, whether they're newspapers, television or radio, is that they don't spend as much money as they should on reporting.

Good reporting is expensive and hard. The reason it's so hard is that half the world is trying to hide the truth from the other half. Too many government officials, business executives, union leaders and ordinary citizens who deal with the public are doing things they don't want anyone to know about, and they're good at concealing them.

It seems as if all the bad guys are caught sooner or later but they are not. It's a safe bet that we've never read about the biggest crooks in business and government because no one ever found out about them. There are not enough reporters.

Most politicians and business people are honest but they're also paranoid about reporters. Maybe it's Mike Wallace's fault. Even when they have nothing to hide, they try to hide it. Once, as a reporter, I tried to find out how they make billiard balls round but the little company that makes a lot of them wouldn't let me in its plant because it said the process was a secret.

The public has a lot of mistaken ideas about reporters. I don't know whether or not reporters and editors are generally more liberal than conservative, as critics claim. Even if they are, it's possible for a reporter who votes Democratic to treat Republicans fairly. A good reporter covering a political story can be as detached, personally, from his work as a gynecologist.

There are other charges people make against reporters that are seldom true, or if they're true, they're meaningless. One is that reporters don't give the whole story. Well, of course they don't give the whole story. Boiling a story down to its essentials is part of a journalist's job. It's the only thing that allows a newspaper to give the essential elements of one hundred stories in the space it has to print them and the time people have to read them. The public assumption that selection necessarily means distortion is ridiculous. Whether it's pictures or words, someone has to choose the ones that tell the story quickest and best.

I'm always surprised that people who distrust newspaper reporters because they say reporters are biased accept Matthew, Mark, Luke and John's reports on the life of Jesus Christ. The gospel writers' stories differ, and they could hardly be called impartial reporters. They wanted everyone to believe what they believed.

It's difficult for a news organization not to spend more on its sales department than on its editorial department. Sales brings in money and editorial spends it.

Each of the three television networks has about one hundred reporters. (Television calls them "correspondents" because all titles are inflated in television.) It seems like a lot but not when you consider that the network news departments are trying to cover the world. They could use twice that many.

The anchormen on the networks each make at least a million dollars a year. The correspondents make substantially less but Dan Rather is a better buy for the networks because he's on every weekday and he attracts a crowd just sitting there being Dan Rather. Good reporters like Brian Ross at NBC or Richard Threlkeld at ABC or Bruce Morton at CBS don't get on once a week because they're spending their time the hard way, being reporters.

The networks would be better news organizations if they each took the million dollars their anchormen make and hired another twenty reporters for $50,000. You wouldn't find the anchormen arguing about that, either. They're reporters and, while they like the money, they're embarrassed to be caught up in the star system that puts ratings ahead of information.

SPENT HENS

This morning, driving to work, I became aware of something white flying around in the air. A mile further along, I could see that whatever it was came from a huge truck up ahead of me. As I got closer to the truck, I realized it was a gigantic tractor trailer loaded with hundreds of crates of chickens.

As I passed the truck, I noted the name painted on the door of the cab: DECOSTER EGG FARM, TURNER, MAINE. Turner, Maine, according to my map, is about 360 miles from where I saw them, so the feathers had been flying for at least seven hours.

I estimated that each crate held twelve chickens. The crates were stacked five high and five across, and from one end of the truck to the other, I think there were twenty crates. It's hard to count when you're driving the car and passing a truck.

If my figures are accurate, there were 6,000 chickens on board.

Now, I'm not unnecessarily sentimental about chickens, but I can't get the birds in the crates on the bottom out of my mind. It seems to me they must have suffocated to death before they arrived at their destination. Many of the birds in the crates on the outside had their heads stuck, half in and half out, between the narrow slats.

Last week I got a letter from a woman who said that after she retired, she became well-known in her town as a person who took care of wounded wild animals. She had, she said, just come back from picking up a robin whose wing had been damaged when it was caught by a cat. She said she saved as many as five birds in a week sometimes.

Yesterday I saw a woman pick up a small dog

she had on a leash and carry it across a puddle near the curb. She kissed the dog several times and then put it down. I watched as she continued on past a sign in a grocery store window: BABY LAMB, $1.59 A POUND.

We aren't very consistent in our treatment of animals. The robin the woman took in was, no doubt, grateful, but chickens must hurt as much as robins. What about the 6,000 chickens? Why does the little dog get so much better treatment than the baby lamb?

Once I passed the chicken truck this morning, I started to get angry. I was going to call the American Society for the Prevention of Cruelty to Animals.

In my office, I decided instead to call the DeCoster Egg Farm in Maine. I spoke to Mr. Matthews, a friendly fellow who answered every question I asked. He didn't sound as though he'd hurt a flea.

They have about a million chickens up there, he said. The ones I saw were what they call "spent hens." What a sad phrase, I thought. The hens, kept all their lives in tiny pens and fed from an automatically replenished trough in front of them, lay an egg a day for about a year, Mr. Matthews told me. He thought the chickens I saw were headed for United Poultry in Newark, New Jersey. I called there, and whereas Mr. Matthews was hard to understand because of his thick and charming Maine accent, the man at United was impossible to talk to because he spoke almost no

English and obviously couldn't hear me with the thousands of chickens I could hear in the background.

"We kill 'em," he said. I tried to find out how many of the DeCoster chickens were DOA but the man at United either didn't know, didn't care or couldn't hear.

DISHONESTY

All right, test time. Is the following statement true or false?

"Corruption appears to be pervasive in our society. I am thinking not simply of the public officeholder who betrays his trust. What also troubles me is the corruption of our ordinary citizens. I am thinking of the children who learn from their parents to cheat the storekeeper, the telephone company and the government. I am thinking of corporations who cheat the consumer. . . ."

This is a statement by the flamboyant mayor of New York City, Ed Koch. Do you agree that most Americans are dishonest?

It would be hard to go about the business of living here if we all thought they were. I think all of us have to lock the doors of our houses, not because we're all dishonest but because about one percent of us steal. If it wasn't for that one percent, cars wouldn't have to be made with ignition keys.

When Mayor Koch talks about cheating the telephone company or the government, he's getting into something else. I think that, given half a chance, a lot of Americans would cheat the telephone company or the government. It's not because Americans are dishonest. It's because they think taking something like a phone call from the telephone company without paying for it doesn't really hurt anyone. They're usually mad at the phone company, anyway. I've often had my change returned in a coin booth after I've made a long-distance call, but I've never called back the operator to say I wanted to redeposit it. It's wrong, but it never made me feel dishonest.

Unfortunately, I suppose my attitude toward the phone company is the same one that allows shoplifters to walk out of a big, impersonal store without paying for an item they've hidden under their coat.

Most people who steal wouldn't take something directly from another person. Stealing from an impersonal entity like the government or a utility company or even a department store doesn't seem dishonest to them. They don't think of themselves in the same league with the mugger who looks someone in the eye, knocks the person to the ground and takes what money he or she is carrying.

Person-to-person, most people are honest. During World War II, I saw American soldiers go into the homes of German citizens who had fled as our Army approached and strip their homes of anything of value. These were not dishonest American soldiers. They were young men with a temporarily suspended sense of decency. It did not seem to them as though they were stealing. The "If-I-don't-someone-else-will" mentality took over.

Dishonesty is a complex thing. Almost no one who steals thinks of himself as a bad person. They've talked themselves into believing they have it coming. Often they feel society has cheated them and owes them something.

It's always amusing to read about Mafia figures responsible for dozens of murders who hold to a firm code of ethics in relation to each other. Between them, a handshake is all that's necessary. They are scrupulously honest on a personal basis and often devoutly religious and dedicated family members.

Several years ago in New York, I was traveling with a camera crew with hundreds of thousands of dollars' worth of equipment in a station wagon. We stopped to park the station wagon in a lot next door to a restaurant in which a notorious Mafia leader had been pumped full of bullets a few weeks earlier.

When we started to lock the car, the parking-lot attendant waved at us.

"Hey," he said, shaking his finger in a gesture that indicated locking the car wasn't necessary, "this is Mulberry Street. Nobody's gonna steal nothing here."

We are not personally dishonest but some of us

need to be reminded from time to time what honesty is.

CHEAPENING THE LAW

The Supreme Court has ruled that lawyers can advertise in newspapers to get customers for specific cases. That means lawyers can run ads to try to get people to sue other people or companies. The lawyers may even suggest whom the people can sue in order to make a bundle.

I like the Supreme Court ruling because if I ever need a lawyer, it's going to help me decide which lawyer to go to. First, I'll eliminate all the lawyers who advertise. I wouldn't dream of going to one of them.

Doctors are allowed to advertise now, too, and I'm no more apt to go to a doctor who tries to sell himself with an ad than to a lawyer who does.

I'm not against advertising. It's okay for Miller to tell us how good its beer is and it's okay for politicians to tell us how great they are, but I don't want to hear it from a doctor or a lawyer.

There are 650,000 lawyers in the United States and 520,000 doctors. You won't find more than a small percentage of either who will take advantage of this ruling and run ads for themselves. It may be legal but not many of them think it's ethical.

The majority of good, honest lawyers and the handful of great ones must be embarrassed to see how many money-grubbing ambulance chasers there are in their profession. It would be wrong to suggest that every lawyer or every doctor who advertises is unethical, but that's the impression such ads leave on most of us.

The persistent suers in the legal profession often seem more interested in money than justice. The really big money for lawyers is in class-action suits. These are cases in which one plaintiff represents hundreds, thousands or sometimes even millions of others. If the lawyer wins one, he wins them all and may collect a part of the payoff from each participant. A thirty-percent fee is considered standard. It helps account for why so many American lawyers rushed off to Bhopal, India, in the hope that they'd get in on a good thing by suing Union Carbide on behalf of a great many Indian victims. More than $35 billion in lawsuits were filed against Union Carbide. Who believes the lawyers' interest was primarily justice for those Indian people? Lawyers claim they are protecting the individual against the giant corporation and, of course, sometimes they are. Sometimes.

Melvin Belli, one of the American lawyers who went to India, filed suit for $15 billion on behalf of two Bhopal residents. If he were to win the suit and get the standard thirty-percent legal fee, Belli would collect $4.5 billion. He could buy a couple of minutes of commercial time on *The Bill Cosby Show* every week for that much money but Belli gets so much free publicity he doesn't have to advertise.

Americans think of criminal trials when they think of lawyers but most of the good and important work lawyers do isn't related to crime. Lawyers do their heaviest work behind the scenes in business. They make business work by keeping it organized and legal.

There are a great many doctors and lawyers who take their principal pleasure in life from doing good things for other people. I have known enough of both to be certain this is true. They get up in the morning and are concerned not with making a living, but with what they can do for their patients and their clients. They are not businessmen, they are professionals. Success for them is not expressed by numbers. They've had a good day if they've done something good for another human being. They like the money but it isn't what gets them up in the morning.

When a lawyer advertises, it cheapens the law. It cheapens our judicial system when money becomes more important than the fundamental principles of justice and fairness.

HOLIDAY NEWS

Don't think for a minute that you're any prouder to be an American than I am. But sometimes we act so irrationally, I worry. I have an example in mind.

245

Until it got dark and we went into town to see the fireworks, the Fourth of July was just like another vacation day for me. I spent most of it in my shop, making some shelves to fit in between the wall and the refrigerator. (I'm always making shelves to put junk on; then I go out and buy more junk, which I put where the junk was that I moved to the shelves.)

We're about 150 miles from New York but I put up a good aerial that's attached to a good radio and I get a powerful New York all-news radio station. About every twenty-seven minutes they start repeating the same stories, the same scores and the same weather. It isn't their fault, of course. That's all the news there is and they figure people don't just turn on the radio and listen to it all day.

Anyone in the news business hates to work on Christmas or Independence Day because there is no news. This year was no exception. The radio kept repeating the same four stories, all related to one another, all day long:

The President started the Firecracker 400 from a radio in his car in Washington when he said, "Gentlemen, start your engines." Later in the day, he planned to be in Daytona to watch the exciting end of the race. The drivers, the announcer said, were averaging 162 miles an hour.

The second story was also about driving and it came from Connecticut. The state police there were arresting thousands more people than usual for speeding. Anyone going more than fifty-five miles per hour was being stopped and given a ticket. The Connecticut police had already arrested twice as many as last year in an effort to get people to drive slower.

The third story was about the big fireworks display they were having in New York. It was going to be louder and more spectacular than anything they'd had before.

The last story was about a man in Carmel, New York, who had been arrested for selling fireworks to children. The announcer said fireworks were dangerous and illegal.

So here were four paradoxical news stories. One glorified driving cars as fast as possible, followed by a grim warning not to drive fast. The third spoke of how wonderfully exciting fireworks are and the last said fireworks are dangerous and illegal.

It must be tough for a kid listening to the radio or looking at a newspaper to know what adults think is right or wrong. One minute the child is hearing that they're cracking down on drivers who drink and the next minute he or she is listening to the beer commercial on the car radio.

The newspaper says Congress is considering making the cancer warning stronger on every pack of cigarettes. On another page, Congress has passed a bill approving millions of dollars of price support to tobacco farmers.

The headline story is about the little old lady who wins a million dollars in the state-operated lottery. On the next page, the police are arresting people involved in a gambling ring.

It is idiotic for any government to arrest people for betting on games or numbers or cards and dice and then set up special places where that same government makes money off people who bet on games, numbers, cards and dice.

We just don't make any sense sometimes.

VII

ECONOMY CLASS

ECONOMY CLASS

What follows is the timetable for my last fourteen hours:

5:00 P.M. Leave midtown New York City by taxi for Kennedy Airport.

5:50 Arrive Kennedy. Pay $18.30 cab fare plus $3.00 tip.

6:00–6:35 Stand in line to check baggage and to allow airline-ticket clerk to check my previously purchased ticket.

6:35 The plane is going to be jammed. I feel claustrophobic. I ask the ticket clerk how much it would cost to upgrade my ticket to first class. Round-trip economy is $552. First class is $3,858. I do not upgrade.

6:45 Public-address system announces that 7 P.M. flight to London is boarding. Capacity is 350 people.

6:50–7:20 Stand in line with 350 people, all carrying too much luggage on board.

7:20 Strapped in, I am lulled into a doze by the gentle vibration of the engines before takeoff.

7:40 I am awakened by the thrust of the jet engines as the 7 P.M. flight takes off.

7:45–7:50 Dozing again.

7:50 Awakened by flight attendant announcing that if there's anything they can do to make my flight more pleasant, please don't hesitate to ask. Ask? They're so busy you couldn't grab one with a hook.

8:05 I doze for the third and last time on the flight. My night's sleep of approximately forty minutes is abruptly ended by the captain's loud announcement that he is the captain and that the flight will take six hours and twenty minutes. We should set our watches five hours ahead, he says. This makes it 1:05 A.M.

1:15 A.M. I strike up a conversation with a U.S. sailor sitting next to me. He decides he wants to smoke a cigarette and climbs over the man on the aisle to go to the back.

1:25 The flight attendant comes by to ask if I want to rent a pair of earphones for three dollars to see the movie.

I say, "You mean to *hear* the movie. No thanks. I read lips." I strike myself as very funny but do not strike the flight attendant that way at all.

It occurs to me, though, that the sailor may want to see the movie when he comes back to his seat. I am Mr. Nice Guy—so I say to the flight attendant, "Here's three dollars. I'll take a pair of earphones for the sailor so he can hear the movie."

1:35 Flight attendant comes by and asks what I'd like to drink. "Plenty," I say, being very funny again although she doesn't think so, again.

I tell her I'll have two of her toy bottles of bourbon. I give her five dollars and then Mr. Nice Guy suddenly realizes the sailor may want a drink too when he comes back so I buy two more. I have now put out eight dollars for this sailor I hardly know.

1:40–2:10 I drink my two little bottles of bourbon.

2:15 It begins to look as though the sailor will not return to his seat. Mr. Nice Guy does not want to waste good bourbon.

2:25 Just two hours and three minutes and four bourbons after boarding, dinner is served. It was a very good, well-prepared meal in its day, but this is not its day.

"Do you always serve dinner this late at home?" I say, as funny as possible, to the stewardess.

"Coffee?" she says, looking at me without a trace of hate in her pretty eyes.

3:15–4:30 I talk with several men who have congregated back by the lavatories to talk, not go to the bathroom.

5:17 Breakfast is served three hours after dinner.

6:00 The captain announces we are about to land.

7:10 We land, indicating the captain uses the word *about* very loosely.

7:15 I get my coat out of the overhead rack and who finally comes back to get his but the sailor I've spent eight dollars on who doesn't even know I'm Mr. Nice Guy. I don't tell him.

"Thank you," the stewardess says to me on the way out. "Please fly with us again."

MACH 2

Through a variety of circumstances I don't want to lie to you about, I have flown from London to New York on the Concorde.

The only thing I'm hiding is who paid for the three-hour-and-forty-five-minute trip. It costs $2,292, or $10.18 per minute.

There are ten Concordes, six British Airways and four Air France. Each airplane holds one hundred people, and I can't imagine where they find that many passengers with that much money. It certainly isn't my kind of money.

At my age I hate to think I may be doing anything for the last time but I suspect I have traveled on the Concorde for the last time. It isn't because of my age, it's because of the price.

British Airways starts right off trying to convince you the Concorde is worth the money. There's a plush red carpet on the floor in the special airport area where you pay for your ticket. That's so if you faint when they tell you how much it is, you have a soft place to fall.

Once you've gone through the security gates and customs, you're ushered into the Concorde waiting room. There are plush chairs all around and coffee tables decorated with flowers, plates of cookies and dainty, expensive-looking little sandwiches. I went to a summer camp once whose management was having a hard time making a go of it. They opened the candy store just before dinner every day and the kids would spoil their appetites and not eat so much at the table, so I wasn't about to be tricked into any snacks in the lounge. I waited for the gourmet fare on board.

Of the one hundred seats on the Concorde, all but four were taken. Most of the people on board appeared to be businessmen in their middle forties. Three passengers were seriously overweight. There were two black men and one very thin woman in a big hat that she had to remove before there was room for her to sit down.

My first impression was how narrow the plane was. There are two seats on either side of the aisle. The aisle is seventeen inches wide and each seat is eighteen inches. I fit in an eighteen-inch seat tight enough so I didn't really think I needed a seat belt.

Seated next to me by the window was a man in his early forties wearing a sports coat and no necktie, whom I judged to be a Hollywood producer. His name, it turned out, was Gerald Isenberg, and he *was* a Hollywood producer. He told me the names of some of the movies he's produced and I said, "Oh, sure," but I'd never heard of any of them. When the flight attendant recognized me she looked at him and said, "This is Andy Rooney."

"Oh, sure," my new friend said, making it apparent my name was as well-known to him as his movies were to me.

There was a digital indicator we didn't understand on the bulkhead at the front of the cabin. When it finally read "M 2.03" Jerry and I realized it stood for "Mach 2," or twice the speed of sound.

"You know," Jerry said, turning toward me, "I'm kind of disappointed with this damn thing. Does it feel as though we're going very fast to you? I paid all this money and it doesn't even seem as though we're going very fast."

We were cruising now at 1,350 miles per hour.

The food and wine on board, including a little pastry boat of genuine caviar, were excellent, but speed is really all the Concorde has to offer. It recognizes, by cutting travel time by one-third, that a long flight to anywhere on a commercial airliner can be a miserable experience. The Concorde may not be a wonderful experience, but because it's shorter, it's less miserable.

You don't do much but eat during the flight. You can't wander the aisles and make friends with any of the rich and famous people on board or even make your way to one end of the toilets no matter how much you have to go because once the fifteen-inch food cart is in the seventeen-inch aisle, even the thin woman without the hat wouldn't have been able to pass it.

DON'T SEND ME PACKING

There are people who can pack a suitcase and people who can't. When I'm going away, I wish I could pay one of those Japanese workers who fit electrophonic equipment into Styrofoam molds to come over to my house for a few hours and help me pack my suitcase.

If practice or experience helped, I'd be a great packer. I travel often and pack a suitcase as many as fifty times a year but I never get any better at doing it.

There are several problems a person can have with packing and I have all of them. I'm not naturally neat and, for the life of me, I can't fold a shirt or a suit the way they come folded when they're new or fresh from the dry cleaner. Anything I pack needs pressing when I get where I'm going. I've watched other people make those quick, deft moves with a piece of clothing and then lay it gently into a suitcase but I can't duplicate their action. Women use tissue paper. Packing with tissue paper baffles me.

257

Worse than being a messy folder, I have a problem with what to take. Some people suffer from indecision. They can't decide what to take and what to leave home. I don't have that problem. I take everything. If I'm going to be away four days, I take five shirts. If the place I'm going could be warm or cold, I take clothes for hot and cold weather. I take rain gear, too. I seldom use more than half of what I've carted with me.

Because of my habit of tossing everything in, I've never yet been able to close any suitcase I've packed without sitting or standing on it. Usually I struggle for three or four minutes with the catches. It's a great relief to me when the catches catch but the feeling doesn't last long. Just as I always put too much in, I always forget to put in one or two things and invariably have to reopen the suitcase and force in the forgotten items.

I own three suitcases now. The most beat-up one is twenty-five years old and is, of course, the one I like best. I've tried to replace it but American Tourister no longer makes that model. Companies that make retail merchandise generally don't like anything that lasts for twenty-five years.

Good packers like suitcases with little compartments and pockets with elastic tops at the front and back of their suitcases. They tuck things neatly into them. All I want is a big empty box for a suitcase, something I can dump clothes in.

The order in which you pack a suitcase has never been clear to me. I usually put my underwear and my pajamas in first, flat along the bottom because it doesn't hurt them to be mashed down.

As good an idea as this seems when I'm packing, I always realize my error when I arrive at my destination, because very often the first thing I want out of the suitcase is my pajamas. To get at them, I have to root around and disturb everything on top.

I always put all my shirts in one place but this may be a mistake, also. I don't wear all my shirts at the same time and they probably ought to be packed at different levels as I layer my suitcase.

Years ago I read one of those Sunday supplement articles with advice on how to pack. All I remember from it is the suggestion that you save space by stuffing your socks in your shoes. I do that but my packing expertise ends there. When I put the shoes in that have been stuffed with socks, I can never keep the shoes clear of the collars on my clean shirts.

One traveling rule I always enforce on myself and my family is simple: No one can take more than he or she can carry. There may be help available at the airport or at the hotel, but at some point on any trip you have to hurry somewhere carrying your own bags.

I wouldn't want anyone to look inside my suitcases but I can always carry them.

TELEPHONE TALK

Every grade-school teacher ought to spend a little time teaching children how to use the telephone. It wouldn't take long and it would save everyone time for the rest of their lives.

There are only a few rules:

1. Keep it short.
2. When you make a phone call and someone answers, say who you are and whom you want to talk to. Never mind the hello.

Ideally, you should say your name when you answer the telephone, too, but these days you don't like to reveal who you are to just anyone who calls.

Most people pick up the telephone and say, "Hello." It doesn't mean anything except, "Here I am, who is it and what do you want?" The French have a better word. They say simply, "*J'écoute*," meaning literally, "I listen."

After a week in a hotel at a convention in San Francisco, I became particularly sensitive to telephone problems.

It seems as though most hotel telephone people have never stayed in a hotel room themselves. They don't understand how small a hotel room is. When they ring your room, the ring is too long, too loud and too insistent. It's as if they thought you might be upstairs or in the basement.

I've never stayed in a hotel room so big that I was more than ten feet from the telephone. All they have to do for me is give it a little tinkle once and I'll hear it.

In San Francisco, the hotels did a pretty good job of handling a huge number of calls every day, but they could have helped themselves do better.

The Hilton, the biggest hotel in San Francisco with 1,900 rooms, handled a lot of calls very well. But someone made the mistake of having the operators answer, "Good morning, San Francisco Hilton, Veronica speaking."

That's more than I want to hear from Veronica and, while I'm sure she's a nice girl, I didn't call the Hilton to talk to her.

The famous Fairmont also had its operators telling you who they were: "Good morning. The Fairmont Hotel. This is Barbara."

I didn't want to get to know Barbara any more than I wanted to break my heart over Veronica. I wasn't even moved by her wish that I have a good morning. The Fairmont could have relieved some of the load on its switchboard simply by having operators answer, "Fairmont."

I called the Hyatt Regency Hotel. Once it rang nineteen times before the operator answered.

"Thank you for calling the Hyatt Regency," she said. "This is Beverly."

Why in the world is Beverly thanking me for

calling the Hyatt Regency? I called because someone I knew was staying there.

Another time I called the Hyatt Regency and got Gloria. She also thanked me for calling. When I asked Gloria for the front desk, she thanked me again and added that she wanted me to "have a nice day."

One Holiday Inn had its operators answering, "Holiday Inn Financial Center. Good Morning." Too long, Holiday Inn. Anyway, you're really in Chinatown, not the Financial Center.

Telephone conversations are almost all unnecessarily long for what gets said, and I especially resent operators who intrude on my phone calls with unnecessary talk.

AT&T is taking up our time with advertising these days, too.

"Thank you for calling AT&T," they say every time you make a long-distance call.

Well, don't thank me, AT&T. You just happen to be the only phone company I'm hooked into. I don't decide to use you each time I make a long-distance call, so no thanks are necessary.

If AT&T handles ten million long-distance phone calls a day, and every operator takes three seconds saying, "Thank you for calling AT&T," and perhaps adds, "Have a nice day," on her own, it takes between three and four seconds. I've done some arithmetic, and three seconds times ten million is 8,333 hours or 347 days that telephone operators would be wasting saying, "Thank you for calling AT&T."

Now I suppose Veronica will never speak to me again.

ELEVATOR ENCOUNTERS

During the 1984 Republican Convention, I found myself bunking in the same hotel with the delegation from North Carolina.

There's something very special about an elevator society. You're trapped, shoulder-to-shoulder—at the very least—with strangers you don't really want to get to know, but if someone is friendly, you can't ignore him.

One day I got on the elevator with a delegate from Raleigh who wanted to be best friends.

"Hey, aren't you Andy Rooney?" he asked. Sometimes I deny it but he was standing there, staring at me, looking me up and down, the way people sometimes do in an elevator, and there didn't seem to be any point in denying it.

He told me how much he liked my writing and I immediately thought more highly of him, and then he said his ten-year-old son never misses me on television. Ten-year-olds aren't the audience I like to think I'm writing for but if you write for a living, you take anyone you can get.

"Thank you," I said.

I was getting off at the tenth floor, but at the sixth he started shaking my hand and telling me that if I ever came to North Carolina to look him up. When the door opened at ten, he was still holding on to me. I was trying to ease my hand out of his. He held on, though, and put his foot in front of the door so it couldn't close while he finished telling me about a story I'd done on television. I knew how it came out, of course, but he wouldn't let go until he completed it. You probably know someone who shakes your hand for too long.

The next morning I got on the elevator after breakfast and a woman standing three to four inches from my nose turned to her husband and said, "Look, Jack. Do you see who this is?"

Because I'd already seen who I was in the mirror earlier in the day when I shaved, I was not interested in having her point it out to everyone else on the elevator.

"You're Andy Rooney," she said.

"Yes," I said, in a manner that I hoped would lead her to drop the issue.

"Do you know," she said, "that my husband here is always being mistaken for you. Four or five times a day people come up to him and ask him if he's Andy Rooney."

Her husband grinned and nodded. He was a man about fifteen years younger than I am, six feet tall, twenty-five pounds lighter and with a brown mustache and long pointed nose.

"I can certainly see why," I said, and was temporarily thankful when the elevator stopped at my floor. I say temporarily because this Andy Rooney look-alike and his wife got off with me.

"Do you mind if I go get my camera and take a picture of you two together?" she asked.

Later, I got on the elevator and was pleased to have Senator Jesse Helms crowd in with the rest of us.

I was pleased because Jesse Helms is a lot taller than I thought and, being both taller and better-known than I am, he attracted more attention from his fellow North Carolinians. I was thinking how nice it was to have an anonymous ride to my room when Jesse turned around, reached over the shorter heads in the car and said, "Mr. Rooney, Jesse Helms. It's nice to meet you."

At that instant I had an idea. I knew how I could keep from ever being spoken to in an elevator by a North Carolina politician again. I could say:

"I don't want to shake your hand, Senator. I dislike you and I don't see why I should pretend to be friendly in this elevator.

"I believe this is my floor, sir. I hope you have a nice trip to yours."

I didn't say that, of course. He was so friendly, so Southern, I just pulled my arm up from where it was pressing against the person next to me, and extended it through a hole in the crowd to shake his.

"Nice to meet you, Senator," I lied with a smile.

If I ever go to heaven, it won't be on an elevator. The elevators I ride don't stop on that floor.

PLACES NOT TO GO
ON VACATION

I love to look at the travel section of the Sunday newspaper because all the ads for faraway places remind me of how much I like to stay at home. There are so many places in the world I don't want to go to that I can hardly wait for the day when I retire so I can sit home and enjoy the money I've saved on not going anywhere.

Just for fun, I made a list of places I don't want to go:

—A Caribbean or a South Pacific island where beautifully browned women lie around on white beaches in bikinis all day. I don't mind the women in bikinis but I don't like lying on beaches and it isn't considered polite to go just to look at the bikinis.

—A bus tour of nine countries in Europe with a busload of thirty-seven other tourists is something I desperately don't want to do. I would pay $5,000 round trip not to go on one of those. I don't go on tours of anything. If I want to see something, I want to look at it at my own pace. I do not want to be told how long to look at one thing and how short a time to look at another.

—Please excuse me from a rafting trip down the Colorado or camping in Yellowstone Park this summer. I spend most of my time in New York

City, and if it's crowds like that I want, we have them right here at home, without the flies. I've seen those tours down the Colorado from the air and there are so many rubber rafts they could use a traffic-light buoy some days. Anyway, I've gotten used to the convenience of indoor plumbing. I got camping out of my system in our backyard before I was fourteen.

—I do not wish to take an old stern-wheeler down the Mississippi, retracing the course of Huck Finn. Even if it's called *The Belle of Louisville*, I don't want to go.

—I do not wish to take "a luxury tour of Yugoslavia for $929, including two meals a day and all hotel rooms." I've been to Yugoslavia, thank you. It's a nice place but I'm just as happy that I have it checked off my list of places that would be interesting to visit.

—Canada's St. Lawrence and Nova Scotia plus New England offer "1,700 miles of unspoiled coastline," according to their ad, but I know for a fact they've been running those ads for years trying to attract tourists, and I'll bet there isn't too much left that's unspoiled. You can say that for most of the world. If it's a place people can get to, it is no longer unspoiled. The only unspoiled places are those that people can't reach with an empty beer can, an orange peel or a cigarette butt.

—Another ad wants us all to come to Israel. "Where on earth could be closer to heaven than Israel?" the ad reads. Never mind whether or not it's close to heaven. What about the food? Even people who love Israel say the food is terrible there. Of course, you never hear anyone bragging about the food in heaven, either.

For most of my life I've traveled more than most people, which may have something to do with the way I feel about travel sections in newspapers. Going somewhere just to move doesn't appeal to me. Too many people are looking for some Shangri-la that doesn't exist.

Many cities that used to be exciting to visit because they were so different from what we're used to in America no longer are different. There's a Shangri-la Hilton everywhere now and you can make reservations by calling an 800 number. Their coffee shop is a McDonald's franchise and everyone on the staff has to speak English so you don't have to wrestle with a foreign language. At dinnertime you can go to their famous Mr. Steak restaurant and have steak, French fries, cole slaw and for dessert, vanilla ice cream with chocolate sauce, just like at the restaurant at home. The gift shop in the lobby has every cute little souvenir you'd want to bring home to anyone so, if you take the 5,000-mile trip to Shangri-la, you won't even have to leave your hotel room this year.

Sounds like fun, doesn't it?

But as Sam Goldwyn said, "Include me out."

SOME THOUGHTS ABOUT VACATIONS

The thing all of us need to get away from for a real rest is impossible. We need to get away from ourselves. There are times when I get sick and tired of being so much like myself every day of my life, including on vacation.

—When you go away on vacation with the children, it isn't much of a vacation for you or them.

—There are too many people at all the good places.

—Maybe we ought to have a national lottery and draw for the weeks of the year that we take our vacations. It would thin out the crowds and be better for all the vacation areas that have either too many people or not enough.

—I don't notice too many bad things about getting older every year except that it hurts more to go barefoot. The water seems colder, too.

—There ought to be a limit to how much time anyone has to spend in a car on vacation. Places that are hard to get to are not necessarily better.

—Boats are not nearly as dependable as cars. There are more things that can go wrong with a boat than with almost anything else I know of.

—There are people who like to talk about having been to every one of the fifty states on vaca-

269

tion, or they talk about having been to all except North Dakota and Alaska or Montana and Hawaii. It always sounds to me as if they've had some pretty terrible vacations just traveling to get someplace so they can say they've been there. Frankly, I don't care whether they've been to all fifty states or not. What did they do that was interesting when they got there?

—It's difficult to break my routine on vacation. I still get up early because of some nervous premonition that the world is passing me by.

—The trick of a real vacation is not in getting over the feeling the world is passing you by, but in not caring whether it does or not.

—The biggest change in my daily schedule during vacation is when I take my shower. During most of the year I take a shower every morning and put on clean clothes. When I'm on vacation I shower before dinner and put on clean clothes then. In the morning, I put on the dirty ones again.

—It's amazing how much money it costs to do not much of anything when you're on vacation.

—Most of the things I do that are healthy for me are not things I do intentionally. I almost always run up stairs, for example, just to get it over with, and I've never liked sitting out in the sun to get a tan. Even before doctors started telling us how dangerous too much sun is, I hated it.

—I eat too much on vacation but, of course, I eat too much when I'm not on vacation, too.

—One of the many things I don't like about vacation is that you always end up counting the number of days you have left.

—There are people who enjoy planning a vacation more than they enjoy taking one. Then the day they arrive, they start talking about when and how they're going home.

—I have more vacation shirts than I have time off to wear them. I keep buying new sports shirts but usually end up wearing my comfortable, old ones. Some years, the right occasion to wear my new shirt never comes.

—The biggest trouble with my vacation this year is that we haven't had enough rainy days. You do things on a rainy day that you don't do any other time. I love a rainy day when you can't go out and you do all those indoor things.

—A picnic sounds like a better idea than picnics usually turn out to be.

—I don't notice that people are any better-natured or any more relaxed when they're on vacation than at any other time of the year.

WALKING WITH HORSE IN HAND

Walking has gone out of style and it's too bad because walking is good for the soul. The best people are walkers. They walk to work, they walk to the store and they take a walk. Walkers are people of substance.

The best cities in the world are walking-around cities. London, Chicago, San Francisco and New York are all good walking cities. You can amuse yourself in any one of them for hours without going far or spending much. In Los Angeles, you need a car to cross the street.

Look at some of the advantages to traveling by foot:

—No one can get you on the phone.

—Every step gives you a sense of accomplishment by bringing you closer to your destination.

—You see things you can't see when you drive. You are free to walk fast, walk slow or stop and start when you feel like it.

—You can walk either way on either side of the street. There are no one-way streets when you're walking.

—Walking is good for thinking. No one interrupts your thoughts. You can ignore the surroundings and just keep going, thoughtfully.

In school, I remember having to read a poem called "Endymion" that I didn't understand.

"It is good walking when one hath his horse in hand," one line read.

It's obvious to me now that the author meant it was better walking when you were doing it from choice and not because you had no other way of getting somewhere.

When most of us walk these days, it's from

choice, not necessity. We have our horse in hand. Our horse is the car sitting in the driveway.

We could use it if we wished.

When all American cities had downtown areas with a lot of small stores along the main street and the side streets, walking was more interesting. Downtown is gone now in most cities. If you're going to do that kind of shopping-walking, you drive to the shopping mall, park the car and walk around the mall. It isn't much fun. There's a sameness to most malls. They're predictable. They all pay the same rent per square foot and they all have the same look. When you've seen a couple of malls, you've seen them all. Even the fancy malls are predictable in their fancy ways.

It's difficult for anyone who doesn't know New York to understand how anyone can love it. That's because they don't know how to walk in it. My office is not in any midtown area but if I feel like taking a walk at lunchtime, I can pass the following places within ten blocks of where I work:

—A store that sells nothing but shoelaces, soles and heels, crepe, glue, shoe polish and other miscellaneous items for boot-blacks and cobblers.

—The Flying Saucer Bookstore. It has every book and article ever written on the subject.

—Two Russian restaurants, three Thai restaurants, half a dozen Japanese, Italian and Chinese restaurants, a dozen restaurants of unspecified ethnic origin and one McDonald's.

—A dreary little hole-in-the-wall that specializes

in old magazines. If you want an October 1946 *Life* magazine, they have it.

—A store for poodles. They don't sell dogs, they sell leashes, ribbons, little sleeping and carrying baskets and a line of canned vegetarian dog food. If you have a dog who's a vegetarian, that would be important. It's not important to me but it's the kind of place in any city that I enjoy walking past.

SPECIAL DELIVERY

The letters I get are divided into five categories. They are:

1. Good letters with a comment about something I've written or with an idea.
2. Letters from someone trying to get me to promote something he has to sell. Also in this category are the hundreds of letters I get from organizations wanting me to donate something for their charity auctions.
3. Angry letters saying I was wrong about something.
4. Communications from old friends or acquaintances I knew in some other section of my life.
5. Really stupid letters.

A small sampling:

From Fairbanks, Alaska, a man writes on lined tablet paper to tell me that millions of Americans "never did buy the Watergate propaganda against Nixon put on us by the one-sided media."

There's no doubt you can't change the media once it makes up its mind. It keeps assuming that the earth is round, too.

Dixie Tullis is a "certified graphologist" and wants a sample of my handwriting.

To tell you the truth, Dixie, my handwriting is so bad you'd think I was illiterate. I type everything except my signature. Sometimes even my typing is hard to read. Can you analyze typing?

A woman in Orrville, Ohio, analyzes trees people draw. She wants me to draw one and send it to her.

I don't have time to draw you a tree, Ethel. If I get a minute, maybe I'll sketch you a bush and see what you can do with that.

A public-relations firm wants me to send them something for a display of celebrity art they're having. They assure me that "such personalities as Dinah Shore, Tony Bennett and Paul Sorvino" are already scheduled.

Am I more or less well-known than Paul Sorvino, and if so, who is Paul Sorvino?

What would you do with a letter like this?

"Please send my husband a get-well card. He

has been an invalid for five years and we are on Social Security. Now he has a light stroke and an infection in his neck from having his voice box removed for cancer and one leg amputated. We don't have a car so I don't see him much. Hope you can read this as I am crippled with arthritis."

Am I hard-hearted if I ignore this request? What about all the people in the world who are in similarly desperate situations who bear their grief quietly? Do I write them get-well cards? To what address?

Lucille Carter writes from Houston to say she heard Arthur Godfrey recite a poem in the early 1950s about a man who had two wives, one named Millie and the other named Tillie. Lucille wants to know where she can get a copy of it.

I'll look through my pockets and the trunk of my car and if I find a copy, I'll send it to you, Lucille, but don't wait by the mailbox.

A retired Presbyterian minister in Pasadena suggests the United States should start all over in the year 2000 by canceling all debts, including the national debt, destroying all paperwork, revoking all subsidies and tax breaks and reneging on all foreign treaties. He also says all government officials at every level should be replaced and the Constitution rewritten so that nothing in it can be misunderstood.

Boy, you Presbyterian ministers from Pasadena are a wild bunch. I'll bet your old church isn't going to like you much when they have to start paying taxes on their tax-exempt property.

A young girl in Mooresville, North Carolina, wants me to send her "some advice about growing up in the world today." I feel terrible about not getting at my mail sooner. She says here that she has to have my answer quickly.

Hers is not the only letter I didn't get around to answering.

The only letters I enjoy are in categories one and four.

THE NEW OFFICE

Because I have never been an executive of any kind, I have never seen the Big Business Bible but there must be one that all business executives read every night before they go to bed.

"Move thy workers to new surroundings as regularly as doth the season change," it must say somewhere in the BBB because there's always someone in a company who decrees that you have to move. It has been decreed that I move to a new office in a new building.

There was nothing wrong with my old office that some paint and a little straightening up on my part wouldn't have fixed. But it was decreed I

277

move because the company built a big new wing and they had to put someone in it.

I've visited my old office twice since I vacated it last week. It looks so forlorn sitting there, waiting for me to come back and go to work clattering away with my typewriter. I never will but it doesn't know. Poor thing. I have forsaken you forever, dear old office. Try to forgive me. Try to forgive *them*, for the corporate world knoweth not what it doth.

There are so many architects, engineers, construction supervisors, unions, government agencies and workers involved in putting up a new building in New York that it's difficult to know who went wrong and where. I feel, though, that I have been part of someone else's learning experience.

What went wrong? Am I quibbling?

Well, for one thing, during the second year of construction, part of the new building fell down and they had to start the building over again.

My complaint is not with the basic construction because I don't know anything about that. My complaint is with little things.

The four big elevators are equipped with a panel of buttons on only one side. If there are six, eight or twelve people in the elevator, it is impossible for the last ones on to get to the buttons, so someone has to play elevator man.

Although there are buttons on only one side, they are braille and a bell rings as the car passes each floor so that a blind person can count the dings and know when to get off. No one objects to this aid to the blind. However, there are no blind people working in the building and I imagine the blind would rather have the jobs than bells.

There are a men's room and a women's room on each floor. (They have been careful not to call it the "ladies' room.") The men's room has three sinks, one designed for a handicapped person. It has two urinals and two toilets, one of which is specially designed to accommodate a person in a wheelchair. A usually well-informed source tells me there is one handicapped toilet in each ladies' room, too. (I still call them ladies' rooms even if the company doesn't.)

There are nine floors and two bathrooms on each floor.

What's wrong with eighteen toilets for handicapped employees? What's wrong is that there are no handicapped employees working in the building. It would be better for the handicapped if they had nine handicapped employees and a toilet for them on every other floor.

Each sink has one spigot and one of those spring-controlled handles you press down. It gives you hot water until the spring flips the valve shut. The faucets on this floor run, from left to right, for two, fifteen and six seconds. Who in the company pointed to a picture in a catalog and said, "We'll take fifty-four of those"? Has he never washed his hands?

Some days I just sit here in my lovely new

office, yearning for my old office, my old elevator, my old bathroom and my old junk.

SUGGESTION BOX

Every couple of years the management of the company I work for sends around a memo saying we've all got to pull our socks up and start saving money. They describe how tough things are in the business, ignoring the fact that the company made a profit roughly the size of the national debt last year.

They often ask for suggestions from employees on ways to save. It's just a trick, of course. They don't take any suggestions from employees seriously. They just think it makes us feel better if they ask us. They pretend we're all in this thing together, which we aren't, of course.

Even though I know they won't take my suggestions, I have some ideas for the company on ways to cut expenses:

—Get rid of the paper-towel dispensers in the men's room in the new building. They're so poorly designed that everyone who goes in there wastes two or three towels trying to tear out a whole one.

—Several executives have company limousines with chauffeurs. The chauffeurs wait out front in the cars in case their bosses come out and want to be driven someplace . . . like to the restaurant across the street. The chauffeurs leave the engines running so they'll have heat in the winter and air-conditioning in the summer. My suggestion is that they could save money with the limousines by using regular instead of high-test gas.

—The expense-account form has hundreds of little boxes on it for entering amounts and explanations. No one can comfortably write that small and even the good typists have trouble making their entries. As a result, a lot of people put off doing their expense accounts. This, in turn, moves management to spend a lot of unnecessary time writing angry letters to employees who haven't accounted for the money they spent. Save money by making the boxes bigger on the expense-account forms so they would be easier to fill in.

—In order to purchase office supplies, like a box of paper clips or a bag of rubber bands, it is necessary to get the signatures of nine different people on the purchase order. If the number of signatures necessary was reduced to five, it might save up to twenty-five percent on each rubber band or paper clip.

—The company has 435 vice presidents.* While we realize that in many cases "vice president" is an honorary title given to salesmen to make their business cards look more impressive, it is difficult for those of us who are foot soldiers in the organization to believe it's necessary to have that many officers.

—We strongly urge that the company stop sup-

*True.

plying notepads to executives that read, "From the desk of. . . ." If the executive wishes to let someone know whose desk the note is from, he or she can write the name on the pad with a pencil and save the company the expense of having it printed.

—The big annual company convention with representatives from company offices all across the country is traditionally held at some of the fanciest hotels in exotic vacation places like Honolulu or Pago Pago. It has never been clear to some of us why these meetings are necessary at all and, if they are, why they couldn't be held at the Holiday Inn in Troy, or the Best Western in Wilkes-Barre.

—For the past six months the company cafeteria has been undergoing renovation and redecoration. Might it not be a money saver and a morale booster if you left the cafeteria the way it was and put half the money you were going to spend on design into better food?

—While I do not have any specific idea for what it might be, the time all employees spend waiting for the elevator should be harnessed for some useful purpose.

BEING WITH PEOPLE, BEING WITHOUT

We're all torn between the desire for privacy and the fear of loneliness.

We all want to be part of the crowd one minute and by ourselves the next.

I have wended my hot, weary way back from a crowded convention to the cool, peaceful quiet of my woodworking shop set in the woods one hundred feet from our vacation home.

Today it is unlikely that I will see anyone at all between breakfast and late afternoon, when I shake the sawdust out of my hair and go down to the house for a cool drink and the evening news.

A week ago, I couldn't wait to get to where the action was. Yesterday, I went to considerable trouble and some expense to move my airline reservation up by just two hours.

A week ago, I anticipated the warmth of friendship; yesterday, I yearned for the chilly silence of solitude. At the convention, I had enjoyed a thousand handshakes, a thousand snippets of conversation on several dozen social occasions, but now I wish to be alone with myself, perhaps to finish in my mind those conversations; perhaps to put them out of my mind completely. The great virtue of being alone is that your mind can go its own way.

It isn't forced to think along the lines of a conversation you didn't start and the contents of which are of no interest to you.

It is amazing how the same brain that juggles words and ideas while fencing with friends in a crowded room can turn its power to figuring the angle of a cut in a piece of cherry wood that will make the sidepiece of a drawer fit precisely into the dovetailed front.

The conversion from convention reporter and part-time well-known person didn't take long once I got into my old khaki pants. These hands with which I hit the keys already have bits of wood chips stuck to the hairs on the back of them. I shook out my shirt before I sat down at my typewriter because I didn't want to get sawdust down in the cracks between the keys. But I am alone now, and after that hectic week, I treasure these moments of blessed anonymity.

I love being alone. I don't feel the need for anyone. I know it won't last, though. Dangle an event in Los Angeles, in Florida or in Seattle in my face again next week, next month or next year and I'll endure the standing in lines, the crowded transportation, the inconvenience, noise and bustle to get there.

There doesn't seem to be any happy medium between too many people in our lives and too few. We look forward to our children coming home for a visit. They come with children of their own and it soon gets to be a crowd rubbing against itself until there's the irritation generated by friction.

They're ready to go; we're ready for them to leave.

I admire people who don't feel the need to see friends on Saturday night or even to mingle with the crowd in the line at the local movie. I associate the desire for privacy with intellect. The people I know who genuinely don't want to go to a party are my smartest friends. We are naturally gregarious creatures and it's the superior people who are so self-contained over long periods as not to need the inconsequential companionship that goes with a party or a night out. We all know a few. They're either superhuman beings or they're a little strange. We need each other and we need to get away from each other. We need proximity and distance, conversation and silence.

We almost always get more of each than we want at any one time.

VIII

KEEPING COUNT

KEEPING COUNT

A great many laws deal in numbers: We can't do this until we're twenty-one; we'll get this when we're sixty-five; we can drive fifty-five here but only twenty-five there; we pay eight percent extra on this and an added four-percent tax there. I was thinking of some other laws dealing with numbers that I wouldn't mind seeing passed:

—No one under the age of twenty-one could smoke cigarettes.

—No one over the age of twenty-one could smoke cigarettes, either.

—Commercial television shows couldn't spend more than ten minutes out of any one hour advertising a product or themselves.

—Noncommercial television couldn't have more than ten minutes of commercials an hour.

—All letters would be limited to one typewritten page; handwritten letters would be limited to two.

—Politicians running for office would be limited to saying the same thing not more than one hundred times during any campaign.

—It would be illegal for anyone to stay on the telephone for more than five minutes.

—No woman over the age of forty would be allowed to dye her hair blond.

—No man any age would be allowed to wear a toupee.

—It would be against the law to price anything $1.99 or $.99. Service stations would have to sell gas in round numbers like $1.10 a gallon, not $1.09.

—All watches and clocks would have numbers on their faces, not dots.

—Announcers for athletic events like football, baseball and basketball games would be given a limited quota of words they could use during any one game. When they talked over that number, they'd be cut off.

—Anyone driving slower than forty-five miles an hour on a major highway would be arrested along with those going faster than fifty-five.

—No number assigned to a person by a bank, credit-card company, government agency, telephone company, power company or employer could be higher than the number 235,000,000. That's the number of people there are in the United States and there's something funny going on with any number more than that.

—After the age of fifteen, birthdays would only be celebrated once every five years. It would be illegal for one person to bake a cake for anyone or sing "Happy Birthday" more often than every five years.

—Model numbers for any new product would have to start with 1, not 110 or 1001. If there's an alphabetical designation, those would start with A.

The first model would be A1. The second model would be B1, not FX1001.

—If the post office is going to continue to insist we put more numbers on our letters for their convenience, they've got to do something for our convenience, like improve the service or lower the cost of stamps.

—It would be mandatory for airlines to use the gates nearest the terminal, not farthest from it.

—Eliminating the thirteenth floor from a hotel's numbering system or in any other way perpetuating the myth that thirteen is an unlucky number would be prohibited.

—Bank depositors who were made to stand in line to get some of their own money out of the bank would be given an extra dollar free for every minute over five they were forced to wait.

Collectively, they would be known as "The Laws of Numbers."

MORE LAWS

There has been a new wave of laws recently designed, not to protect us from each other, as laws always have in the past, but to protect us from ourselves. The legal necessity for wearing an automobile seat belt in many states is such a law. It may be good but we've never had a law like it.

If we're going to start a whole new kind of law, I have some suggestions:

—Declare a ceiling on laws. Neither Congress nor any state legislature could pass a law without first rescinding an old one to make room for the new one.

—Car manufacturers would be banned from building cars that can go faster than it's legal to drive in this country. This would probably lead to a change in the legal speed limit.

—Make it illegal for anyone to go to a dirty movie without his or her mother. This would include mothers. Even a mother couldn't go to one without her mother. These would be known as MOM-rated movies.

—Last year 6,824 Americans were killed in pedestrian accidents. Add a sentence to the seat-belt laws passed in some states, making it illegal to cross the street.

—Set up police roadblocks and have officers check for junk in the glove compartments of cars. Anyone found with old, outdated road maps, broken pencils, unmatched gloves or dark glasses with one lens missing would have to return to "go."

—Part of the driver's test would be a seat-belt time trial. Anyone who could not fasten or unfasten a seat belt in less than a minute would be denied a license.

—The post office would start charging a nickel for a stamp for a personal letter and five dollars for a stamp on any piece of mail that contained advertising the recipient didn't want.

—Young children would travel for half fare on

the airlines only if strangers who got assigned seats next to them also went for half fare.

—Nothing is more repulsive to a nonsmoker than cigarette butts in an ashtray on a dinner table. A line on every package of cigarettes sold would advise smokers that in a restaurant they'd have to eat their own cigarette butts when they finished smoking them.

—When there are more than five people in any line, it would be mandatory for the airline, the bank or the checkout counter at the supermarket to open a new counter or window. If anyone had to wait in line more than six minutes for anything, that person would get it free.

—Drivers who turn on their right-turn blinker just as they start to turn right would have to go back to driving school.

—Anyone advertising something as "free" when it really isn't would get an all-expense-paid trip to Beirut.

—Everyone would have to get a driver's license for a shopping cart. Anyone who blocked the aisle in a supermarket would have his or her shopping-cart driver's license revoked for ten days for the first offense, a year for the second and lose it for life for the third offense.

—People who take their shopping carts to the parking lot and leave them so they block a parking space would be ticketed.

—No company would be allowed to reduce the size of a box, a bottle, a can or a tube of anything without announcing it in full-page advertisements as big as the one announcing the product was "new and improved!"

—It would be illegal for a television network to promote the idea that a sporting event begins at three-thirty when it means the show begins at three-thirty but the actual event doesn't start until five P.M.

—Batteries would be included as part of the package with everything that needs them.

—Anyone keeping another person's name in a computer storage bank would have to inform the person whose name was stored there and advise him or her of the purpose. If the person didn't want his name in the computer, it would be removed.

—A depositor would have the right to ask a bank to keep his or her money separate from everyone else's, in cash, if the person chose to have it that way.

YOU CAN'T TEACH AN OLD DOG NEW PROGRAMS

It's sometimes difficult not to take pleasure from someone else's failure. The home-computer business has taken an unexpected turn for the worse and I can't suppress a smile.

I know why I feel that way. All of us hate to be out of it, no matter what the latest thing is, and I was beginning to feel out of it because I didn't have a home computer. Now that I've learned that millions of Americans didn't buy one either, I feel much better.

I saw ads listing all the ways a home computer would help simplify my life and solve all my problems, so, naturally, being an all-American boy, I didn't want to be the last kid on my block without one.

I hadn't bought a new car in several years so I decided I had enough money to buy a computer. Week after week I kept going into the places that sold them. The salesman would start by telling me how I could learn to write my own programs. I listened to all the program talk and then I realized I didn't know what a "program" was.

"You just set up your own program . . . the one you need," they'd tell me.

"Program?" I'd say.

You see, to me a program is either a show I watch on television or the magazine I buy on the way into the stadium to see a football game so I'll know the names and numbers of all the players. Any other use of the word *program* is foreign to me.

The computer salesmen would tell me how I could use my home computer to keep my accounts straight, to save my telephone numbers, to store recipes and to keep our Christmas-card list. I could even keep track of the people who sent us cards that we didn't send cards to, so we wouldn't be embarrassed again next year.

The computer salesmen knew a lot about their particular lines of computers but almost nothing about any other. There has been very little cooperation on standards within the industry. It's as if gas for a Ford wouldn't work in a Dodge.

Even when the salesmen knew a lot about computers, they didn't know anything about me. They didn't understand, for instance, that I don't have what you'd call "accounts." I have money in the bank and I get bills. I pay the bills with money out of the bank. That's it. There isn't any computer program that would help me. I'd be killing a fly with a sledgehammer.

As for telephone numbers, I keep them in a small black book that works just fine and doesn't have to be plugged into an electrical socket.

In the kitchen I like to cook but I don't use recipes very often. If I need to know something, I go directly to Fannie Farmer or *The Joy of Cooking*. They satisfy my need for culinary education. I certainly wouldn't start fooling with an expensive computer if I had flour and butter all over my fingers.

As for the Christmas-card list, we keep last year's cards until we've made out next year's.

It's apparent to me and must now be apparent to the makers of computers that they were trying to sell a piece of equipment that didn't really have a purpose in the average home. People were properly amazed at what a computer could do but they didn't need to have it done.

When computer companies figure out what it is

Americans would like to have done for them by home computers and then start making one that will do those things, computers will catch on.

I like the convenience of being able to get someplace quickly by flying on an airplane but I don't feel the need to buy one and learn to fly it myself. That's the way I feel about computers. I recognize their importance but I am not interested in becoming an expert in their use.

A lot of educators are saying that anyone who doesn't know how to operate a computer will be a computer illiterate. Count me in. One educator said anyone who didn't learn how to operate a computer would be handicapped.

Maybe I'll be able to park in one of those spots reserved for the handicapped right near the door of the supermarket then, because I'm going to be a handicapped, computer-illiterate person.

COMPUTERS ANONYMOUS

Poor Ralph!

I've known Ralph for fifteen years. Wonderful guy. Bright, good personality, capable, hard-working . . . but he's out of it now. Ralph just sits there staring all day. He sits there at the little screen in front of him hitting an assortment of keys on the dashboard of his computer. I hate to say this about a friend, but . . . well, Ralph's a computer junkie.

Ralph works in the library of a large private company in New York and we often have lunch together. After lunch he'll say:

"Hey, you wanna see something amazing? Come on over to my office for a minute."

I don't want to hurt Ralph's feelings, so I tell him yes, I'll go. We go to his office. Ralph sits down in front of his computer and I watch over his shoulder, feigning interest.

"Look at this," he says, pressing, in rapid succession, a series of keys on the typewriter-like machine in front of him.

The screen lights up and a long series of mixed numbers, letters and symbols appears in luminescent green.

XY#$$749$$290%%

"Now we're into the system," Ralph says. "What would you like to know? Anything you want to know how to spell or anything? How about the polite way to address the Queen of England if you should ever meet her? I have software on manners."

I sort of hum, meaning, "I'd rather not know."

"How about Reagan?" Ralph asks. "The library is into a news system. I'll get you everything on Reagan."

Without giving me time to hum at him again, Ralph hits more keys and more numbers and finally one line ends with the letters REAG.

"That means Reagan," Ralph says. He puts a little moving dot next to REAG, pushes more keys

298

There was one secondhand-car place that said they'd give anyone "a free quartz watch just for coming in." A place that offers a free watch is the last place I'd buy a secondhand car.

There was a 1974 Cadillac for $1,000 and a 1980 Lincoln Mark V for $7,335. The Lincoln is sort of a status car but you wouldn't drive a six-year-old car if it was status you wanted. I'm surprised all Mark V's aren't thrown away when they're six.

The most amazing two-line ad was for a 1975 Mercedes. They wanted $15,900 for that car. Even assuming they'd come down a thousand dollars, that's a lot of money for a car that old.

Some of these secondhand-car dealers ran ads reading, "No credit, bad credit." That means they'll sell you a car with time payment even if the bank says you aren't good for it.

There were big ads trying to talk me into leasing a car. You can get an Oldsmobile Regency for $244 a month but you have to rent it for sixty months or five years. That comes to $14,640. I called an Oldsmobile agency. To buy one new would cost $16,700. Is that a good deal? There must be some tax angle to it that most of us don't understand.

I hit the "Lost and Found" columns briefly on my way to "Help Wanted." Someone lost a gold bracelet "in the vicinity of Constitution Hall." The little ad said, "Reward." Lots of luck. Adding that word "reward" was a mistake. Anyone who'd return a gold bracelet he found would do it because he was honest.

I finally got to "Help Wanted" but I didn't see any job I wanted that I could do. All the good jobs wanted someone better than I am at whatever it was, and all the bad jobs were terrible. I don't want to be a "Sales Trainee."

Two jobs under "C" interested me. "Cabinet-maker. Must be experienced." I'd love to work as a cabinetmaker but I know I'm not good enough. I'm probably not even good enough to be a "cabi-netmaker's assistant." There was an opening for that, too.

"Executive Chef needed for luxury hotel kitchen." I like to cook but I have quite a few disasters, so a big hotel couldn't depend on me. I don't like to cook the same thing twice, either, and big-hotel menus don't change much.

I'm about as good a chef as I am a cabinet-maker and in both cases it's not very.

I'd have to be pretty hard up for an article before I'd give up writing to take some of the jobs listed: "Dry Clean Spotter," "Carpet Installer wanted," "File Clerk to $400/wk." (When they say "to $400 a week," it usually means you start at $160.)

There sure are a lot of openings these days for security guards. It doesn't seem to take much experience, just a uniform and a badge.

Here's one: "Security Guard. To work unarmed. Must have secret clearance."

I'd like the idea of having all the power those

security guards have but I notice that several of these jobs pay only $4.50 an hour. I've often wondered if security guards are any more honest than the rest of us.

A look through the classifieds is therapeutic for me. I feel better already. By the time I've finished reading about other jobs and other wonderful opportunities, I'm a lot happier just going back to doing what I do.

GARLIC INCREASES SEX POTENCY!

There's a conspiracy among the newspapers of this country to suppress information. All you have to do to confirm this is to read the headlines of the things that look like newspapers in the supermarket while you're waiting in line to pay for your groceries. Then you will understand what a poor job your regular newspaper is doing.

It's very likely that your own newspaper has failed you miserably in providing information about what's going on in the world. Did you read in your paper, for instance, that a three-headed baby was found alive and well on an island in the South Pacific and that it may have been dropped off there by a UFO? You didn't read that in your newspaper, did you? For that kind of news you had to read those headlines in your supermarket.

Why is your newspaper trying to keep this information from you? Don't we all have a right to know about the three-headed baby and the UFO without going to our supermarket? Are the editors un-American or something?

It's incredible what my newspaper doesn't tell me. Linda Evans, I think it was, or perhaps Farrah Fawcett, is thought to be the daughter of Clark Gable, possibly by Marilyn Monroe or Carole Lombard. Did you know that? Of course you didn't if all you read is your newspaper. Linda and Farrah probably didn't even know it themselves and may never because I doubt if they eat home enough to do their own shopping in a supermarket.

There's more, too. A baboon has recently given birth to a polar bear, Winston Churchill's aunt once gave a birthday party in Buckingham Palace for Adolf Hitler when he was four and known as Schicklgruber. Hitler was always grateful and never failed to send her a Christmas card with a nativity scene on it until the mails were interrupted by the war.

I had to find out all these things while the woman in front paid for a full cart of groceries worth forty-seven dollars minus $1.38 in coupon refunds. In the time that took, I read almost every sheet on that rack without buying one of them.

These supermarket publications don't give people the same dull old information. They tell it like it is:

304

I SOLD MY BABY FOR A LITE BEER!
BIONIC MAN MARRIES MOTHER-IN-LAW!
GARLIC INCREASES SEX POTENCY!

You'll have to read farther down in this last story to find that while garlic may increase your potency, no one will come near you.

It isn't only world news like this that the publications provide. They regularly print medical information that you can't even find in the *New England Journal of Medicine*.

EATING RUTABAGA KILLS CANCER!
TEN WAYS TO EAT ALL YOU WANT AND STILL LOSE
    12 POUNDS A DAY
VOODOO DRUG MAY BRING BACK JACK KENNEDY

The stories themselves are as tastefully written as their headlines, and while they may not always live up to the headline's promise, what's a headline for, anyway?

They don't miss anything in these publications and it's difficult to understand why, if they can do it, other newspapers can't. When it comes to politics or the international situation, no one who doesn't read them from cover to cover can be really well-informed. Look at this sampling:

HOW REAGAN'S STARS GUIDE HIM IN FOREIGN POLICY
I TURNED IN MOTHER TO THE KGB
RUSSIAN COUPLE HAVE FIRST BABY IN SPACE!

305

We are all indebted to the supermarkets of America for carrying this fine line of journalistic literature. Sometimes you can even find a real newspaper somewhere in the store. When I'm through reading and just before I pay, I often look skeptically at the things I'm buying. I think to myself, I hope these groceries are better than the reading matter.

SWEEPSTAKES MALARKEY

Just as soon as my $2 million comes from *Reader's Digest*, I'll probably be retiring.

It seems almost certain that I'll be a winner, according to the postcards I've been getting from Betty B. Glass at the Reader's Digest Bureau of Control in Pleasantville, New York. In addition to the $2 million in checks to be drawn on The Bank of New York for deposit in my account, I'll be getting an additional $15,000 a day as a bonus award if I'm the Grand Prize Winner. There may be some misunderstanding here because I estimate that if I live another thirty years or 10,950 days, that would come to $164,250,000.

That isn't all, either. I could qualify for an extra prize of $100,000 cash if I find a gold seal attached to my Sweepstakes cards. You probably got one of these cards yourself from Betty, who is "Sweepstakes Director" for the *Digest*.

Because I wanted to get a little better idea of what my chances are, I called *Reader's Digest* and asked for her. A very pleasant, British-sounding woman answered the phone.

"Betty Glass," the voice said.

"Hi," I said. "I'm Andy Rooney."

"Andy Rooney!" the voice said. "Are you for real?"

Well, she had taken the words right out of my mouth because I had called fully expecting to find that the "Betty Glass" who signed my Sweepstakes card was not a real person. Wrong. Betty Glass is real and sounds very capable. She came to the United States from England thirty-five years ago, went to work for the *Digest* almost right away and has worked there ever since. I think Betty ought to be ashamed of herself but she's proud of her job at the *Digest*.

After talking with Betty, I was less hopeful of getting the whole $2 million plus the $100,000 plus the $15,000 a day. It turns out that the most anyone has ever won is not $2 million plus those extras but only about $350,000. Whoever wins the Sweepstakes this year will get an annuity of $167,000 a year, even though it says in six places on this card they sent me that the Grand Prize is $2 million.

The *Digest* doesn't actually do the details of this so-called "$2,000,000 Sweepstakes" itself. It hires someone else to do that. That company must subscribe to the old maxim "Never underestimate the stupidity of the average person."

They've done everything they can to borrow the appearance and wording from legitimate documents to make the Sweepstakes card look official and important. If you inspect it carefully, it looks about as honest and trustworthy as a card game at a carnival.

"Urgent Notification" (in red)
"This Is To Certify . . ."
"Record of Registration"
"Not for Transfer"
"Documentation of Prize Eligibility"
"Retain for Your Records"

The only thing the card doesn't say is, *"Hogwash!"*

I don't know what's gotten into the *Reader's Digest* anyway. I bought a copy because it has an article of mine in it, and I was surprised to read on the flap covering the front of the *Digest* the title of one of the articles: "What Men Call Extraordinary Sex."

Is this the dependable, all-American, old *Reader's Digest* we all know and love? Does it need this kind of Presbyterian pornography to attract readers? Are sweepstakes and sex what it has to do for circulation?

The *Digest* not only tried to attract readers to this issue with the promise of something sexy but then it failed to produce. "What Men Call Extraordinary Sex" is about as sexy as leftover spaghetti.

It's sad that *Reader's Digest* can't survive by doing what it started out doing; that is, editing an interesting, populist little magazine that opened up new avenues of interest to millions of Americans.

If I win the $2,000,000 Sweepstakes, I'm going to buy Betty Glass a bus ticket to Atlantic City and a subscription to *Playboy* so she can tell her editors about real long-shot chances and real sexy articles.

THINGS HARD TO DO

The following things are hard to do:

—Get in your car when someone has parked too close to you on the driver's side.

—Tear something along the dotted line when the instructions read, "Tear Along Dotted Line."

—Carry a couch upstairs if you're the one walking backward.

—Draw a circle freehand.

—Let down a venetian blind the first time without pulling the cord this way and that.

—Tie a necktie so it comes out even at the ends.

—Put the ice-cube trays back in the freezer without spilling water.

—Replace the screens with the storm windows . . . or the storm windows with the screens.

—Get the color right again on the television once you've messed it up.

—Cut the fingernails of your right hand with your left hand if you're right-handed or vice versa.

—Reach for the towel when you get out of the shower without getting water all over the bathroom floor.

—Turn over the mattress.

—Get the car in the garage without hitting some of the junk you've got stored along the side.

—Take something out of your eye without your glasses on . . . which you've had to take off to get at what's in your eye.

—Get off a crowded elevator at the second floor of an eight-floor store when you were the first one on.

—Keep from getting distracted by another newspaper story when you're looking for the continuation on page nine of a story you started on page one.

—Open the back door when you're carrying two bags of groceries.

—Get up and go to bed if you fall asleep on the couch watching television.

—Swallow a pill by taking a drink from a fountain you have to bend over to get at.

—Remember when you last put a battery in your watch.

—Get anything out of your pants pocket when you have your seat belt fastened.

—Find the light switch in a dark room.

—Keep your hands from smelling like gas when you help yourself at a self-service gas station.

—Take all the pins out of a new shirt.

—Pack a suitcase for warm weather when you're starting from a cold place.

—Get all the peanut butter out of the jar.

—Get rid of the toothpick after you've eaten an hors d'oeuvre at a cocktail party.

—Quit a job you hate if the money's good.

—Know what to do with all the wires from two lamps, a record player and the television set.

—Clean a paintbrush so you can use it again.

—Not to lose some in the sink when you strain the water off the pasta.

—End a telephone conversation politely with someone you don't want to talk to any longer.

THE ART OF PARKING

A lot of people who know how to drive don't seem to know how to park. There are drivers who can put a nineteen-foot car in a twenty-foot space on the first try. Others will take ten minutes trying to park a Volkswagen in a space a tractor trailer just pulled out of.

Poor parkers are divided up into two categories: (1) the people who just plain don't have a good sense of how to jockey a car into a parking place, and (2) the inconsiderate drivers who don't care about anyone else.

If there are 250 cars parked in the lot of a mall or supermarket, you can bet that fifty of those cars are taking up two spaces. The people who park with their tires across a diagonal line in a lot force the next person to edge over, too.

One of the chief menaces in a parking lot is the person who pulls in and parks too close to you on the driver's side. He doesn't have any problem. He gets out the other side. He doesn't have a passenger so he doesn't leave any room on his right, your left. Then you return to your car, often with your hands full of packages and have to squeeze in.

Parallel parking at a curb is an art that few people have mastered. I know it's a sexist opinion, but I hold it nonetheless: Women do not park as well as men. Sue me, take my license away or jam my seat belt, but it's the truth. Tell me that women are smarter, nicer, better-looking than men. Tell me they're compassionate, sensitive and intuitive . . . but don't tell me they can park a car.

If everyone who drove knew how to park and was considerate, we could get twenty-five percent more cars into the available places. We need those places, too. It's the shortage of parking spaces that's killing cities. Everyone wants to drive to the door of the store he's shopping at. You can't do that in the American downtown built between 1900 and 1940.

Most American downtowns are either dying or dead. Fortunately, many of the dead ones are beginning to revive because they were torn down and rebuilt—with parking space.

I like downtown better than the shopping malls spreading out over the countryside. A real downtown gives a place focus. Every city should have one.

I'm waiting for automakers to invent a small car with wheels fitted to the underside of the car, like casters on a rollaway bed. When you got alongside a parking place, you could drop your casters, lock them in place and shift into a gear that would roll the car sideways into the spot. The space would only have to be an inch longer than the car to accommodate it, and you wouldn't have to fight the steering wheel for five minutes to get the car into place.

I hesitate to bring up the sensitive matter of handicapped parking. There aren't many people so mean as to think it isn't a good and civilized idea to provide the handicapped with easy access to stores and offices. My complaint is that too many stores are using the "Handicapped Parking" signs as a way of keeping people from parking where they don't want them. People have been good about observing the "Handicapped Parking" signs but sometimes stores abuse them. In five years I don't think I've ever seen all the handicapped parking places taken at any of the stores I go to. Most often, there is no one in any of them.

In New York City it doesn't bother me to walk eight or ten blocks to a store from my office. I don't know what gets into me when I'm home out in Connecticut. I'll cruise the parking lot for ten minutes looking for a space up near the door of the store. Even though the space in the lot farthest from the store is less than the length of a block in the city, I won't take it. I cruise like a hawk circling a field looking for movement.

Hunting for a parking place is an art in itself. You have to size up the people coming out of a store. You have to be a good judge of where they're going and how far their car is so you can position yourself to take their place when they drive off.

Parking spaces are an endangered species in America.

THE JOY OF KISSING

Joy Cartier from Honolulu has written me a good, sensible letter suggesting I write something about kissing. I am so taken with Joy's name, her stationery and her attitude that I think I'll do it.

Joy seems to feel that kissing has gotten out of hand. She doesn't like the idea of being kissed by someone she hardly knows, nor does she approve of the "explicit, deep kissing (eating up!) in today's television and movies." Joy says she comes from a family "who kiss normal."

Kissing is probably suffering from the same kind of escalation that everything else in our society suffers from. Things aren't considered to be worth as much as they once were so we need more of whatever they are. Dollars aren't worth as much so we need more money. Titles aren't worth as much so the top job in a company is no longer the president's because he has a boss called the "CEO," chief executive officer. Our language suffers from inflation. To say a simple "thank you" is no longer enough. We say, "Thank you very much."

A kiss on the screen in the movies used to be a pretty sexy, exciting thing . . . not any longer. Escalation has set in. If the couple doesn't get into bed and do it while we're all watching, it's considered a movie for children.

It occurs to me, reading Joy's letter, that I may be one of the people she's complaining about. I don't do any "deep kissing" but I do kiss a lot of people, all women and mostly on weekends.

Years ago when we'd go to a party, there were always a few men who kissed some or all of the women when they met. For a while my friend Tom Jackson and I were the only ones who didn't. Now Tom is the only one who doesn't. Tom's refusal to go along with me on this doesn't seem to have diminished his social standing in our crowd.

Kissing seems like a nice, friendly custom but I have the same feeling Joy Cartier has. We're trivializing kissing by doing too much of it or doing it when a handshake would come closer to expressing the relationship we have in mind.

I think, too, that Joy is probably suspicious of

prolific kissers for the same reason most of us have learned to be suspicious of the man who greets us a little too warmly and with a hearty handshake. Experience has taught us that he's probably a phony, or, at the very least, intent on selling us something.

Kissing habits have not only changed over the years but they're different in different countries. The French, for instance, kiss and shake hands more than we do. Two French men who work together, perhaps even doing manual labor, will usually shake hands every morning when they first see each other. It seems natural and nice.

The kiss on the cheek that's such a popular French custom seems less satisfactory. For one thing, it isn't really a kiss because neither person's lips ever touch the other person's cheek.

I always thought the old-world custom of a man kissing a lady's hand was nice. I wouldn't think of doing it myself but when court figures bowed and kissed milady's hand, there was something well, *courtly* about it.

"Kissing normal" is a nice custom and I hope we don't lose it. A kiss expresses something at the moment you first see someone you like or at the time you part company with someone you like that would be difficult to express any other way. A kiss is our most tender gesture.

So there it is, Joy. That's just about everything I've ever thought about kissing. If I get to Honolulu and we meet, I'll be pretty disappointed if you don't make an exception in my case and give me one. You can skip the lei.

SCHOOL DAYS

Some thoughts about teachers:

—Great teachers are usually a little crazy.

—Just plain good teachers aren't at all crazy. They know their business; they hold steadfastly to traditional values and try to impart them to children. They get more satisfaction from helping and shaping the minds of young people than others get from the money they're paid.

—It's important that a teacher get students interested in a subject. It doesn't make much difference what the subject is.

—A teacher doesn't have to be a perfect person to teach what is right. The teacher doesn't have to know everything about the subject being taught, either.

—The teachers who have plugged away at their jobs for twenty, thirty and forty years are heroes. I suspect they know in their hearts they've done a good thing, too, and are more satisfied with themselves than most people are.

—Most of us end up with no more than five or six people who remember us. Teachers have thousands of people who remember them for the rest of their lives.

—When I started learning arithmetic, I fell behind because Miss Shute was teaching faster than I could learn. Teaching dumb kids in the same class with smart ones must be a problem for teachers.

—Some parents want their children to be taught practical subjects that they can use in later life. I don't approve of children being taught practical subjects in school. They ought to learn about literature, arithmetic, history, geography, writing, art and music. If they don't get to know something about those things in school, they never will. There's plenty of time for learning how to make things or keep house.

—The argument about whether better teachers should be paid more comes up every year. It's easy to say that better teachers should make more money. The hard thing is picking who gets to decide who the best teachers are. The principal of the school I went to didn't like the teacher that all the students thought was best.

—Kids don't necessarily prefer the easiest teacher. They're more aware of who's good and who isn't than most teachers think.

—Teaching and babysitting are two different things.

—The teacher who knows the most about a subject isn't necessarily the one who can teach it best.

—It's impossible to teach writing. The best a teacher can do is read what a student has written and point out what's wrong. No teacher can explain how to write well.

—I'm not used to teachers striking for more money. They almost always deserve more but my image of a teacher doesn't fit my image of a striking worker walking the picket line. Teachers were making an average of $25,000 last year. It's not great, but it's not terrible.

—A school-bus driver has a tough job but he does not deserve to be paid as much as the teachers at the school to which he brings the kids.

—This is the age of numbers but we need a lot of teachers who don't know anything about them. Children are going to have to learn how to use computers in school but if numbers get any more important in our civilization than they already are, they're going to become the enemy. Numbers tend to give the impression that there's more order in the world than there is. As many good things come out of disorder as out of order and they're usually more interesting.

—Whoever said, "He who can, does. He who cannot, teaches," was unfair to teachers. It's unfair because it assumes teaching is nothing. Being a good teacher takes an ability as special as being a lawyer. A teacher needs to know how to teach more than he or she needs to be expert or accomplished in the subject. A great arithmetic teacher doesn't have to be a great mathematician. A great art teacher doesn't have to be a great painter.

MAY I PLEASE BE EXCUSED?

The principal of a school in Warwick, Rhode Island, made a rule that kids can only go to the bathroom twice a day during school. They can go once during a ten-minute break in the morning and again at lunchtime but they won't be excused from class to go.

I'm shocked. Freedom to go to the bathroom is a God-given right that no principal can take away. Asking to be excused to go to the bathroom is a child's escape hatch and safety net.

French and geometry made me have to go to the bathroom worse than any other subjects. I don't think a day went by that I didn't ask Mr. Sharp, my French teacher, if I might please be excused. Mr. Sharp might have suspected that there was no pressing biological need for me to leave the room but he never told me I couldn't.

Several of the easy teachers in our school didn't want to be bothered being asked about going to the bathroom. They told us at the beginning of the year that we should just get up and go. This was my first experience with progressive education. It took some of the fun out of it because asking the teacher was a way of challenging him or her. You knew you didn't really have to go and the teacher knew you didn't. You were daring the teacher not to let you.

Going to the bathroom during French class probably accounts for all the trouble I've had ordering dinner in French restaurants over the years. I seem to be pretty good with the names of things like *poulet, poisson* and *légumes* but if I try to speak to a French waiter and use verbs and tenses, I'm very weak. Mr. Sharp must have taught verbs and tenses when I left the room.

Doctors have never explained, to my knowledge, why it is that smart kids don't have to go to the bathroom during class as often as dumb kids. I don't think I ever recall Wayne Wilkins having to leave the room during French, and he was the brightest boy in our class.

Mr. Miley, the school principal who put this rule into effect, obviously feels that leaving the room has nothing to do with the learning process. How wrong you are, Mr. Miley!

As a result of raising my hand to be excused as often as I did in school, I developed a very good sense of timing. I knew exactly how long I could stay out without having the teacher come look for me or yell at me when I did come back. There's no question that, to this day, I know more about that sort of thing than Wayne Wilkins does. He, on the other hand, probably has less trouble reading the menu in French restaurants once he passes the *poisson*, the *poulet* and the *légumes*.

Mr. Miley says he thinks there's a link between bathroom visits and failing grades. You've got it all wrong, Mr. Miley. Bathroom visits don't *cause* bad grades, they are a *result* of bad grades. Bad grades come before being excused to go to the bathroom, not after.

Usually when I left the classroom during French, I never even went to the bathroom. I walked down the hall to the water fountain and spent maybe a minute taking a lot of very tiny sips of water. Often I'd see if, by turning the faucet handle quickly, I could make the stream shoot up over the sink of the fountain onto the floor.

Actually, the school halls were not a pleasant place to be during class. They were very lonely and I was never comfortable being out there even though I liked them better than being in class.

One bad thing about Mr. Sharp's classroom was that, in order to get to the boys' room, you had to pass the principal's office. There was a little bit of Mr. Miley in Dr. McCormick, too, so you couldn't walk too slowly past his office door. Every once in a while he'd pop out unexpectedly and, if you weren't walking as though you really had to go, he'd ask you where you were going.

When you gotta go, Mr. Miley, you gotta go, even if it's just to get out of class for a few minutes.

NOTES ON THE ENGLISH LANGUAGE

—In 1850 fewer than half of all the people in the United States could read or write any language.

—The ten ugliest words in the English language were once listed by a national association of teachers of speech as: *gripe, plump, plutocrat, crunch, phlegmatic, flatulent, cacophony, treachery, sap* and *jazz*. You can tell this list is twenty years old because the word *sap* as slang for a dumb, ineffectual person, is hardly ever used anymore and the word *plutocrat* is almost dead.

I'd argue about other words on the list. I agree about *flatulent*, but *jazz* isn't an ugly word. It's a wonderfully descriptive, onomatopoeic word.

If I were making a list of ugly words, I'd certainly put *cuspidor* on it, not to mention *flaccid*.

—The ten most beautiful words, according to Wilfred Funk, the dictionary writer, are: *dawn, hush, mist, murmuring, lullaby, tranquil, luminous, chimes, golden* and *melody*.

I don't mind those words but most of them are soft and mushy. I prefer stronger words like *redundant* or *preposterous*. They have a ring to them.

—When I write the name of our country, I write "The United States." An editor always makes it "the United States." Capital T–h–e is part of the formal name of our country. I spell country with a capital C, too. I also refer to "the President." I capitalize the P when I'm referring to Ronald Reagan. Editors always cut my C down to a c and sometimes lowercase my capital P. I've never understood why.

—Words go in and out of style. I remember twenty years ago there was a big run on the word *charisma*.

For a while you couldn't read a newspaper without running into the word *unilateral* several times. About five years ago the word *perception* became popular and is still being overused.

The current language fad is the ubiquitous s. People are making everything plural. No one has *skill* anymore. He or she has *skills* or *talents*.

—*A Manual of Style* by The University of Chicago Press recommends capitalizing celestial objects unless some generic word is part of the name. They capitalize both words in *Milky Way* but only the first in *Halley's comet*. I think a comet has just as much right to be capitalized as a Way. How come we don't capitalize the sun and the earth?

—There is an increasing tendency in newspapers to start sentences with "But." From my memory of the definition of a sentence as a free-standing idea, it's weak and wrong.

—No matter what any of the grammar books or English teachers say, punctuation is an arbitrary matter. It should be used to make sentences clear. Rules about punctuation don't help much.

Most writers are using fewer commas than they

used to and almost no colons or semicolons. You can go too far cutting down on punctuation. Short paragraphs give more eye-catching indentations to a page, and commas, dots, dashes, colons and semi-colons decorate and lighten a page of print. They call attention to what might otherwise look like a block of concrete.

—Some phrases I'd retire from the language for a while are: "at this point in time," "ballpark figure," "bottom line," "between a rock and a hard place," "double-digit inflation," "meaningful dialogue," "value judgment," "that's your opinion," "world-class," "what can I tell you" and "no problem."

—People aren't using as many funny words meaning *drunk* as they once did. It's probably because being drunk doesn't seem as funny anymore.

GAINING ENTRANCE

The best colleges are faced with a dilemma every year: They need a lot of freshmen to pay for their buildings and teachers but they have to keep the place hard to get into if they want good students.

College-entrance administrators, the people who stand at the college gates letting some come in and keeping others out, are depending more on essays written by the applicants than they did a few years ago.

It's good. College entrance, like everything else, was beginning to depend too heavily on statistics. The best things in our lives, things like love, family and health, can't be expressed in terms of numbers, and yet we insist on assigning numbers to everything. I suspect it's because numbers save us from having to think about things.

I didn't get into the college of my first choice, Williams, because my numbers weren't high enough. I always liked to think that if they'd judged me by something less tangible than my math scores or the addition of my right and wrong marks on the multiple choice tests, I'd have done better.

I don't envy the college-entrance people who have to read all those essays, though. Correcting a math exam is easy but judging anything as intangible as the merits of a piece of writing is complex.

Colleges are bucking a worldwide trend, too. The scientists and the engineers with their computers are making most of their decisions with numbers. They enter a big batch of them in the computer, press some keys and out comes an answer. Computer experts talk as if they have the answer to everything within their grasp, but no one can assign a number to such intangibles as taste, beauty, art, honesty, goodness or to an essay by a student.

Numbers are popular because all of us are so unsure of so many things in our lives that we feel better when we know something for certain. Numbers are the most certain things we have. It probably accounts for why sports are such a popular pastime. When the game is over, we're left with two numbers. The athlete or the team with the biggest number is the winner and that's that. It's over. No indecision.

The world is divided between people whose work is judged by counting and people whose work is not. A political candidate who gets fewer votes than his opponent has been judged in numbers. An insurance salesman is judged by the amount of the policies he sells.

People whose work is judged by counting, like factory workers who turn out so many widgets an hour, masons who lay so many bricks or field workers who pick this number of bushels, take some comfort from the certainty of their occupation. They're in no doubt where they stand.

People whose work isn't judged in numerical terms live a life of uncertainty. No computer and no set of numbers ever devised could help the Supreme Court dispense justice.

There's no area in which differences of opinion of the quality of work vary so much from numbers as in art. This includes painting, literature, music, dance and theater. If we could assign figures to the acting of Meryl Streep or Jessica Lange there wouldn't be any suspense about who would win the Oscar for best actress.

College-entrance examiners, without the wisdom of Supreme Court justices, are going to have to make some difficult judgments about excellence and potential.

Because of my bitter experience, I naturally like seeing colleges using written essays as part of the entrance requirement. Thomas Jefferson, talking about the virtues of public education, said that if we were all educated "twenty of the best geniuses will be raked from the rubbish annually."

No writer these days would dare suggest that there was any human rubbish in America to be raked over, but I think it would be okay to say that this new trend in college-admissions standards might uncover some good students who might otherwise have been missed.

A HOMEMADE THANKSGIVING

One of the best things about Thanksgiving is that it isn't commercial. We don't give presents to each other on Thanksgiving, and even Hallmark hasn't been able to talk us into sending each other cards saying, "Happy Thanksgiving."

Thanksgiving is a uniquely American day, but it could use a little focus. We ought to do things that would remind us of the virtues we admire in the Pilgrim Fathers, not to mention, of course, the Pilgrim Mothers. The centerpiece of most of our Thanksgivings is the Thanksgiving feast, so that would be the place to express these all-American attributes and return to basic ways of doing things.

I propose that we go back to preparing the meal and cooking it the old-fashioned way. I propose, for this one day, that we abandon all mixes, all frozen food, all canned food and anything done for us in advance by a big food company. We'd keep in mind there were no supermarkets in Plymouth in 1621. Here's how it would go if we were all to honor the Pilgrim Fathers with a real, homemade Thanksgiving dinner:

—There'd be no frozen turkey. Frozen turkeys aren't bad. They just aren't as good as fresh-killed turkeys and the turkey people ought to be made more aware that we know the difference. (I'm not too keen on the term "fresh-killed"; I don't like to be reminded.)

Frozen birds are pumped up, trussed and wrapped in plastic that shrinks tight around them. They look great in the supermarket case, but they look better than they taste.

Some of them say "prebasted." That means they've been injected with vegetable oil.

—Don't buy stuffing. Don't even buy the bread you put in the stuffing. Make a few loaves of bread. Cut one of them up, let the bread get stale and use that in the stuffing. You can put almost anything good in stuffing and the stuffing will be good. I put eggs, butter, and usually the leftover sausage from Thanksgiving breakfast in it. Moisten it with orange juice.

—Make your own cranberry sauce and cranberry jelly. The big difference is you strain one and don't strain the other. You can put other stuff like almonds in cranberry sauce, too, but the jelly should be a beautiful, crystal-clear red.

—Don't put anything fake in the gravy. When the bird is cooked, take it out of the pan, pour off most of the fat and then scrape the dark brown goo off the bottom of the pan with a spatula. Make a roux of a few tablespoons of flour with some of the fat and then mix the whole mess together with water. The best place to do that is in a blender. After it's mixed, bring it to a boil in a pan until it thickens a little.

—Don't be caught using anything for mashed potatoes except potatoes you've peeled and cooked yourself. Mash them with warm milk and butter. Thanksgiving dinner takes a lot of butter. This isn't a diet I'm prescribing.

—If you had a garden, you should have been able to save a few of your own squash from late fall. The Pilgrim Fathers would appreciate your having grown your own vegetables.

—Make a pumpkin pie. Don't buy a can of pumpkin, even though the other ingredients you put in are probably more important than the pumpkin in pumpkin pie. Don't buy a frozen pie crust, either. Pie crust is messy but satisfying to make. If it isn't messy and hard to roll, it probably isn't any good.

—If you plan to have ice cream, make it. Get an electric freezer and make the ice cream out of cream, sugar and vanilla or some other flavoring, nothing else.

—If you've gone this far getting together an all-homemade Thanksgiving dinner, you might as well go all the way and grind your own coffee beans. You can do it in an ordinary blender.

—After Thanksgiving dinner, put the dishes in the dishwasher. The Pilgrim Fathers will forgive you that.

CAN I HELP YOU?

We all spend more time in stores in December than at any other time of the year. A little shopping goes a long way. I start out with enthusiasm but cool off after thirty minutes.

There's a big difference between the way stores treat us at Christmas and the way they treat us the rest of the year.

In March, June or September, you walk into a store and a salesperson comes up and says, "May I help you?"

You want to take a quick look at what they have and how much things cost. You don't want to be sold anything yet but the salesperson is determined to give you more help than you want. He hovers over you. You can't show the slightest interest in an item or he tells you all about it.

"Just looking," you say.

As soon as the first salesperson gives up on you, a second heads your way.

"Is there something I can show you?" she wants to know.

You're perfectly capable of seeing it for yourself. You don't need someone to "show" you anything.

Salespeople who want to know if they can help make me uneasy. If I take one on and spend a lot of his or her time, I feel obligated to buy something and I usually go home with an item I don't want.

"Are you looking for anything special?" a clerk wants to know.

"What do you have?" I ask.

This puts them on the defensive.

"It depends on what you're looking for," he says.

It's a standoff now. He won't accept the fact that I don't have anything specific in my mind that I want to buy. I won't accept his offer of help.

At Christmastime you're more apt to have the opposite experience. Say you go into a store, fight your way through the crowd and actually find something you want to purchase. You may even have the item in your hands so you start looking for someone to take your money. *Quid pro quo.* Finding a salesman can be the hard part.

One saleslady has ten scarves all over the counter. She's spent the last ten minutes with a fussy customer who can't make up her mind but won't let the clerk go. The phone behind the counter is ringing but no one is answering it. A second salesperson has disappeared into the never-never land backstage at the store to "see if we have it in stock." She won't sell the one they have in the display case.

A third clerk is about to check on the authenticity of an American Express card. A sixty-year-old woman with a fur coat and a rich look about her has offered the card for a thirty-seven-dollar purchase and the clerk's attitude is that the woman is a thief whose card is either forged or stolen. The salesperson has seen too many American Express commercials.

You stand there, impatiently, wondering where to take up your position so that you'll be spotted and waited on next. The minute you decide to move to a register that looks better, the clerk at the first place finishes and waits on someone who came along five minutes after you did.

Once you've trapped a salesman into waiting on you, you have to resign yourself to another five or ten minutes of paperwork. A twenty-dollar item plus tax can be like buying a house with a mortgage. The paperwork seems endless.

Stores are even more suspicious of checks than of credit cards.

They assume the checks are written on accounts with insufficient funds. Even though I know I have enough money in my account to cover the purchase, I always stand there nervously imagining a negative report when they make that mysterious phone call.

After an ominous wait, the salesperson hangs up the phone. In my imagination, she then picks up the speaker for the store's public-address system.

"Attention, attention!" she says. "Mr. Andrew A. Rooney, standing in front of me at the scarf counter, has just tried to pass a bad check. Please leave the store, Mr. Rooney. There he goes now, folks, the man slouching out of the store in the brown overcoat."

Buying Christmas presents is harder than deciding what to buy.

A GUIDE TO CHRISTMAS SHOPPING

Things to consider when it's time to shop for Christmas:

—If you're going to be out shopping for several hours, remember to buy the heavy presents last.

—Don't buy anyone socks for Christmas.

—The best Christmas present for a kid usually can't be wrapped.

—Some people like anything you give them just because *you* gave it to them. Other people never like anything you give them and there's nothing you can do about it.

—It's difficult to keep from buying Christmas presents for other people that you'd like to have for yourself. For instance, I've been thinking of buying a Makita band saw for someone, but I know she'd only take it back and exchange it for a cashmere sweater.

—It's hard to buy things in some stores. I always give up when I have to deal with more than one salesperson. A lot of places ask you to pick out what you want, go somewhere else to pay for it and then return to the original place to pick it up. I go somewhere else to shop.

—Department stores could save a lot of money if they didn't keep their places so hot. Make the clerks wear coats.

—It might be worth it for the big stores to go to the trouble of providing coat-check rooms or lockers. When I enter a store from out of the cold, I'd stay a lot longer and probably buy more if I could get rid of my coat while I'm in there.

—I'm surprised perfume is still considered a Christmas gift. It seems old-fashioned. When you can smell the perfume, someone's wearing too much.

—Bedroom slippers used to be more popular as Christmas presents than they are now. I never wear them myself. On the occasions when I ought to, I go barefoot. Someone always says, "You'll catch cold," but I never have.

—I never got over the delight I felt riding an escalator when I was a kid. If I have to go to the eighth floor of a department store today, I still take the escalator even though the elevator's faster.

—The Santa Clauses seem a lot seedier than they used to.

—Asking salespeople if the item you've selected would fit them or what size they take never helps you get the right size for someone else.

—If you buy several Christmas presents early and have them wrapped or wrap them yourself, it's possible to forget whose present is in which box. You can't always tell what something is by the shape of the box, either.

—When I was a kid, I always felt sorry for grown-ups because they got such dull presents. My mother always got slips, usually pink.

—I get tired a lot faster walking around a big store than I do running around the tennis court.

—No matter how many presents you buy, you're always going to be worried you didn't buy enough or the right present for someone.

—You often see ten things you'd like to buy for one person, but nothing seems right for someone else.

—Two weeks before Christmas, I always think of a good present for someone but it has to be ordered three weeks in advance.

—I'm always surprised how many people in my family give me presents I like when I consider how few things I see that I'd buy for myself.

—If I worked behind the counter of a store that played Christmas music over its loudspeakers, I'd want to be paid extra for having to listen to it.

There are just so many times anyone can stand to hear "Jingle Bells," "Rudolph, the Red-Nosed Reindeer" or even "Silent Night."

—The closer it gets to Christmas, the quicker I make decisions about buying presents.

—I spend more money on presents than I used to but people don't seem to like them any better.

—A lot of stores are selling telephones now. I hope no one gives me one. I have no interest in getting a decorator telephone for Christmas. Our two phones are heavy old black ones and they work just fine.

—Stores ought to give customers a choice of wrapping paper. I don't like it to look as though I bought all my presents in one store.

—When you're Christmas shopping, it's best not to think of the sales the stores will have after the holidays.

BEWARE OF CHILDREN BEARING GIFTS

We have been conducting an interesting experiment at our house over Christmas. The place has been a virtual viral and bacterial laboratory, a hothouse of cold cultures from various cities in the United States whence our children descended on us along with their children, each carrying a native disease.

If a group of scientists wanted to study a cold culture from Boston, a flu bug flown in from Chicago and a virus brought from Washington, D.C., they should have been at our house.

Martha and Leo arrived first from Washington. A six-hour drive with two small children is no one's idea of a wonderful time, and after getting something to eat they all went to bed early.

The following morning I got up about seven and went to the kitchen to start breakfast. I was trying to remember how to make muffins when Justin came padding downstairs in his Dr. Denton's. He seemed subdued but he's one of those people who awakens slowly, so I didn't think much about it. He stood there while I combed his hair, then he said, "I'm thirsty."

Normal enough, I thought, but he didn't say it with much spirit.

I gave him a little glass of water with one ice cube in it.

He drank it slowly, without his usual gulping gusto.

"I don't feel so good," he said, staring straight ahead.

Finally, I thought to myself, it's Christmas at last. One of the kids is sick. When our four children come home with three grandchildren, several of whom are snuffling, sneezing, coughing or wheezing, I'm overcome with Christmas spirit. Colds and the flu are as much a part of Christmas in our house as the Christmas tree.

Later in the day, Emily called to say she and

Kirby would arrive from Boston about noon Christmas Eve.

"Alexis has a cold," Emily said just before she hung up, "but she's had it for several days. Maybe the worst is over."

That was wishful thinking. Grandchildren always save their most contagious days for when they come for Christmas so they can share their diseases with the rest of the family.

I came into the living room early in the afternoon before Christmas and Martha was lying on the couch with a coat over her.

"Isn't it cold in here?" she asked.

"It's seventy," I said. "Do you want me to shove the heat up?"

"It feels cold to me," Martha said. "Maybe I'm having a chill."

A "chill" is a prelude to a fever and, of course, she was having a chill. She was bringing an entirely different viral culture to our house from the government office where she works in Washington. When everyone leaves this week, I'm sure we'll be left with Justin's flu bug, Martha's virus and Alexis's cold. They're just what I wanted for Christmas.

As far as I know, there's no report in the Bible about the baby Jesus catching cold because he slept in a chilly stable during the early days of his life. If there was ever any doubt about Jesus being the son of God, one only has to look at his apparent immunity to colds and the flu. For Jesus to have gone through those early days of his difficult childhood without passing on a bad cold to either Mary, Joseph or the Three Wise Men is enough to make a believer of the most doubting Thomas. Of course, the Wise Men may have been smart enough not to get too near him.

When children come home for Christmas with colds, there's nothing a family can do but accept it as part of Christmas. Over the years, we've passed so many germs to other members of the family that I'm surprised colds don't come gift-wrapped.

CHRISTMAS TREES

If Santa Claus wants to do something useful during his time off from December 26 this year to December 24 next year, he could take down Christmas trees.

I don't know of any work I hate more than dismantling the Christmas tree. There's no job for which I'm less suited than untangling the lights from the ornaments and the ornaments from the branches, but I know my reluctance to untrim the tree is part sloth and part sentiment.

It seems so sad that Christmas is over. When the tree comes down, it's a reminder of passing time and of a wonderful Christmas we'll never see again. Justin will never be six again, Ben and Alexis will never be three again.

Taking down the Christmas tree is a thankless job. No one says how good the tree looks after you've taken all the lights and ornaments off it and dragged it out into the yard by the driveway.

Taking down the outdoor lights and decorations is even harder because it's usually cold, often wet, and the job involves a ladder. We had a blue spruce in front of our house for years but it got so big we didn't have a ladder tall enough or pocketbook full enough to cover it with lights. Our outdoor decorations have been makeshift ever since we stopped decorating that tree. I'm never satisfied with what we do but I wouldn't think of not having any. The outdoor Christmas lights that decorate the neighborhood are evidence of an outgoing friendliness we feel at Christmas. Outdoor lights shout "Merry Christmas" at every passerby.

Last Sunday morning I took our outside lights down. Later that afternoon, just after dark, I had to do an errand and I noticed a lot of people still had their Christmas lights up. The weekend after New Year's seemed like the logical time to remove them but now I think I may have done ours too early. In the little village of Lake Placid, New York, the custom is to leave Christmas decorations up until the snow melts.

There's always an argument in our house about when the tree should come out of the living room. The forces in favor of taking it down soon after Christmas cite the mess it makes as it begins to dry and drop its needles. Its potential as a fire hazard is always mentioned. Some people fight dirty in our house.

Sentiment aside, taking down the tree in the

living room and removing the outside lights isn't an easy job. We move a desk out of the living room into a temporary place in the hall to make room for the tree, and once the tree goes out the four-drawer desk has to go back in.

I can handle the hauling and lifting. It's the packing I'm weak on. On Christmas Eve, when I go down cellar to get the boxes containing the lights and ornaments, I'm irritated if they aren't neatly packed away with layers of paper between the ornaments and with the strings of lights untangled and separated so they can be wrapped easily around the tree. On the other hand, I have no patience for packing anything away neatly at dismantling time.

Throwing away the Christmas tree is no easy job, either. If you don't take it to the dump yourself, the tree lies on the ground out back like a corpse. Bits of tinsel cling to it and it can stay out there for weeks. Before we realized we shouldn't foul up the atmosphere by dumping smoke into it with burning trash, I used to enjoy hacking off the branches of the Christmas tree and starting a fire with them. I watched as each new branch thrown on the fire exploded into a crackling flame.

Now the tree just sits there and I look wistfully in the newspaper every day, hoping for some notice that the trash collectors will pick up dead Christmas trees on our street tomorrow. Trash collectors are very picky about what they take these days. You can't leave any old junk out any old day.

Trash collectors aren't as sentimental about old Christmas trees as I am.

IX

CYCLES

COCOA ON MY MIND

This morning I got up early and went to my basement office to do some work. I say "office." That's just for tax purposes. What it is, is a typewriter on a small table between two longer tables that I made. One is cherry, the other walnut. Sometimes I call them "desks." They're simple but I made them myself and I like sitting between them in front of my typewriter even when I can't think of anything to write.

It was before six o'clock and I wasn't ready for coffee yet, but for some reason the idea of a cup of cocoa had crossed my mind as I'd started downstairs. I'd decided not to make a commotion in the kitchen and wake everyone.

I rolled a piece of paper in my typewriter and sat there staring at it. All I could think of was cocoa. I hadn't thought of a cup of cocoa in nine years and now I couldn't get it out of my mind.

You know, of course, what I did. My most serious character flaw is that I don't deny myself much. I went back up to the kitchen, found some good Dutch cocoa that had been in the cabinet for years and made myself some.

Downstairs again, sitting between my wood, in front of my trusty typewriter with my cup of cocoa, I thought how good life was. The cocoa was delicious and I found myself wondering why more people don't drink cocoa instead of coffee in the morning. I concluded that, like almost everything else in life, it has something to do with either calories or money.

It was sleeting outside and as I drank the cocoa I could hear the little pellets of wet ice hitting the ground-level windows. It made me feel better than ever. Here I was in a house I loved, warm, dry and surrounded by my books, the tools of my trade, in a room filled with friendly souvenirs of my life.

The first cup of cocoa was so good and it was so pleasant sitting there, dreaming, that I went back up to the kitchen to get what was left in the pan.

I do not understand the cycles of life, the ups and downs of the spirit. From the moment I came back into the kitchen, the day that had begun so well started downhill. I cannot tell for sure whether the deterioration in my attitude toward life from that moment on was caused by actual events or whether it was some chemical change in my brain that made things seem less good than they had seemed a few minutes before.

The cocoa left in the pan had a skin on top of it now. I had forgotten that cocoa did that. I heated it and poured myself what was left and headed back downstairs. One of the screws on the knob to the cellar has loosened and it caught my index finger as I opened the door with my free hand. It was a very light pain but it made me jerk back and I spilled a little of the cocoa with the scum on the rug.

I continued downstairs, put the cup of cocoa on one of my wood tables and came back up to the kitchen to get a wet sponge to clean up what I'd spilled.

By the time I got back to my typewriter, the cocoa was cold and it was almost seven o'clock. I noticed a little water was coming in at the top of one of the basement windows that needed new caulking. The oil burner in the next room went on and I got thinking about our oil bill.

At about seven-fifteen I made a few hits at the keys of my typewriter and noticed right away that my fingernails needed cutting and the ribbon in my typewriter needed to be changed. Within a few minutes I'd begun to think of all the work I had to do in the next week. I've got to get that tax stuff together, too.

I don't care whether I ever have another cup of cocoa or not.

LOST AND NOT FOUND

There are days when I just look for things. I don't find them, I just look.

Looking for things I can't find seems to be something I do in spells and right now, I'm in a long, frustrating spell.

It started last weekend. I could swear I bought

an extra bulb for the light over the garage door six months ago when the last one burned out, but I couldn't find it. The shelf in the garage would have been the logical place for me to put it but it's not there. Or, at least, I don't think it's there. Maybe I'll take one more look.

That's the way it is with looking. You start with the place that seems most likely. If it's an item of clothing, I'll usually go to my bedroom closet. If I don't find it, I'll look through my dresser drawers and then I'll go downstairs and look in the closet where we keep the coats. We also keep the vacuum cleaner in the coat closet and that doesn't make it any easier when you're looking for something.

After I've looked in three or four places, I decide I didn't look carefully enough in the first place and I return to the bedroom closet. You'd be surprised how often I find something in the place I've already looked. That's why maybe I ought to look on the shelves in the garage once more for that 150-watt outdoor floodlight bulb.

Last evening I was looking for the book of instructions for a little calculator I bought a year ago. It was out of paper and I wanted to put in a new roll but I couldn't get the cover off. That damn book of instructions has been on the book-shelf, on top of the television set, in the drawer of the table next to my chair in the living room or in the basket on the kitchen shelf for a year. I've seen it a thousand times but last night when I needed it, I couldn't find it anywhere.

Usually when I'm looking for one thing, I find something else I was looking for a week ago and don't need any longer. For instance, if I go out and buy a new bulb for the outdoor light over the garage door this week and then start looking in the cellar for the small hammer next week, you can bet I'll find the light bulb.

The unexpected pleasure of finding something by accident a week after you needed it doesn't make up for the angst you felt at the time. When you want something you know you have and can't find, you want it bad.

This all comes to mind because just now I was searching through my desk drawers for an attachment that lets me charge the batteries in my small tape recorder. I couldn't find the charger but I did stumble on the envelope containing my October 1985 bank statement. Three weeks ago when I was scrambling to get my tax stuff together, I looked everywhere for that envelope because there were some important tax deductions among my canceled checks. I didn't find it at the time and had to go to my accountant with only eleven bank statements.

Looking and not finding is certainly one of the most frustrating ways to spend time. You don't know whether to get mad and kick someone or sit down and cry. I usually try to think of someone other than myself to blame it on.

A week seldom goes by that I don't search the pockets in the clothes in my closet for some piece of paper I've lost. There are days when I make

351

five trips between the cellar, the living room and the upstairs bedrooms looking for something. When I'm downstairs, it always seems most likely that what I'm looking for is upstairs. When I'm at the office, I seem to remember where I may have put that piece of paper at home; when I'm home, I can visualize it in the office.

If there's any young person out there just getting out of college who majored in finding things, I might have a job for him. I'd want someone who specializes in closets, shelves and pockets. That's where I lose things.

REPAIR FEVER

It would be easier to fix things if something else didn't always break while you were fixing the first thing.

I don't ever recall starting one repair job that didn't lead to another. I think this accounts for why so many people are afraid to go to a doctor. They aren't worried about what they know they have. They're worried about what the doctor might find.

Around the house this is especially true. This morning the bulb burned out in the overhead fixture in the kitchen. It's an easy thing to change a light bulb so I went to get the small stepladder hanging on two hooks in the garage.

As I took the ladder down, I noticed one of the

hooks was loose and made a mental note to fix it before I put the ladder back. I set up the ladder in the kitchen but as I put my foot on the first step I noticed a screw was missing from the metal hinge that flexes open and keeps the ladder's legs a fixed and safe distance apart.

It seemed best to fix that before putting in the new bulb so I went to the kitchen drawer where I keep a small assortment of emergency tools and hardware. I found a screw that was the right size but it was a straight-slotted screw and all I had in the drawer was a Phillips screwdriver. I went to my shop and got another screwdriver.

On my way back, I came through the screen door that opens into the dining room and noticed the door wasn't closing tight. I realized that's why we've been getting so many flies and mosquitoes in the house. The screen door has one of those automatic door closers on it that I hate and it needed adjustment.

If it's simple, I thought to myself, I might as well do it right now and get the door problem out of the way while I have the screwdriver in my hand. I reached up for the adjusting screw in the door closer but it was a little too high and I couldn't quite get my hand in the right position to turn the screw.

"Okay," I said, "first I'll fix the ladder so I can change the bulb, then I'll bring the ladder into the dining room and fix the screen door."

I fixed the ladder, got into an argument about what size bulb to use and replaced the burned out bulb with a 100-watter. The light fixture has a globe that's held to a metal rim on the ceiling with three setscrews. I took the globe off and juggled it in one hand while I balanced myself on the ladder and unscrewed the dead bulb with the other hand. In the process of getting the new bulb out of my pocket, I dropped one of the three setscrews on the kitchen floor so I climbed down the ladder, threw the old bulb in the wastebasket and got down on my hands and knees to look for the missing screw.

It was so dark in the kitchen without the light on that I couldn't find the screw so I went to the living room where I thought I'd left my glasses. While I was looking for my glasses, the telephone rang. The call was from a second cousin who lives in Eugene, Oregon. He wanted to talk about a mutual relative who's sick.

We bought a new telephone recently and I've been trying to fix up a system so I could have it ring in my workshop. Obviously, I'd done something wrong with the wires because I could barely hear my cousin's voice.

"I'll have to call you back," I yelled, trying to reach Oregon without wires. "I'll call you back on the other phone," I yelled again and hung up.

The downstairs telephone is in a tiny, closetlike cubbyhole off the dining room, and for a moment after I hung up I just sat there, staring. What should I do first? Do I call back right away or do I continue looking for my glasses in the living room so I can go back to the kitchen to find the screw I dropped on the floor so I can replace the globe on the light fixture and take the ladder to the screen door in the dining room?

Sometimes my world falls apart faster than I can fix it.

FORGETFULNESS

All four kids came home for the Christmas holidays and after they'd departed all we had left to remember them by was one hat, a pair of running shoes, two sweaters, a nightgown, a raincoat, three socks, a blue jacket and a bad cold.

The only mystery is the blue jacket. We've called all of them except Brian and none of them claims the jacket. It wouldn't fit Brian. The feeling is that it belongs to one of their friends who came over to the house to visit while they were home.

Leaving things behind when they're home for a few days is a tradition with the kids in our family. Brian often brings a bag of laundry to do and once he even left that in the dryer.

Forgetting things is something the children come by naturally. I've taught them everything they know about it. I've left things all over the world.

—Once I left a camera on the top of Barry Goldwater's car when we were filming a show with him near the Grand Canyon.

—Several years ago I turned in a rental car at the airport in Frankfurt, Germany, and left my suitcase in the trunk. I was halfway to New York before I remembered it.

—The Thursday before Christmas I stopped at the information booth in Grand Central terminal to pick up a timetable. I put down a shopping bag I was carrying while I looked at the train schedule. After seeing what train I could catch, I rushed off, leaving the shopping bag with two hundred dollars' worth of Christmas presents in it in the middle of one of the busiest places on earth. I got to the train, took off my coat and sat down to read the paper before I remembered it. I rushed back and the bag was still sitting where I'd left it, having been passed by several thousand people in the meantime.

—The following day I stopped at a good electrical supply store to buy two dozen extra Christmas tree replacement light bulbs. After I'd bought and paid for the bulbs, I saw some batteries I needed. I told the clerk I wanted those, too. He put them in a bag and rang them up. I paid for them and walked off, leaving the bulbs I'd come to get in the first place on the counter.

When I take a shower in a hotel room in the morning, I often hang my pajamas on the back of the bathroom door. I get out of the shower, dry off and open the door. The pajamas are then hidden from my view and I often pack without them. I suppose I've lost half a dozen pairs of pajamas that way. I get very attached to pajamas, too. Some of the ones I lost were real favorites but they'd seen so much service and were so well-worn that I was too embarrassed to write the hotel and ask that they send them to me.

If I hadn't been leaving things behind since I was about nine, I'd think I was losing my mind with age. There's never been a time in my life when I wasn't forgetting things. During my early days in the Army at Fort Bragg, we used to have to fall out in the company street for a roll call at six A.M. We were supposed to be properly dressed and carrying our rifles.

On three mornings over a period of two weeks, I lined up on time but on each occasion I forgot my rifle.

"How do you like that," Sergeant Fischuk said to the assembled company, pointing me out as a horrible example of what an education can do to a man. "Rooney's got a college education and he don't even remember to bring his rifle."

One of the most distressing things I do regularly is forget where I've parked the car. In November I drove my car into the city one morning, parked it and went to work. At 5:25 P.M. I left the office, hurried to the railroad station for a train I often ride and took it home. I never remembered I'd driven in until I got to my destination and realized I didn't have a car parked there to drive home in.

Last night I made some notes I was going to use when I wrote this but I forget what was on them and unfortunately, when I came to work this morning, I'd left the notes on my dresser.

NAPPING

You're certainly not interested in how I sleep, but I'm going to tell you only because you'll relate it to yourself or to the people you know well enough to know how they sleep.

There aren't many things I do really well but when it comes to sleeping, I'm one of the best. If sleeping was an Olympic event, I'd be on the U.S. team.

Coming home from a trip recently I got on the plane, strapped myself in and fell asleep before takeoff. As always, I didn't wake up until the flight attendant shook me to ask if I was comfortable. Keep in mind, the flight was at nine A.M., and I'd just had a good night's sleep.

Nothing seems to bother some people when they sleep, and I'm one of them. I can eat dinner, drink two cups of strong black coffee and drop off thirty seconds after I hit the pillow. One of the few things that keeps me awake is decaffeinated coffee.

If the village fire alarm goes off in the middle of the night, I awaken easily, try to determine where the fire is and then drop back off to sleep in a matter of seconds.

Some people sleep faster than others. I'm a very

fast sleeper. I can nod off for three minutes and wake up as refreshed as though I'd had eight hours. Some people can lie around in bed for nine hours and get up sleepy. I awaken instantly, going full speed.

We probably ought to sleep more often and not for so long. The trouble is, once the bed is made, we can't get back in it, and during the day most of us get so far from our beds that it wouldn't be practical, anyway. It might pay off for a company to have a room with cots where employees could take a nap. Companies have cafeterias and bathrooms, why not a dormitory bedroom? If employees got an hour for lunch, they could divide it any way they liked between eating and sleeping.

Naps are underrated. I don't know why we dismiss napping as an inconsequential little act. The word itself doesn't even sound important. I think everyone should get off his or her feet and lie down for a few minutes at some point during a long day.

Staying in bed for eight hours a night, on the other hand, seems wasteful to me. It's like overcharging a battery. At some point, it doesn't do any good. Most people who sleep eight hours stay in bed because they don't want to get up, not because they need the sleep. Taking all your sleep in one piece doesn't make any more sense than eating too much but only eating once a day.

Napping got a bad reputation somewhere along the line and I resent it. For some reason, people who don't nap feel superior to those who do.

Nappers try to hide it. They don't let on that they drop off once in a while because they know what other people will say.

"Boy, you can really sleep," or, "Look at him. He sleeps like a baby." It isn't much, but there's just a touch of scorn in the voice.

People who are awake feel superior to people who are asleep because sleeping people usually don't look so good. It's a rare person who looks or acts as well asleep as he or she does awake. You don't have any control of your face muscles, your jaw is apt to drop open and your hair is a mess. You look just the opposite of the way you look standing in front of a mirror with your hair combed and your clothes all together just before you leave the house for work. You can bet the President doesn't look too good when he's asleep. Even Miss America would probably be embarrassed to have a picture of herself taken while she was unconscious.

I'd like to form an organization of good sleepers and nappers. We'd demand the respect we deserve. We are people who dare drop off for a few minutes in the middle of the day. We're an oppressed minority and we're tired of it. Nappers of the world, unite!

IT WAS A DARK AND STORMY NIGHT . . .

It was cold and dark when I awoke, a little too early to get up but too late to take a chance on going back to sleep.

Lying there, in the few moments I give myself to rally to the idea of starting a day's work, I suddenly had an awful feeling. It was a premonition of disaster, almost as though some unearthly power was whispering a warning to me.

"Something terrible is going to happen today," I thought to myself. I don't often whisper words under my breath but I whispered those.

It nagged at me as I showered and dressed. It was a cousin to the feeling I have when I've forgotten something. I've never thought I might have forgotten something when I have not so I wasn't treating this premonition lightly.

My mind started checking, computer-like, through things that could happen to me.

It stopped on "accident."

The train would be safer than driving to work, I thought to myself . . . except, I continued in my head, if something's going to happen, there's nothing I can do to prevent it.

I'd better be careful crossing the streets today, though, I thought, not giving in completely to predestination.

361

On the train I tried to concentrate on the news-paper but every bit of bad news in it reminded me of something awful that might happen to me. I put down the paper and searched the faces of other commuters for some clue. I saw no tension on any face. It's going to be a personal tragedy, I thought, not a national catastrophe that touches everyone . . . not a nuclear bomb.

One dread thought led to another. I was ob-sessed. I knew that I could not deny so strong a sense that something was going to go wrong. On the other hand, I tried to be rational. I'm not a person who believes in fairy tales, mysticism or magic. I'm not a person who gives a second thought to the report of a flying saucer.

Still, there it was and I couldn't get rid of the thought. When I got to the office, I immediately called each of the four children, in order. I asked how they were and what their plans were for the day. I told them nothing about what I felt was going to happen.

Much of my day was spent thinking of worst cases. What would be the worst thing that could happen? Was I going to discover a lump some-where on my body? Was I going to feel a sudden stabbing pain in my chest?

I worked intermittently and by the end of the day I was relieved to notice that nothing had happened yet. The premonition of disaster was still there but I'd gotten through most of the day. Now if I could make it home and find everyone safe and the house still standing, perhaps I could relax a little. Maybe, I thought, I'm just kidding myself. The sense of foreboding was too strong to dismiss, though.

We had an uneventful dinner but at exactly 7:45, while we were sitting in the living room watching a bad television show, the phone rang. It seemed louder, more insistent than usual and my heart sank. Margie went to answer the phone. I sat, staring at an open book but not reading anything. I turned down the television sound. I didn't want to hear but I couldn't keep from listening. It was one of Margie's friends looking for her to substitute in a tennis group.

At nine-thirty I realized I was too anxious to concentrate on reading or television so I went to my basement workshop. As I switched on the overhead lights, the teeth on my power saw glistened. I stood for a moment as my eyes scanned a variety of sharp and dangerous tools. I switched off the light and went back upstairs.

Shortly after ten I went to bed. I turned off the light and lay there for a moment in silence. Suddenly I heard a small creaking noise. It seemed to come from downstairs. First it was almost inaudible but it grew louder and came with greater frequency.

That's the last thing I remember before I fell asleep that day.

So much for premonitions of disaster.

FINDING THE BALANCE

This morning I was driving to work at about 6:45, enjoying my own thoughts and the warm red glow just below the horizon, when the weatherman on the radio said the sun would be coming up at 7:14.

"It's gradually getting lighter earlier," Herman said gleefully, as though it were good news.

There's no way to predict what's going to depress us but I suddenly found myself depressed. There were emanations of the arrival of spring in that earlier sunrise. I realized a new season was coming and I hadn't finished enjoying this one.

I savor seasons. I enjoy a good, cold winter with plenty of snow. I don't want a wimpy winter. I don't want winter to last into March but I'm disappointed when we don't get enough cold weather to freeze all the ponds solid or enough snow for skiing and sledding.

It struck me, as I drove with less enthusiasm, that Christmas and New Year's were really over. They'd joined the memories of our past.

We all spend more time preparing for pleasure than we do enjoying it, but still, it's disappointing that we cease to take pleasure from so many things before they're over. Often when I'm in the middle of doing something I've looked forward to doing for weeks, I suddenly realize the enjoyment is over before the event. I'm thinking about what's next.

At a party I'm thinking about going home to bed. In San Francisco I'm thinking about getting back to Connecticut. Monday, I think of the weekend and by Saturday night I'm looking forward to Monday.

At dinner, I often get up from the table before the meal is over to make the coffee because I've already started thinking about dessert.

This morning the first thought of the approaching spring was depressing to me because it reminded me, not of warm weather, but of the passage of time.

I like spring because, among other good things, it means I'll soon be able to get back to my summer workshop, but please, don't rush me. The idea of spring now, in the middle of winter, does nothing but make me think of how short life is. It seems as though I just left my workshop, went to a few football games, did my Christmas shopping and the New Year's party. I'm not ready for another summer so soon.

Maybe we'll get a foot of snow next week that will put these depressing how-time-flies thoughts out of my mind.

It's difficult to get time to pass at the right speed. Sometimes, in the middle of the night, I think time will never move on to morning. Some days, on the other hand, I can't hold time still long enough to do all the things I want to do.

The trick is to get a good balance of activity

and inactivity in your life. You need high points to look forward to and back on but you need plenty of time in between for not doing much of anything. Not doing much of anything can be the greatest pleasure of all, if you know how to do it.

The art of living well has its geniuses just as certainly as music, painting and writing well have theirs. The greatest Old Master in the art of living that I know is Walter Cronkite. You know him as a respected newsman but believe me when I tell you his ability to live and enjoy life exceeds his greatness as a journalist. He fills all the days of his life with events, any one of which would satisfy most people for a year.

Walter works and plays at full speed all day long. He watches the whales, plays tennis, flies to Vienna for New Year's. He dances until two A.M., sails in solitude, accepts awards gracefully. He attends boards of directors' meetings, tells jokes and plays endlessly with his computers. He comes back from a trip on the *QEII* in time for the Super Bowl.

If life were fattening, Walter Cronkite would weigh five hundred pounds. He disproves the theory that you can't have your cake and eat it too.

I wish now I hadn't driven in to work this morning and gotten into this whole mess.

TRADING PLACES

The other day I was riding the crosstown bus in New York. There were about fourteen other people on the bus and I didn't have anything to read so I got to looking at them. I tried not to get caught but I looked at each one of them for ten or fifteen seconds.

The game was to decide whether there was any one of them I'd trade places with . . . me be they, they be me.

It's our ego, I suppose, that keeps most of us from seriously wishing we were someone else. There was no one on the bus I'd rather have been than myself. I was aware, while making the decision, that if any of them had been looking me over, they wouldn't have swapped either. For one thing I had my coat on with the missing buttons and the frayed cuff on the right sleeve.

Even if we aren't satisfied with who we are, what we do or what we're like, most of us wouldn't change persons and places with anyone else if we could. I'm not satisfied with myself and I don't understand why I'm not more willing to make some changes that would at least alter my appearance. It wouldn't be hard . . . not like losing weight.

The trouble is, we all get set in the way we look. I've been parting my hair on the right side since my mother started doing it for me at age four. I've tried parting it on the left side but when I look in the mirror, it just isn't me and I can't leave the sanctity of the bathroom until I've undone it and put the part back where it belongs. It's just a notion, of course. There's no evidence at all that I look any better with my hair parted on the right than on the left.

We've all known women who fall in love with their hair when they're twelve and can't bring themselves to cut it. Many young women grow into their middle twenties before they chop it off, usually during some life crisis.

Son Brian chipped a front tooth playing hockey when he was seventeen. He must have studied the mirror and decided to cover it with a mustache because he grew one and he's had it ever since. I don't think of myself as having a son with a mustache but it looks so normal on him that he'd look strange to me if he ever shaved it off. Not that he ever will.

Women play with the shape and color of their hair more than men but you can tell they've made the decision to change with great reluctance. A woman who has been dying her hair blond since she was twenty and realizes it's beginning to look a little funny by the time she hits fifty goes through all sorts of torture before she allows her hair to grow out from its roots in its natural color, which, in all probability, is gray.

No one thinks of me as well-dressed, but in my own little mind wearing anything but the type and style of clothing I do would make me look silly.

The fact that it has been made clear to me by certain family members and assorted close friends that I already look silly in what I wear does not deter me. I have a very clear idea of what clothes are best-looking and which of the clothes in that general style look best on me. I even think I know which make me look thinner, which fatter. I think that's true of all of us and I'm surprised we could hold so firmly to such erroneous convictions. I wouldn't change my clothes for anything even though I'd accept a critic's observation that I was poorly dressed.

Looking around the bus I was tempted to accept being one tall young man in his early thirties who looked successful, but I thought to myself, If he's so successful, how come he didn't take a cab instead of the bus? I excused myself from this judgment.

The only thing that ever attracts me to consider a swap with someone is youth. I look at a young person and say to myself, If I knew what I know and had as many years left as he does, I could be president.

By then the bus usually gets to where I'm going and I climb off. I don't want to be president anyway.

THE DREAM PARTY

Should auld acquaintance be forgot and never brought to mind?

Sometimes it probably should. There are a few auld acquaintances most of us have that we never want to see again. The fact that they're auld doesn't necessarily make them good.

It's difficult to say why we drop some old friends. Usually it's because our paths have diverged. Our interests are different from what they were when we understood each other. We moved apart either physically or mentally and sometimes both.

It would be fun if each of us could have a party of the hundred or so people who have meant the most to us as friends in our lives. I'd like to have just the friends, new and old, that I really want to see. I'd exclude everyone else, even if we owed them. No one would be at my party because of any social obligation, business connection or because he or she was married to a friend.

It would be an impossible party to have. Some of the people I'd like most to see are married to people I don't ever want to see again. We'd either have to skip a friend or have someone at the party we didn't like. There goes the perfect party.

At my dream party, geography would be no bar to an invitation. I'd collect my friends from all the places in the world they've disappeared to. Just as examples, there's one in Columbus, one in Bonn, three in London, two in San Francisco. Ben and Jane are in Vermont and others are scattered around the globe. Round-trip tickets would be enclosed with each invitation whether the friends could make the trip or not. Inasmuch as this is only a dream, money is no object.

There'd be friends from each of the six parts of my life: childhood, high school, college, war, neighborhood and business. Even though auld friends are not necessarily the best friends, there's no doubt that we usually have a special feeling for someone who has shared with us the experiences of a special part of our lives.

Many of my friends from one part of my life have never met the friends from another. I have an idea they'd like each other as much as I like them. I suspect the friends each of us chooses have characteristics in common that would lead them to getting along together. There's almost always a trick of thought you share with a friend. You have to have a common way of thinking about things.

"Madam," the nineteenth-century writer Sydney Smith said, "I have been looking for a person who disliked gravy all my life; let us swear eternal friendship."

When you know someone feels the way you feel about basic things in life, it gives you a warm sense of fellow-feeling that's hard to beat. None of us, though, can be very specific about why it is we like some people and dislike others. It doesn't pay to analyze a friendship. Something happens between two people who are friends and you can't put your finger on exactly what it is . . . nor should you try.

The only difficulty I can think about with my dream party is what to do about Don and Fred. I like both of them a lot. They've been important friends in my life. They, unfortunately, detest each other and for good reasons but I couldn't have a dream party without having both of them. I'm at a loss to explain how it is that I could like both Don and Fred with all their virtues and all their shortcomings while they can't stand each other.

I guess I'll probably never have my dream party. Too many problems. I'd only make a lot of enemies of my friends.

THE LONG AND SHORT OF IT

It seems as if everything is too long these days. With the exception of my shoes, I wish things were shorter. Very often I'm ready to go to bed before the TV program I'm watching is over but I can't because I don't know who the murderer is.

Driving to work takes too long and when I get there, it seems like forever before the elevator comes to take me to the seventh floor.

People call me on the phone and we've finished saying anything that makes any difference ten minutes before we hang up. Some of these things may be just a matter of my own impatience but I know the average telephone call lasts longer than is necessary. People repeat themselves as if they didn't really believe you heard what they said the first three times they said it.

"Why don't we meet tomorrow at noon?" someone will say to me.

"Fine," I say, "tomorrow at noon."

"Okay, then," they'll say, repeating what we both just said. "I'll see you tomorrow at noon."

It takes too long to buy things in a store. It's not unusual to wait in line at the supermarket checkout counter with eight or ten people ahead of you with full shopping carts. In the department stores it's often difficult to find a salesperson, and then no matter how you want to pay for your purchase it always seems like the clerk has to fill out a lot of forms. They're even suspicious of cash.

A few small grocery stores survive in most neighborhoods even though they charge a little more because if all you want is a pound of coffee, a quart of milk or a jar of peanut butter, it isn't worth the time you have to spend standing in line at the big store to get it. It has been my experience that the "Express Checkout" counter can be the slowest of all because there are often more people in it. (There is a difference of opinion about whether you stand "on" a line or "in" a line. I stand in one.)

One problem we all have is saving some periods of free time when we don't really have to do anything. In order to have that time, we have to save it by getting through the rest of the day quickly. Every time during the day that we have to wait for something, we're cutting down either on the work we accomplish or the time we have free at the end of the day.

In the past year I've been to three funerals and two weddings. All five seemed endless. Nothing that was said or done at any of them couldn't have been done better and more memorably in half the time.

Business meetings are tedious and interminable. I've only been to half a dozen business meetings in my life but I sympathize with the president. They say he has a tendency to doze off during long meetings. Not being president, I've always made a desperate attempt to stay awake in the meetings I've attended but it wasn't easy. If weddings and funerals could be cut in half, the average business meeting could be cut by seventy-five percent. There are very few meetings that should take more than fifteen minutes After that it's repetitious hot air.

Company banquets at annual meetings are among the longest things in life. I attend three or four of these a year and they are endless. They almost always run behind schedule from the very beginning. If cocktails are supposed to be served from six P.M. to seven P.M., they last until seven-thirty. If dinner is supposed to start at seven o'clock, it begins about 8:10. If the first business is supposed to be conducted at nine P.M., the master of ceremonies doesn't start things until 9:45. If the principal speaker is supposed to talk from 9:15 to 9:45, he isn't introduced until 10:15 and he talks until eleven. After the speaker they usually give out awards to company employees, and this can take longer than getting a mortgage loan from the bank.

The older you get, the more precious time becomes to you. I'd like to have some time-wasters eliminated.

IMPRACTICAL WISHES

Every kid wants a pony. I wanted a pony when I was eight but the desire didn't last long. I think it went away when I realized there was no chance my parents would ever get me one.

That's a great defense mechanism we all have against bitter disappointment. When there is no chance of getting something we want, we don't agonize over it for very long. We change what we want. I changed from wanting a pony to wanting a bicycle, a more practical wish that was fulfilled.

Since giving up on the pony, I've had the same fleeting sensation of desire for a thousand things that I never got, and almost certainly never will. I've made a list of a few of them:

—The movie star of the 1940s Audrey Totter and the Olympic swimmer Eleanor Holm were the only celebrity women I ever wanted, passionately. I must have felt the way young women my age felt about Frank Sinatra or the way the next generation felt about Elvis Presley.

—Through my twenties, thirties and forties I wanted a motorcycle. I don't like motorcyclists or the way they behave on or off their machines but I always wanted to own a motorcycle. During World War II, I found one abandoned by a German soldier by the side of the road leading into Cherbourg. I managed to get it into the back of my jeep but I only rode it once before the Army moved on and I had to leave the motorcycle behind.

—I've never priced one but so many people have swimming pools that I suppose I could afford one. The idea of a swimming pool in the backyard doesn't appeal to me. I don't want leaves in my pool. What I have always wanted is an Olympic-sized pool, fifty meters long, *inside* my house. Unfortunately, that would be something like three times as big as my house, so the pool would stick out.

—Some of the things I've wanted are things I could have had but made a conscious decision not to get. I don't know why. For instance, I've always wanted to own a Volkswagen Bug. It seemed like the ultimately practical little car for around town. Every time I see an ad for one in the "Used Car" section of the paper, I'm tempted to call the phone number listed. I never will.

—Ever since I saw the first heated sidewalk in front of a store in New York one snowy day, I've wanted to run heated cables or hot-water pipes under my sidewalk and driveway. When it sleets or snows I often look out the kitchen window and think how wonderful it would be if I could just turn on the heating coils and have the snow or ice melt the minute it hits the driveway.

—Several years ago I was a guest in Senator Barry Goldwater's home in Scottsdale, Arizona. Barry's a kid with a lot of toys. We watched a movie in his living room and I've forgotten the movie but I've never forgotten the setup he had for showing it. The ceiling of his living room is built with attractive six- or eight-inch boards, probably redwood. When Barry flips a switch at one end of the room, one of the wood panels opens up and drops a large motion-picture screen into the room.

I don't really want a motion-picture screen in my living room but I often think of Barry's gadget as an example of the kind of thing I don't know how to have done in my own home. I don't know where anyone finds the workmen who know how to install something like that. I'd like to have a variation on the same idea that would lift a small closet filled with groceries up into the kitchen from the basement at the flip of a switch. When we didn't want it, it would be out of the way and covered by the part of the floor that opened up when you called for it.

I've got about as much chance of having a screen that drops into my living room as I have of getting the pony, the motorcycle or Audrey Totter.

THE VANISHING DRUGSTORE

"The good old days" have never interested me much. Most days, both old and new, are good. I like remembering familiar and pleasant old things but it doesn't pay to spend much time thinking about them. You can probably guess what's coming. I'm going to talk about "the good old days."

I saw a picture in the paper of a lot of kids hanging around a video-game parlor and I got to thinking that they're missing one of the best places there ever was to hang around in, the drugstore. The drugstore I knew as a kid had nothing to do with medicine. The drugstore to us was the place with the stools, the soda fountain and the wire-legged chairs around a few white marble tables. It was where my mother sent me to buy Cliquot Club ginger ale or a quart of hand-packed chocolate ice cream.

There were lots of things we did in the drugstore. We weighed ourselves on the scale, twirled around on the high stools in front of the fountain and drank sarsaparilla, root beer or Coca-Cola. Pepsi wasn't in the picture yet.

Each of us distinguished himself by ordering his Coke a different way. We never had it just plain. We'd order "a cherry Coke," "a lemon Coke" or "a vanilla Coke." When someone wanted to be different, he'd order "a chocolate Coke." That was a terrible combination.

At one point some of the older kids, real tough guys, we thought, started whispering among themselves. After they ordered their Cokes, they'd furtively slip something else into the glass. The rumor had spread that adding an aspirin to Coke would make you high, and that's what they were doing. It was as close as we ever got to the drug scene.

Some of the drugstores had a magazine counter and kids would stand there for hours looking at racy publications like *Photoplay*, with pictures of Bebe Daniels or Dolores Del Rio in bathing suits.

All druggists were called "Doc." They hated their ice-cream fountains because they attracted people who just hung out there, but having one helped pay the bills so they kept them. "Doc" provided services for which he'd be sued out of business today. If you got something in your eye or a splinter in your hand, you didn't go to a doctor then, you went to "Doc" and he removed it. Today a pharmacist hardly dares recommend a cough drop for fear he'll be accused of practicing medicine without a license.

My friend Clint McCarty's father was a druggist

in a small town in Alabama. Clint has a sad story of why his father went out of business.

There were two drugstores in town. One of them was down by the school. Clint's father's was at the other end of town. When the kids came out in the afternoon, they'd stop in and buy an ice-cream cone or a candy bar from the drugstore near the school and then walk through town toward home. By the time they got to Clint's father's drugstore, they were thirsty, so they'd go in and get a free glass of carbonated water. Druggists didn't charge for carbonated water then.

There was one disastrous event, though, that did him in. Clint's father rented his upstairs rooms to one of the two doctors in town. Both the druggist and the doctor often had a lot of free time during the day and they'd get together and play dominoes in the back room.

It was a good arrangement for Clint's father. He bought prescription pads with the doctor's name on them and the doctor, in return, recommended to his patients that they have the prescription filled right there.

During the course of the domino game one day, the doctor started using one of the prescription pads to keep score on. Since the pads cost money, Clint's father objected and they got into a violent argument.

The result was that they stopped speaking, the doctor moved out and that was the end of this business relationship. Between that and the free carbonated water, Clint's father just couldn't stay in business.

I don't buy medicine in Baskin-Robbins but I miss buying ice cream at the drugstore.

THE GLORIES OF MATURITY

I don't do as many things I don't like to do as I had to when I was young.

Except that you have more years ahead of you, youth isn't necessarily a better time of life than any other. When I was young, I was always having to do things I hated.

School was harder than work has ever been. I enjoy working and I never enjoyed studying. I liked learning but found the process of education tedious. There are still nights I dream I'm back in school with an exam the next morning. The scenario is always the same. I haven't read any of the books and I skipped class most of the time so I'm totally unprepared for the exam.

Staying up all night to study for an exam was a terrible experience, and I did it a lot in college. My parents and all the teachers said cramming didn't work but they were wrong. It may be the wrong way to learn but cramming is a good way to pass an exam. It just hurts a lot while you're doing it.

I no longer stay up all night for anything. If I

have something I should have written and haven't, I go to bed and try to get it done the next morning. If I don't get it done? Sue me.

There is no single thing in my adult life so regularly unpleasant and burdensome as homework was in my youth. If I bring work home from the office now, it's because the work interests me. It is not drudgery and if I don't feel like doing it, I put it off.

There are still things that come up in my life for which I'm unprepared but they don't bother me the way they did when I was a teenager. They no longer seem like life-or-death situations. If my income-tax stuff isn't all together when I go to my accountant, so what?

Love is more pleasant once you get out of your twenties. It doesn't hurt all the time. I no longer fall in and out of love. I have my love.

As a grown-up, I don't eat things that are good for me if I don't like them. My mother was always insisting that something was good for me and I had to eat it. Now the most I do is try to avoid things that are bad for me. I'm not doing much for the carrot farmers.

Shoveling snow is my idea of hard fun so I shovel snow in the winter, but I've always hated cutting the grass so in the summer I pay someone to do that.

On Saturdays, I always had to stop playing with the other kids and have lunch at twelve o'clock. I still play a lot on Saturdays but I quit playing and come in for lunch when I feel like it. I don't care what time it is.

They can write about the glories of youth but there are advantages to maturity, too. I don't read anything I don't want to read, I don't go places I don't want to go, I don't spend a lot of time talking to people I don't feel like talking to.

I feel no need to wear what the other fellows are wearing, listen to the music other people listen to or go to movies I don't want to see.

Every other Sunday my father and mother would put everyone in the car and drive to Troy to see some relatives. I liked the relatives but I hated ruining Sunday to go see them. I sat on the floor and looked at books while the adults talked. I'm glad I don't have to go to Troy anymore.

When I was drafted into the Army, I detested the discipline. When First Sergeant Hardy M. Harrell ordered me to get rid of the books I kept under my bunk at Fort Bragg, I made the mistake of telling him he didn't like books because he couldn't read. This turned out to be the wrong thing for a private to tell a first sergeant and I spent the next thirty days doing a great many things I didn't like doing.

Now there are books under my bed again.

I'm happy not doing all the things I had to do in the Army.

I offer all this to young people who are wondering about life. Don't think things keep getting worse. Youth can be a terrible time of life just because of all the things you hate to do, but have to do anyway.

GRANDFATHERHOOD

It seems to me that grandfathers are a lot younger than they used to be before I got to be one.

When I had a grandfather, all grandfathers and grandmothers were born at that age. It seemed as though they had always been what they were, grandmothers and grandfathers. They were kindly old folks and their grandchildren could do no wrong in their elderly eyes.

I guess I haven't taken naturally to being a grandfather. I have no interest whatsoever in being a lovable, gray-haired old codger who approves of everything his grandchild does.

Up until last week, I thought of Justin as my daughter's son. I had seen him for a day or two five or six times a year since he was born six years ago, but I'd never spent an extended length of time with him. Either his father or his mother had always been present when Justin was at our house.

Last week was different. Margie and I had this cute little blond, brown-eyed person with us all week. I seemed to have him more than Margie when I was there because he wanted to do what I was doing. I was trying to enjoy what little's left of my vacation in my workshop. If I was in the workshop, Justin wanted to be in the workshop.

If I hammered, he wanted to hammer. If I sawed, he wanted to saw. It's one-hundred-percent impossible to accomplish anything in a workshop with dangerous tools and a grandchild who insists on being there with you.

"Are we going to do our work?" he asked as soon as he got up every day. Some work.

I kept waiting to feel like a regular grandfather. I kept waiting to excuse him when he did something dumb or thoughtless. Instead, I found myself treating Justin more like a person than a grandchild. I was liking him more and more as a little friend.

The only thing this kid seemed to remember me for from last summer was that I got up early and made him pancakes for breakfast. Naturally, everyone else thought that was cute so I had to get up early this year and make him pancakes for breakfast, too.

Elephants and grandchildren never forget.

I spent quite a bit of time with Justin, trying to break him of his eating habits. He must have gotten them from my daughter Martha, or his father, Leo. He never got them from me. I never saw a young boy so interested in fruit and vegetables and so uninterested in candy, soft drinks or junk food. I don't know what's wrong with him, anyway.

He doesn't want ice cream. The next thing he'll be telling me is he doesn't want anything for Christmas. I queried Martha about his aberrant behavior in regard to food, trying to determine how in the world this kin of mine ever got off on the wrong foot by not liking ice cream. Can they get government help for a condition like this?

I remember enough old Art Linkletter shows to know that kids ask a lot of cute questions, but I was unprepared for those Justin asked.

During a long drive over country roads to the grocery store, the sun shone in his eyes. I had a baseball cap with a long peak on it in back of the car and suggested he put it on. First, he put it on straight but the sun was still hitting his face so directly that he pulled the cap down over his eyes and was looking through the woven fibers of the dark blue material.

"Hey, Granddad!" he said suddenly. Even though there were only two of us in the car, it took me a minute to realize he meant me.

"What's all these colors?" he asked. "I see all colors. What makes all the colors, Granddad?"

I knew instantly I was about to fail my first quiz as a grandfather. I know that the light from the sun contains every color in the spectrum and I know that under certain circumstances it's possible to bend light beams so that the colors break down and separate. The process is called refraction. I know that but I can't explain it.

I can't figure out how Justin learned how to be a grandchild faster than I learned how to be a grandfather.

MEMORIES

My interest in anniversaries is limited. By the time you get to be sixty, you've accumulated enough memories, good and bad, to last a lifetime. The way lifetimes are going these days, you still have quite a long way to go, though, and it's my feeling that those of us who have reached that age ought to push on to acquire new memories instead of sitting back to consider the old ones. No one should spend too much time on memories. Some people start doing that when they're twenty and never get over living in the past. The most interesting people I know don't spend much time reminiscing.

The trouble with most memories is that too many of them are sad. They involve friends or events that are gone.

Someone asked me what year my father died and I couldn't remember. The date never seemed like one to commit to memory, and I don't think of him any less often for having put it out of my mind.

There are people who make a hobby out of remembering all the birthdays, anniversaries and important dates in the lives of their friends and relatives. I don't mean to be a skeptic all the time but I have the feeling that Hallmark has had as much to do with the increase in overtly expressed sentiment on these occasions as true love.

It's easy to overdo the celebration of anniversaries and birthdays. If I'd had my last birthday party when my mother invited six neighborhood kids in for cake and ice cream when I was nine, it would be okay with me. I am no longer pleased to be reminded that I'm a year older. I like someone having a birthday party for me about as much as I like champagne—which is not at all. If I never had either again I'd be pleased and I'd certainly sleep better that night.

I've returned to a couple of class reunions at both my high school and college. I enjoyed them but there's a limit to how much reunioning there's time for. You have to face the fact that the number of people you liked in school was no greater, by percentage, than the people you've met and liked anywhere else. Most of us make more good friends in a lifetime than we have the time to remain friends with.

The memories invoked at a reunion, whether it's a war reunion, class reunion or a family reunion, are not usually as satisfactory as the ones you can call up by yourself when you're alone. The trouble with reunion memories is that they have edited out so much of what happened and forgotten so many details that the crowd is usually left with a few broad, basic stories that are repeated year after year. The memories get to be of the last reunion.

Even when I'm really carried away by my memory and become engrossed in reenacting, in my mind, some pleasurable event from the past, I am almost always brought up sharply by the desperately unhappy thought that the moment is gone forever and no amount of wanting will bring it back. That's more than I can take.

Fortunately, memory is controllable. You can turn memory off and on. An editor once asked Clifton Fadiman to write about his memories of England. At first Fadiman said he couldn't do it because he'd never been to England but then he realized this was a weak excuse and he proceeded to write.

At its worst, memory is a sad reminder of what's all over. At its best, it's a guideline for a better future. But remembering how old I am on my next birthday isn't going to make the future better for me or anyone else.

THANKS, PAL

Ernie Pyle, who wrote the book *Brave Men,* was the best kind of brave man I ever knew. He didn't have the thoughtless, macho kind of bravado that is sometimes mistaken for bravery. He was a war correspondent who was afraid of being killed but did what he had to do in spite of it.

Mostly, Ernie stayed right with the infantrymen who were doing the fighting and the dying. On the scrubby little island of Ie Shima, Ernie was moving up with the infantry when he was shot dead by a Japanese machine gunner forty years ago.

Almost everyone has heard of Ernie Pyle but in case you don't know why he was so widely read and so much loved, I thought I'd offer a little toast to the memory of this gentle, talented little man by telling you.

Unlike most correspondents, Ernie never offered any opinion about who was winning or losing the war. He just told little stories about the men fighting it. He drew vignettes with two fingers on his typewriter keys that told more about the victories and defeats of World War II than all the official communiqués ever issued.

I have an Ernie Pyle kind of story about Ernie Pyle. One day sometime in July of 1944, I was sharing a tent with Ernie and two other reporters in Normandy. Ernie had decided not to go to the front that day, and he was lying on his cot when I came in and sat down on mine. I took off my boots, preparing to lie down for a while when I was dive-bombed by an angry bee.

My cot was almost directly over a hole in the ground that the bees were using as a nest. There must have been hundreds of them down there and, because it was impractical to move either my cot or the tent, I scuffed dirt over the hole so they couldn't get in or out.

The two of us lay on our cots, watching an occasional bee come into the tent looking for home. I started thinking about the bees trapped underneath the dirt.

We watched, silently, for perhaps two minutes. Ernie broke the silence.

"Aw, Andy," he said, "why don't you let 'em out?"

Ernie never seemed to be in much of a hurry. He didn't rush to the scene of some particular bit of action with the other reporters. He made his own stories with little things others of us hardly noticed. His stories about soldiers were as apt to be about loneliness or boredom as about blood and danger.

Ernie never seemed to be interviewing anyone, either. It was more as though he were talking to the soldiers as a friend. You only realized he was working when he took out his notebook and meticulously wrote down the name and full address of every soldier near him. An infantryman could be telling Ernie a story about how his squad of eight guys wiped out a German machinegun nest but Ernie would be as interested in getting all the names and addresses of the eight men as he was in the details of the action.

"Whereabouts in Wheeling, West Virginia?" he'd ask.

Ernie started covering the war in North Africa, and even though he didn't deal in The Big Picture, he knew North Africa was only the beginning.

"This is our war," he wrote, "and we will carry it with us as we go from one battleground to another until it is all over, leaving some of us behind on every beach, in every field. We are just

391

beginning with the ones who lie back of us here in Tunisia. I don't know whether it was their good fortune or their misfortune to get out of it so early in the game. I guess it doesn't make any difference once a man is gone. Medals and speeches and victories are nothing anymore. They died and the others lived and no one knows why it is so. When we leave here for the next shore, there is nothing we can do for the ones underneath the wooden crosses here, except perhaps pause and murmur, 'Thanks, pal.' "

Ernie Pyle gave war correspondents a reputation not all of them deserved. All that those of us who shared that reputation can do for Ernie now is to say, "Thanks, pal."

E. B. WHITE

If you plan to die anytime soon and wish the world to note your passing you'd be wise to become a movie star before you go.

When Simone Signoret and Rock Hudson died, the newspapers and television-news broadcasts were filled with their pictures and remembrances of their careers.

E. B. White died the same week. His passing did not begin to attract the space in the papers or the time on television that Simone Signoret and Rock Hudson got. White was my hero as a writer and my sadness over his death was mitigated by my anger over how briefly it was noted by many newspapers and by two of the three networks. John Hart did a fine piece for the *NBC Nightly News.*

Many of you may not know E. B. White's name and may not be familiar with his work. William Shawn, the editor of *The New Yorker*, for whom E. B. White wrote, said, "Because of his quiet influence, several generations of this country's writers write better than they might have done."

I desperately hope I can be included among the writers who write a little better because of the influence of E. B. White.

Each of us wants the whole world to know the things we know and to like the things we like. I'm not sure why that is but I want the whole world to know and like the writing of E. B. White because, of all the writers I have ever read, he's the one I admire most.

E. B. White is the only major hero of mine I ever got to know personally. He was called "Andy" by his friends and, for a while after I first met him I felt a little presumptuous calling him that, but after he wrote me several letters and signed himself "Andy," I felt easier with it.

I once had lunch with A. J. Liebling, James Thurber and E. B. White. Joe Liebling had been a friend of mine for many years and he knew both Thurber and White so well that he was less awed in their presence than I was.

When Joe and I left the restaurant together, Joe

said, "They're hard to eat with. Jim always has scrambled eggs because he can find them on his plate but he can't see so he never knows when someone else wants to talk. Andy always orders oysters and he makes me nervous because he looks at every one of them as if there was something wrong with it."

My favorite books of White's are *Second Tree from the Corner, One Man's Meat* and a little collection of poems called *The Fox of Peapack.* I never cared much for *Charlotte's Web* or *The Elements of Style.*

Andy White was the grand master of English prose. In *Here Is New York,* a long magazine article later published in book form, he wrote about an old willow tree in the backyard of the house he lived in on Forty-ninth Street near the United Nations. I couldn't get the passage out of my mind as I read his obituary.

It is a battered tree, long suffering and much climbed, held together by strands of wire but beloved by those who know it. In a way it symbolizes the City; life under difficulties, growth against odds, sap rise in the midst of concrete, and the steady reaching for the sun.

Whenever I look at it nowadays, and feel the cold shadow of destruction, I think: "This must be saved, this particular thing, this very tree."

If it were to go, all would go . . . this City, this mischievous and marvelous monument which not to look upon would be like death.

Motion picture fans publicly mourn the loss of Simone Signoret and Rock Hudson. In relative obscurity, a great many writers mourn the loss of a giant among them.

The publishers hope that this
Large Print Book has brought
you pleasurable reading.
Each title is designed to make
the text as easy to see as possible.
G.K. Hall Large Print Books
are available from your library and
your local bookstore. Or, you can
receive information by mail on
upcoming and current Large Print Books
and order directly from the publishers.
Just send your name and address to:

G.K. Hall & Co.
70 Lincoln Street
Boston, Mass. 02111

or call, toll-free:

1-800-343-2806

A note on the text
Large print edition designed by
Bernadette Montalvo.
Composed in 16 pt Plantin
on a Xyvision 300/Linotron 202N
by Genevieve Connell
of G.K. Hall & Co.